KU-226-647

Active
Training

Fourth Edition

Active Training

A Handbook of Techniques, Designs, Case Examples, and Tips

Mel Silberman & Elaine Biech

Assisted by Carol Auerbach

WILEY

Cover image: Faceout Studio
Cover design: Wiley

This book is printed on acid-free paper.

Copyright © 2015 by ebb associates, inc. All rights reserved

Published by John Wiley & Sons, Inc., Hoboken, New Jersey
Published simultaneously in Canada

No part of this publication may be reproduced, stored in a retrieval system, or transmitted in any form or by any means, electronic, mechanical, photocopying, recording, scanning, or otherwise, except as permitted under Section 107 or 108 of the 1976 United States Copyright Act, without either the prior written permission of the Publisher, or authorization through payment of the appropriate per-copy fee to the Copyright Clearance Center, 222 Rosewood Drive, Danvers, MA 01923, (978) 750-8400, fax (978) 646-8600, or on the web at www.copyright.com. Requests to the Publisher for permission should be addressed to the Permissions Department, John Wiley & Sons, Inc., 111 River Street, Hoboken, NJ 07030, (201) 748-6011, fax (201) 748-6008, or online at www.wiley.com/go/permissions.

Limit of Liability/Disclaimer of Warranty: While the publisher and author have used their best efforts in preparing this book, they make no representations or warranties with respect to the accuracy or completeness of the contents of this book and specifically disclaim any implied warranties of merchantability or fitness for a particular purpose. No warranty may be created or extended by sales representatives or written sales materials. The advice and strategies contained herein may not be suitable for your situation. You should consult with a professional where appropriate. Neither the publisher nor the author shall be liable for damages arising herefrom.

For general information about our other products and services, please contact our Customer Care Department within the United States at (800) 762-2974, outside the United States at (317) 572-3993 or fax (317) 572-4002.

Wiley publishes in a variety of print and electronic formats and by print-on-demand. Some material included with standard print versions of this book may not be included in e-books or in print-on-demand. If this book refers to media such as a CD or DVD that is not included in the version you purchased, you may download this material at http://booksupport.wiley.com. For more information about Wiley products, visit www.wiley.com.

Library of Congress Cataloging-in-Publication Data is on file.

9781118972014 (hbk)
9781118972038 (ePDF)
9781118972021 (epub)

Printed in the United States of America
10 9 8 7 6 5 4 3 2 1

Contents

207898
UCB

Acknowledgments

A requisite for this book was to create a tribute to Mel Silberman. Thank you to those who took the extra time to tell us how you knew Mel or how he touched your life. You will find their words throughout the book: Carol Auerbach, Jean Barbazette, Ed Betof, Jane Bozarth, Marlene Caroselli, Barb Crockett, Karen Lawson, Teri B. Lund, Gale J. Mote, Sophie Oberstein, Lisa Owens, and Kathy Shurte.

Matt C. Davis, senior editor at John Wiley and Sons, suggested the idea of revitalizing Mel's work. It's been an honor to meet with all the people whose lives Mel touched. Even more, it was exhilarating and exciting. Thank you to Carol Auerbach who assisted in the revision of *Active Training*. Her thoroughness, experience with previous editions, and wise counsel have been incorporated in this book. Thanks to the editing prowess of Chaitanya Mella. Thanks to my partner in all these writing projects, Dan Greene, who keeps me fed and sane.

Support came in the form of contributions from several colleagues who provided activities, inspiration, and content: Wendy Axelrod, Halelly Azullay, Dianna Booher, Jane Bozarth, Wendy Gates Corbett, Jo Lynn Feinstein, and Cindy Huggett. Thank you.

And finally, training professionals and graduate students who contributed tips, designs, and case examples in the first three editions made it possible for this edition. They include Jackie Agostini, Marie Amey-Taylor, Sharon Balaban, Jean Barbazette, Jeff Brown, Sharon Bowman, Meghan Burke, Marion Burns, Gretchen Castle, Claire Conway, Karen DiNunzio, Karen Johnson Dugger, Germaine Edwards, Kevin Eikenberry, Jody Gandy, Allan Geller,

Chris Gillespie, Neal Goodman, Linda Guerra, Freda Hansburg, Dan Harvey, Ann Houser, Cathleen Hulce, Linda Hyman, Maryann Keenan, Jeff Kindler, Steve Krupp, Janice Engler Marks, Monica McGrath, Rick McKnight, Elaine Mendelow, Chrissa Merron, Lee Miller, Gale Mote, Leigh Mundhenk, Karla Nurcyzk, D. J. O'Loughlin, Cindy Perkiss, Bill Pinchuk, Whit Raymond, Sandy Saville, Milt Silver, Scott Simmerman, George Spence, Bill Stieber, Fay Stokes, Maria Sudeck, Karon West, Susan Wheelan, Vicky Whiteling, Charlotte Zaback, and Ruth Zasloff.

And, especially, thanks to Mel Silberman for your contribution to the profession.

Preface

This fourth edition is built on the same solid foundation of active training originated by Mel Silberman. It's been an honor to be asked to revive the active learning work that Mel started. My goal is to continue to acknowledge his work throughout the book by respecting his voice, celebrating and expanding his ideas, and engaging others to pay tribute to Mel.

One of Mel's personal guidelines was, "It's not what you give them; it's what they take away that counts." Mel believed that it didn't matter how much information you disseminated. If the learner was unable to retain it, learning had not occurred. I followed Mel's advice as I edited this book. I tried to revise and add things that would make the content something you can take away.

Mel and I started in this field at about the same time, and although Mel coined the term "Active Training," both of us believed, practiced, and expounded identical philosophies throughout our careers. For a few years before I was solidly grounded in the history of learning and development, and before I'd heard of Malcolm Knowles, I thought I'd invented Adult Learning Theory. Mel and I had a good laugh about that when I first met him.

It's been twenty-five years since Mel's first edition of *Active Training: A Handbook of Techniques, Designs, Case Examples, and Tips* made its way onto our bookshelves. So it is fitting that 2015 has been selected for the fourth edition.

THE GOALS OF THIS BOOK

Mel's staunch advocates still follow his active learning concepts. Many are represented throughout this and his *101 Ways to Make Training Active* books. Mel's unwavering support is based on the fact that his concepts work. Training is "active" when the learners do most of the work. Learners consider the content, solve problems, make decisions, and practice the skills. This ensures that they are ready to apply what they learned once they return to the workplace or wherever they intend to use their newly acquired skills and knowledge. Like its predecessors, this fourth edition of *Active Training* has three goals:

1. To explore all aspects of training

Training has a front, a middle, and an end. The front involves all the activities involved before the first slide or exercise is ever developed. Foremost are the assessment of the training need and the establishment of training objectives. The middle contains the detailed planning and delivery of the training program. The end focuses on the events that encourage back-on-the-job application, ongoing performance support, and the evaluation of training outcomes. This edition of *Active Training* provides a comprehensive examination of these three phases of training.

2. To promote an active approach to training

The active approach to training involves a commitment to *learning by doing*. Everything we know about adult learners suggests that participants must be actively engaged during a training program for results to occur. If there is little activity, participants will forget or fail to apply what they are taught and will be bored by the material presented. This new edition of *Active Training* continues to define what is meant by the active approach to training and how it can be practiced effectively. It goes beyond the classroom and presents active learning ideas for virtual online classes, using social media, m-learning, and other exciting processes available to our profession.

3. To provide a practical handbook of techniques, designs, case examples, and tips

As *Active Training* promotes learning by doing, it shows how to acquire these skills through *learning by example*. It not only describes several active training techniques but also illustrates how they are applied in actual training situations. Designs and case examples drawn from private and public sector training professionals are presented to give readers ideas for their own situation. One of the special features of *Active Training* is the wide variety of training topics from which its examples are pulled. All of the examples are flexible enough to be customized to the topics and groups any reader might be training.

Since 1990, the year the first edition was published, much has happened. Training continues to be delivered in classroom settings but now is also delivered in new ways that were only a vision in 1990. The view of training as something that only occurs in classrooms has been broadened to include the concept that training means supporting learning wherever it occurs in the organization—in meetings, on computer screens, through mentors, during work team projects, or on your smartphone.

Many examples of training activities and designs are incorporated in this fourth edition. You will find case examples from a long list of training topics in *Active Training*. They include topics such as career development, change management, childcare, coaching, communication skills, conflict management, cultural diversity, customer service, leadership development, problem solving, project management, sales, succession planning, team building, train-the-trainer, and others. They also come from a variety of industries including banking, government, health care, insurance, manufacturing, real estate, and others.

HOW THIS BOOK IS ORGANIZED

This book is organized into five parts: starting at the beginning with understanding more about active training and ending with new roles and realities for trainers.

Part One defines and contains a rationale for an active approach to training. It has been updated to reflect the latest theory, research, and practice. Among other things, it examines the case for active training. It contains a discussion of the nature of adult learning, exploring the reasons why adults learn best when they are active in the learning process. It also identifies the frequently asked questions people concerned with the introduction of active training techniques most often ask. Finally, it examines the contexts in which active training is delivered. While most training takes place in classroom-type settings, an active approach to training can be incorporated online, on the job, or in other delivery modes.

Part Two considers all the steps needed, from the opening to the closing elements, to create an instructional design for an active training program, course, workshop, virtual classroom, or session. You will find these names interchangeable throughout the book. You may find yourself needing to just tweak a course a bit or you may be in complete control over a course design. It is in this situation, when trying to make multiple design decisions that make up a professional training program, that the many tips, designs, and case examples described become especially useful. You will find examples for online learning sprinkled throughout the entire book, but may notice them here more than ever. Chapter 10, "Incorporating Active Training in All Learning," has been revamped and includes additional discussion about online learning and an expanded discussion of social media and m-learning.

Part Three covers every aspect of training delivery, including climate setting, enlisting participation, managing participant behavior, and staging experiential activities. This fourth edition of *Active Training* emphasizes what you can do to create an experience for your participants. You will find new examples and templates throughout.

Part Four examines how to extend the value of training through follow-up activities and evaluation. You will find both of these chapters expanded. The follow-up activities tap into the expanded Kirkpatrick model to include return on expectation (ROE) as a measurement tool.

Part Five is an entirely new section. It presents two chapters. "The Expanded Roles for Trainers" looks at how you can use Active Training methods in your onboarding programs, when you are called upon to lead change, when and why you coach managers, and several other roles. A second all-new chapter, "New Business Realities for Trainers," provides ideas when your job calls on you to do more with less, participate in globalization or vendor management, work with a multigenerational workforce, and other new focuses.

If you are new to the training environment or a student studying the field for the first time, reading *Active Training* can help you to learn the reasons why trainers make the design and delivery choices they do when creating an active training program. In addition, you will learn a variety of facilitation techniques that can help you to conduct any training program professionally. The examples help you to make sense out of the components of a good active training program in a way that straight text never could.

I hope that *Active Training* will continually provide you with specific guidance as you reference the book throughout your career, whether you work in a business, governmental, or educational setting. The book is meant to be practical and helpful for you.

Norfolk, VA   Elaine Biech
April 2015

Active Training

Part One

Introducing Active Training

*T*raining is a method of enhancing human performance. Whenever a person's ability to perform a job is limited by a lack of knowledge or skill, it makes sense to bridge that gap by providing the required instruction.

Sounds simple, doesn't it? Not really. The problem begins with the notion that learning something you don't already know requires another person (a trainer) or medium (a book, a computer) to provide it.

One of Mel's favorite exercises was to cover a wristwatch with the opposite hand and ask those who are observing, "What am I doing?" Immediately, someone would say, "You're covering your watch." He would then request a synonym for the word *cover*. Typically, suggestions such as *hide, obscure,* or *block* are given. With this opening, he would say, "The next time *you* have something to cover with a person whom you are training, you might be hiding the information, obscuring it, or completely blocking it from view. That's because, at that moment, it's *your* information and *your* understanding of it. It does not belong to the *other* person." Mel's point was that as trainers we need to think about "how" we are "covering" the topic, making sure that we do not prevent the learner from "uncovering" it; this "uncovering" process only happens by virtue of the learner's own activity. Ultimately, you—or a book or a computer—cannot do the work for the learner.

Active training occurs when the participants do most of the work. If you neatly package the information or elegantly demonstrate the skills, you, not the participants, are doing "the work" for them. No one

1

is suggesting that well-designed instruction is unnecessary. The key to effective training, however, is how the learning activities are designed so that the participants *acquire* knowledge and skill rather than merely *receive* them.

Yes, there is a whole lot more to training than "show and tell." Learning is not an automatic consequence of pouring information into another person's head. It requires the learner's own mental involvement and doing. Lecturing and demonstrating, by themselves, will never lead to real, lasting learning. Only training that is active will.

In order for people to learn something well, they must *hear* it, *see* it, *question* it, *discuss* it with their peers, and *do* it. They may even *teach* it to someone else in order to solidify their understanding of the information or skill. An active approach to training requires a variety of strategies that promote all six processes—*hearing, seeing, questioning, discussing, doing,* and *teaching.* Let's consider more fully why.

THE NATURE OF ADULT LEARNING

Over twenty-four hundred years ago, Confucius declared:

> What I **hear**, I *forget*.
>
> What I **see**, I *remember*.
>
> What I **do**, I *understand*.

These three simple statements speak volumes about the need for active learning. As only Mel could do, he modified and expanded the wisdom of Confucius into what he called the Active Learning Credo:

> *When I only* **hear***, I forget.*
>
> *When I* **hear** *and* **see***, I remember a little.*
>
> *When I* **hear***,* **see***, and* **ask questions** *and* **discuss** *with someone else, I begin to understand.*
>
> *When I* **hear, see, question, discuss***, and* **do***, I acquire knowledge and skill.*
>
> *When I* **teach** *someone, I master what I have learned.*

Why Is This Important?

Hearing and Seeing. You've probably read "pop data" that insists that participants retain less when listening to lecture and more when what they hear is paired with a visual; they retain even more when they practice by doing. There are several reasons why most adults tend to forget what they hear. One of the most interesting has to do with the rate at which a trainer speaks and the rate at which participants listen.

Most trainers speak at about one hundred to two hundred words per minute. But how many of those words do participants hear? It depends on how they are listening. If the participants are really concentrating, they might be able to listen attentively to about half of what a trainer is saying. That's because participants are thinking while they are listening. It's hard to keep up with a talkative trainer. Even if the material is interesting, it's hard to concentrate for a sustained period of time. Participants probably hear at the rate of four hundred to five hundred words per minute. When they are listening for a sustained period of time to a trainer who is talking more slowly they are likely to get bored and their minds will wander. The upshot? A steady diet of lecture is problematic, because the lecturer and the listener are often not in synch.

To alleviate the audio bombardment of lecturing, master and trainer and CPLP Fellow, Bob Pike, recommends that participants should be given a chance *every eight minutes* to internalize what they have been hearing before it's simply supplanted by the next wave of information (Pike 2003). Ruth Clark (2014) points out that still visuals are helpful to learning; they generally impose less mental load than animated visuals. Still visuals have been shown to be more effective to teach general content (animated visuals are better for procedures).That could be true because between 80 to 90 percent of all information that is absorbed by the brain is visual (Jensen 2008).

When teaching has both an auditory and a visual dimension, the message is reinforced by two delivery systems. It not only helps to use presentation slides along with meaningful words, but several other sources of visual information can be utilized, such as objects, documents, and vivid stories. Some of us prefer one mode of delivery over the other. By using both you have a greater chance of meeting the preferences of more participants.

But merely hearing something and seeing it is not enough to learn it. Let's explore the reasons why.

Ask questions and discuss. The adult brain does not function like an audio or video recorder. The brain doesn't just receive information; it processes it. The brain is suffused with a vast number of networks through which it sorts out all incoming information. Thus, any information already stored influences how and what we understand and eventually learn. Your brain tries to make connections.

If adults discuss information with others and if they are invited to ask questions about it, their brains can do a better job of connecting with information they've already stored. That's because the act of learning begins with a question. The brain starts the work of learning because it has a question about information it is obtaining from the senses (hearing, sight, touch, and taste) that feed it. If the brain could talk, it would say things like: *Where does this information fit? Does it confirm what I already know? Does it challenge what I already know?*

If the brain isn't curious about incoming information, however, it takes the path of least resistance and attends to something else. Therefore, getting participants to ask questions puts them in a seeking mode rather than a passive mode. Their brains are activated to obtain answers rather than merely "logging in." If participants are asked to listen to a lecture or view presentation slides and they come to it with few or any questions, their brains treat the information superficially. If they are trying to find out something, their brains treat the information carefully.

Better yet, if adults can discuss the information with their peers, they can obtain feedback about how well they understand it. Learning is enhanced if people are asked to do the following with their peers:

- State the information in their own words
- Give examples of it
- Have an opportunity to reflect on the information
- See connections between it and other facts or ideas
- Practice higher-order thinking, such as analysis, synthesis, and evaluation
- Apply it to case situations

Even better is the opportunity to do something with the information. Research conducted at Stanford University (Levin 1996) suggests that the optimal environment for learning allows people at different times to be partners, teammates, and teachers. In a training context, this occurs best when learning teams are organized to engage in "action learning" tasks. They challenge participants to solve problems and apply what they know to real work situations. Furthermore, giving participants the opportunity to learn information or a skill and then teach it to peers allows them the opportunity to discover what Aristotle declared many years ago, "Teaching is the highest art of understanding."

In many ways, our brain is like a computer and we are its users. A computer needs to be "on" in order to work. Our brain needs to be on as well. When learning is passive, the brain isn't on. A computer needs the right software to interpret the data that are entered. Our brain needs to link what we are being taught with what we already know and how we think. When learning is passive, the brain doesn't make these linkages to the software of our mind. Finally, a computer cannot retain information that it has processed without "saving it." Our brain needs to test the information, recapitulate it, or explain it to someone else in order to store it in its memory banks. When learning is passive, the brain doesn't save what has been presented.

What occurs when trainers flood participants with their own thoughts (however insightful and well organized they may be) or when they rely too often on "let me show you how" demonstrations and explanations? Pouring facts and concepts into participants' heads and masterfully performing skills and procedures actually interfere with learning. The presentation may make an immediate impression on the brain, but without a photographic memory, participants simply cannot retain very much for any period of time, even though they think they will never forget it. As Eric Jensen, author of *Brain-Based Learning*, explains, "The traditional stand and delivery approach is brain antagonistic. The brain is not very good at absorbing countless bits of semantic (factual) information."

In any case, real learning is not memorization. Most of what we memorize is lost in hours. In order to retain what has been taught, participants must chew on it. Learning can't be swallowed whole. A trainer can't do the mental work for participants because they must put together what they hear and see to form a meaningful whole. Without the opportunity to discuss, ask questions, do, and perhaps even teach someone else, real learning will not occur.

Further, learning is not a one-shot event; it comes in waves. It takes several exposures to material to understand. It also takes different kinds of exposures, not just a repetition of input. For example, a software application can be taught with manuals, through classroom exercises, and through an asynchronous online class. Each way shapes the participants' understanding. Even more important is the way in which the exposure happens. If it happens *to* the learner, there will be little mental engagement *by* the learner.

When learning is passive, learners comes to the encounter without curiosity, without questions, and without interest in the outcome. When learning is active, learners are *seeking* something. They want an answer to a question, need information to solve a problem, or are searching for a better way to do a job.

David Rock is the director of the NeuroLeadership Institute and author of *Your Brain at Work*. He uses an AGES model that identifies four requirements to embed ideas:

1. Attention must be very high; multitasking dramatically reduces recall. The chemical processes to encode memory are activated when we are very focused.

2. Generating a mental map around the new ideas; participant can't just watch or listen.

3. Emotions need to be high; we only remember things we feel strongly about.

4. Spacing learning is critical.

A high AGES score is required for participants to recall ideas. Attention, generation, emotion, and spacing form the AGES model. Practicing in the form of small group work, gamification, contests, or team teaching can all increase a learning event's AGES score.

Practicing. Quite a few studies have compared learning outcomes among individuals playing a game with individuals assigned to a more traditional instructional method such as lectures or computer tutorials. In these studies the same content is presented in a game version and in a traditional version and learning is measured with a test. In her book *Evidence-Based Training Methods*, Ruth Clark (2014) reports that results aren't clear cut; however, in one study simulation games resulted in learning gains 9 to 14 percent higher than comparison groups. However, the comparison groups learned more than the game groups when taught with active instructional methods. The game groups learned more than the comparison groups when the comparison group was taught with passive instructional methods. Ruth states, "My conclusion from the review is that active engagement leads to learning and any method that incorporates relevant active engagement (with feedback) will lead to better learning than a method that relies primarily on passive learning environments such as lectures or reading."

The bottom line here? Telling is NOT training. As Harold Stolovitch and Erica Keeps suggest in their book, *Telling Ain't Training*, there's much more to it.

THE SOCIAL SIDE OF LEARNING

We all face a world of exploding knowledge, rapid change, and uncertainty. As a result, participants may be anxious and defensive when they show up for training. Abraham Maslow taught us that human beings have within them two sets of forces or needs—one that strives for growth and one that clings to safety. A person who must choose between these two needs will choose safety over growth. The need to feel secure has to be met before the need to reach out, take risks, and explore the new can be entertained. Growth forward takes place in little steps. According to Maslow, "each step forward is made possible by the feeling of being safe, of operating out into the unknown from a safe home port."

One of the key ways people feel safe and secure is when they feel connected to other people and are included in a group. This feeling of belonging enables participants to face the challenges set before them. When they are learning with others rather than alone, they have available the emotional and intellectual support that allows them to go beyond their present level of knowledge and skill.

Maslow's concepts underlie the development of the small-group learning methods that are popular in training circles. Placing participants in teams and giving them tasks in which they depend upon each other to complete the work is a way to capitalize on their social needs. They tend to get more engaged in learning because they are doing it with their peers. Once they have become involved, they also have a need to talk with others about what they are experiencing, which leads to further connections.

Collaborative learning activities help to drive active training. Although independent study and large group instruction also stimulate active learning, the ability to teach through small-group cooperative activities will enable you to promote active learning in a special way. Remember that what participants discuss with others and what they teach others enables them to acquire understanding and master learning. The best collaborative learning methods (see, for example, "Jigsaw Learning" in Chapter 5) meet these requirements. Giving different assignments to different participants prompts them not only to learn together but also to teach each other.

As you begin to practice active training, remember:

- Learners follow a hierarchy to take in information.
- Use a variety of delivery methods to support participants' learning.
- Adults have a need to feel safe and a part of the group.

CONCERNS ABOUT ACTIVE TRAINING

If this is your first introduction to using an active approach to training and development, you may have questions. These FAQs may answer them.

Is active training just a bunch of "fun and games"? No, it's not just fun, although learning can be fun and still be worthwhile.

Actually, many active training techniques present participants with unusual challenges that require much hard work.

Does active training focus so much on activity for its own sake that participants don't reflect on what they are learning? This is a real concern. Much of the value of active training activities comes from thinking about them when they are over and discussing their meaning with others. Don't overlook this fact. You will find many suggestions in *Active Training* to help participants reflect on what they have experienced. Ensure that you design time to process each activity; that's where the real learning often occurs. Add value by giving a few comments after an active training activity to connect what the participants experienced to the concepts you want to get across.

Doesn't active training require a lot of time? How can you cover course material using active training methods? Isn't lecturing more efficient? There is no question that active training takes more time than conventional lecturing, but there are many ways to avoid a needless waste of time. Furthermore, even though a lecture can cover considerable ground, you have to question how much is really learned. Also, remember the "coverage" trap. The more you try to cover, the more you may be hiding.

Can active training methods spice up dry, uninteresting information? Absolutely! When the subject is interesting, it's easy to train. When it is dry, often the excitement of active training methods catches up with the participants and they become motivated to master even boring material.

When you use groups in active training, how do you prevent them from wasting time and being unproductive? Groups can be unproductive if an opening does not include introductions and a warm up at the beginning of the session and group work is not carefully structured from the outset. Participants become confused about what to do, organize themselves poorly, and easily get off task. Or they may do the work as quickly as possible, skimming the surface rather than digging into the material. There are several ways to facilitate participants how to learn in groups, such as assigning roles to group members, establishing group ground rules, and practicing group skills. Many tips and techniques in *Active Training* are geared to this problem.

Can you "group participants to death" using active training? Yes, it can happen. Some trainers overuse groups. They don't give participants enough chance to learn things individually and they don't bring the entire group together enough for teaching and discussion. The key is variety. A variety of learning modalities is the spice of good training. Several techniques in *Active Training* will give you alternatives to small-group learning.

Is there a danger that participants will misinform each other in group-based active training methods? That certainly could happen, but the advantages of giving learning a social side far outweigh the disadvantages. Anyway, a trainer can always review material with the entire group after participants try to learn it on their own and teach it to each other. And most questions or misinformation should come out when you debrief the activity.

Doesn't it require more preparation and creativity to teach using active training methods? Yes and no. Once you understand the process, the extra preparation and creativity will not feel like a burden. You will feel excited about your training and this energy will transfer to your participants' learning. Until then, you should find that creating ideas for active training can be challenging. At first, you will wonder how in the world you can teach certain topics actively. This is where *Active Training* comes in. It is intended to ease the transition by providing you with several concrete ways to build activity, variety, and participation into your training. These techniques are useful for virtually any subject matter.

I'm sold on active training, but I wonder if my participants will be. Millennials will enthusiastically embrace active training because they are good at learning by doing. They also don't mind the fast pace of activity. If you have other participants who are less accustomed to active training, they may be uneasy initially. They may be used to trainers who do all the work and to sitting back and believing that they have learned something and will retain it. Some participants may also complain that active training is a "waste of time." In the long run, all will benefit from active training. In the short run, they will be less anxious if you introduce active training gradually. If you don't, you may get some resistance.

Your participants need to know what to expect if your approach is new to them. Following is a statement you may wish to use to convey how the training will be conducted.

Welcome to Active Training!

This training session is based on the principles of active learning. The methods we will use are designed to

- Increase participation
- Enliven learning

- Deepen retention

- Encourage application

You will be asked lots of questions, urged to take a stab at an answer, explore, and try things out. You will also work, at times, with others and will be asked to test yourself periodically to see for yourself what you have learned and what skills you possess.

At all times, this session will be guided by the idea that it's not what *I tell you* that counts; it's what **you take away**.

In addition, I will not cover everything about our topic. I want you to feel that you have *really learned something* rather than having been *exposed to everything*. If I do a good job focusing on the most important topics, you will be able to learn the rest of what you need on your own.

THE DELIVERY OF ACTIVE TRAINING

Active Training is based on the assumption that you are training a group of participants at one site in either a physical or virtual classroom setting. An active approach to training, however, is not limited to this delivery mode but can be incorporated into other modes. Since the instructional design principles are essentially the same regardless of how training is delivered, the ideas in *Active Training* can be easily applied to a wide range of training approaches.

The use of e-learning is revolutionizing the way people obtain learning. The advantage of computer technology is its ability to provide more training, delivered sooner, in more places, and potentially at a lower cost, than traditional classroom-based instruction. The value of e-learning is enhanced when it is designed for maximum interactivity. Straightforward presentation of information even if it is replete with visual graphics, limits the learning experience. The use of questions, case problems, and simulations and the inclusion of interactive exercises expand the quality of learning that will be obtained. Such activities can be built into individuals' interactions in e-learning instruction through user input options that enable them to "talk" to the material. To add the social side of learning, it is also possible to bring together, both face-to-face and virtually, people who have experienced the same instruction and give them group activities to reinforce what they learned individually.

What makes learning exciting today is that learners can make their own decisions about how they best learn the material. They can learn in a synchronous physical or virtual classroom or in an asynchronous setting. Classroom-based instruction is linear; participants learn point A before point B. Nonlinear learning in an asynchronous learning situation allows participants to repeat material, skip material, and, in fact, begin and end whenever they want. Simply creating a technological version of a linear lecture would be a waste of the learner's time.

The issue of ensuring that learners have a chance to practice interpersonal behaviors used in areas such as presentations, coaching sessions, and sales calls is still a concern. Such skill-based learning includes input of the knowledge necessary to perform the skill, demonstration, preparation, practice application, feedback, and reapplication. The most critical of these steps are the quality and delivery of coaching and feedback and the reapplication. It is difficult for technology to deliver these steps as well as human beings can—at least for now. However, using blended learning or a flipped classroom for these topics is an excellent solution.

Using a blended learning solution is the best solution for many situations—not just those where practice is required. From an active training perspective, there are many exciting possibilities. Classroom instruction can be followed by e-learning activities or vice versa. Or the two can be mixed together so that periods of activity in both settings are alternated.

Classroom training can also be blended with other ways to foster learning, including mentoring, coaching, and informal learning.

Another delivery mode for active training is the use of "self-directed learning teams." In this approach, small groups of learners meet face-to-face at their convenience and experience training that has been designed by an "absent" trainer. Guided by materials that do not require a "live" trainer or outside facilitator, teams learn by themselves. The self-directed learning team has the following benefits:

- It promotes high levels of active learning.
- It develops a sense of "ownership" of training.
- It provides built-in social support for learning.
- It allows for different perspectives.
- It is based on a common language of understanding.
- It minimizes training costs and maximizes convenience.

In order for learning teams to be self-directing, well-organized learning packages are needed. Learning team participants benefit from professionally designed training program materials that not only have clear, useful content but also contain directions for active learning activities that promote involvement, retention, and application. While we do not address self-direct learning teams in *Active Training*, you can easily adapt many of the activities to materials provided to these teams.

According to the 2014 ATD State of the Industry Report 20 percent of all training delivered is instructor-led. Whether the training is online or in a classroom, participants must be actively involved. Active training requires the participants to use their brains, studying ideas, solving problems, and applying what they learn. The training is fast-paced, fun, supportive, and personally engaging. Often, participants leave their seats, moving about and thinking aloud. Or online instructors may ask participants to join a group in a breakout "room." This data emphasizes how important it is that all of us ensure that our organizations and employees receive the most out of all training that is delivered. We need to integrate the best active training techniques we have available.

Active training is a way to enliven classroom and virtual learning. Some of the techniques are fun and some are downright serious, but they are all intended to deepen understanding and retention. *Active Training* includes strategies to get participants active from the start through activities that encourage involvement and clarify participants' expectations. It also has strategies for conducting full-group and small-group learning, stimulating discussion and debate, practicing skills, prompting questions, and even getting the participants to teach each other. Finally, *Active Training* has techniques to help you review what's been learned, assess how participants have changed, and consider the next steps to ensure that the training sticks.

"I use 101 Ways as a course text."

Jane Bozarth
Author, *Social Media for Trainers*
and *Better Than Bullet Points*

Part Two

Designing an Active Training Program

Many exciting things have happened in learning and development since the third issue of *Active Training* was published in 2005. Even with the introduction of m-learning, massive open online courses (MOOCs), social learning, numerous tablets, and a host of other tools, techniques, and gadgets, *organizations continue to rely heavily on instructor-led training (ILT). According to the ATD State of the Industry Report (2014), instructor-led training accounted for 70 percent of training available, down about 10 percent over the past ten years. Organizations are beginning to utilize online ILT more often.*

An active training program is characterized by **activity, variety,** and **participation**. More specifically, eight qualities set it apart from other program designs. You will find that these eight qualities are required in all training events: ILT or self-directed, synchronous or asynchronous, in a webinar or classroom. The eight qualities that create successful active training include the following.

1. Moderate Level of Content

In designing training programs, too often the tendency is to cover the waterfront by throwing in everything possible about a given subject. After all, you only get one shot at these participants, so you'd better make sure you have covered it all. You may fail to realize, however, that participants will forget far more than they will ever learn. The best approach is to be selective, choosing the "need to know" before the "nice to know." Training programs that promote active learning have a lean curriculum. They concentrate on the critical learning areas—those elements of the subject that provide the essential basis for building later. When the content level is kept moderate, the trainer has the time to design activities that introduce, present, apply, and reflect upon what is being learned.

2. Balance between Affective, Behavioral, and Cognitive Learning

Active training involves a three-pronged approach: fostering attitudes, developing and practicing skills, and promoting understanding of the concepts and models behind the subject. Although some training programs tend to focus on one of these areas to the exclusion of the others, you want participants not only to know about something, but also to be able to do it. Furthermore, you want them to look at themselves in relation to what you are teaching and to consider how it works for them.

3. Variety of Learning Approaches

Active training employs a wide assortment of training methods. A variety of learning approaches keeps interest alive and can help to minimize the downtimes when energy levels are low. Another and even more important argument for variety is that adults learn in different ways. Using different learning approaches is likely to be more effective than a single approach that may work for some but not for others. Time allocations, group formats, and the physical setting can also be varied to heighten the training experience.

4. Opportunities for Group Participation

Group participation has advantages in any training program. Involving the group moves training from the passive to the active. Group activity engages participants in the learning process and makes them working partners with the trainer. Lecturing is held to a minimum as highly participatory methods like role playing, simulated exercises, and case discussions are featured.

5. Utilization of Participants' Expertise

Each participant in a training program brings relevant experiences to the learning event. Some of these experiences will be directly applicable; others may involve analogies from previous jobs or situations.

In either case, much of the active learning in a training program comes from one's peers. You can build into your design many opportunities for participants to learn from each other.

6. Recycling of Earlier Learned Concepts and Skills

Programs that feature active training have designs that are continually referring back to and incorporating earlier skills and concepts. In effect, the curriculum spirals. Participants get the chance to review what they have already learned and apply it to more challenging tasks. What has previously been taught is rarely passed over, never to appear again. Instead, key concepts and skills get reintroduced as the program becomes more advanced.

7. Real-Life Problem Solving

Active training designs emphasize the real world. Opportunities are set up for the participants to utilize course content to address and help solve actual problems they are currently experiencing. Application is not only something that happens after training; it is a major focus during training. Participants learn best when they get to work on their own material, cases, and examples. This gives the information immediacy and enables participants to assess its utility on the spot.

8. Allowance for Future Planning

At the conclusion of any training program, participants will naturally ask, "Now what?" The success of an active training program is really measured by how that question is answered—that is, how what has been learned in the course is transferred to the job. An active training design ends with consideration of the next steps participants will take and the obstacles they will face as they implement new ideas and skills.

STEPS FOR DESIGNING ACTIVE TRAINING

When you go about the task of designing a training program that reflects these eight qualities, you face a creative challenge not unlike an artist's. Many decisions are ahead, and there is no right way to make them all. There are also different ways to create the same effect. Consequently, there is no orderly way to proceed. Many instructional designers, in fact, don't always function their best by proceeding in a step-by-step progression. The following sequence of steps, however, should serve as a general guide to designing an active training program.

1. Assess the Need for Training and the Participants

The first step in designing an active training program is to determine what, if any, training need exists and to find out as much as possible about the participants who will be affected. If this information cannot be collected prior to training, assessment activities should be incorporated into the beginning of the program. The more assessment data you can obtain, the better it is for planning, customizing, and modifying a design.

2. Set General Learning Goals

With the assessment data in mind, identify potential learning goals for participants. In general terms, describe their needs in the areas of affective awareness, cognitive understanding, behavioral skill building, real-life problem solving, and on-the-job application.

3. Specify Objectives

Get specific about the kinds of learning you want the participants to experience and the results you want to achieve. Each general learning goal will have one or more objectives that, when met, will signal accomplishment of that goal. State these objectives in a form that will make them effective tools for managing, monitoring, and evaluating the training.

4. Design Training Activities

Now that the objectives have been clearly and explicitly stated, you design training activities to achieve them. At this stage, it's sufficient to generate the broad outline (method and format) of all the activities you think will be necessary for each objective in your program. List the possibilities in pencil, on index cards, on a personal computer, or in any other medium in which you can easily change, rearrange, or eliminate them.

5. Sequence Training Activities

Play with the order of activities until you obtain a sequence that has a good mixture. Consider which designs are needed for the beginning, middle, and end of your program. Adjust activities to improve the flow.

6. Start Detailed Planning

Now begin working on the details, specifying how to conduct each activity in your overall design. Decide on timing, introductory remarks, key points and instructions, materials, setting, and ways to end.

7. Revise Design Details

Mentally walk through the overall design, visualizing the participants' experience. Revise any details (particularly timing and instructions) so that each activity complements the ones that precede and/or follow it. Delete any designs that now seem unnecessary, impractical, or ill conceived. Develop contingency plans in case time runs short or the group is more or less skilled than you thought, as well as for any other turn of events you can imagine.

8. Evaluate the Total Result

Examine the program to see if it has the eight characteristics of an active training program. If you see flaws at this point, redesign to achieve a better result.

Designing is never static. It's an ongoing process in which you try things out, perhaps making revisions even as the program is being implemented; obtain feedback from participants; evaluate participant performance; and then modify the design for the next time around. The continuing challenges you'll face in designing an active training program are their own reward. The process is creative, exhilarating, and reinforcing, and the outcome is not only something in which you can take pride in but also a real benefit to the people you are training.

WHAT'S IN THE PART TWO CHAPTERS? The ten chapters that comprise Part Two have been sequenced in order to assist you, step by step, in the process of designing an active training program. The chapters are filled with examples drawn from real-life training situations to illustrate every point made. Here is an overview of their contents.

Chapter 1 explains and illustrates how to assess a training group prior to the start of a program in order to help determine course content, obtain case material, and establish an early relationship with participants.

Chapter 2 tells how the development of training objectives drives the design of a training program and illustrates how objectives are specified, expressed, and presented to participants.

Chapter 3 shows how to create opening exercises that promote team building, on-the-spot assessment, and immediate learning involvement. It also suggests ten ways to obtain participation in the opening phase of a training program.

Chapter 4 describes ways to gain interest in a presentation, maximize understanding and retention, invite audience participation, and reinforce what has been presented.

Chapter 5 discusses and illustrates strategies to avoid or reinforce a lecture presentation.

Chapter 6 shows how role playing, games and simulations, observation, mental imagery, writing tasks, and projects can be utilized to achieve affective and behavioral learning.

Chapter 7 demonstrates how training activities are formed around a purpose, method, and format. It further provides guidelines for detailed construction of active training activities and criteria for including those activities in an overall design.

Chapter 8 suggests ways to sequence training activities in order to achieve an effective mix and flow.

Chapter 9 illustrates the overall structure and flavor of an active training program and outlines the steps you should take to plan one of your own.

Chapter 10 focuses on the role that active training plays in e-learning. You will notice that we have incorporated e-learning examples throughout the book, just as it occurs in our organizations. We still felt e-learning also deserves a chapter of its own to highlight social learning and m-learning.

As you navigate each chapter, avoid being a passive reader. Identify a design problem you are currently facing or anticipate facing in the future and keep it in mind as you read. By maintaining a problem-solving mindset rather than an information-receiving one, you will be an active reader.

To further encourage your participation, you will find a worksheet at the end of each chapter in Part Two that will give you an opportunity to apply what you have learned. You may also find questions and brief exercises. Each of these ensures that we are providing you with the tools required of an active trainer.

"Mel was an inspiration to us all. This book is the perfect remembrance to Mel."

Teri B Lund
Strategic Assessment & Evaluation LLC

Chapter One

Assessing Training Needs

All too often, the training needs in an organization are viewed in isolation from the bottom-line results that the organization is seeking. As a result, training courses are not part of an overall strategy for performance improvement that supports organizational goals. When this occurs, the design of a training program is often approached on a hit-or-miss basis. Some trainers decide what they want to teach (or receive orders from management) without sufficient regard for what the participants need to learn so that the organization can succeed. All this can be avoided by making an effort to assess the need for training and the training participants prior to training. Gathering information about the training need and the actual or potential participants is the first step in designing an active training program from scratch or tailoring an existing one for a specific group.

Sometimes the opportunity to assess the training situation is limited by time constraints and a lack of availability of data. Even in less than ideal circumstances, however, some assessment is necessary before finalizing the design. At the very least, it is helpful to obtain whatever information you can to answer the following questions:

1. What is the nature of the roles and tasks performed by the intended participants? What competencies do these roles and tasks require?

2. How many participants will there be?

3. How familiar are the participants with the subject matter of the training program?

4. What are the ages, sexes, or other important descriptive factors of the participants?

5. What are their attitudes and beliefs relevant to the training topic?

6. What successes and problems have the participants encountered?

7. What is the competence level of the participants?

8. Is the training voluntary or mandatory?

9. How well do the participants know one another?

10. What, if any, expectations do the participants' supervisors have with regard to the training program?

WHY DO ASSESSMENT?

When a problem exists within an organization, the first impulse is often to solve it with a training program. But training is not always the right solution, because the root cause of the problem is not always a lack of knowledge or skill. Instead, according to Gilbert (1996), it might also be any of the following:

- Unclear performance expectations and poor performance feedback
- Lack of tools, resources, and materials to do the job
- Inadequate financial and other rewards
- A poor match between employees' skills and the requirements of the job
- Lack of assurance of job security

Consequently, before even thinking about developing a training program, you need to determine whether training is the answer to the concerns being addressed. This requires an assessment process that, at its minimum, involves three steps:

1. **Pinpoint the problem** by interviewing the client, uncovering underlying issues, and identifying key stakeholders.

2. **Confirm the problem** by interviewing stakeholders, assessing the effect of the problem on the organization.

3. **Seek solutions** by identifying possible actions and gaining consensus on an action plan.

If the problem can be solved with training, some form of assessment is needed to **help determine the training content.** For instance, your group may need certain information or skills more than others. Perhaps the group has some prior exposure to the training topic and now requires more advanced knowledge and skills. Or possibly the group faces certain problems that will affect how much they can apply what you are going to teach them. Without such assessment information, it will be difficult to gear your program to the participants' needs.

Here are some examples of how assessment work completed prior to the training program paid off.

EXAMPLE: A bank manager felt that his customer service personnel needed further product knowledge training. An assessment survey revealed that what they needed more than additional product knowledge was training on how to sell the bank products to potential customers. The subsequent training was well received by the participants and led to increased sales figures for the branches.

EXAMPLE: A trainer in a large retail organization was about to deliver the company's standard course for store managers. She learned from exit interviews of store employers that their biggest reason for leaving was a lack of recognition by managers. She decided to add a module on employee recognition, a topic that had not been previously included in the standard course.

There are other good reasons to do assessment prior to the training program. When designing training activities, it is extremely helpful to **obtain case material** directly from the workplace or personal situation of the participants. If you do this, your designs can be based on real issues participants actually face rather than on simulated or "canned" material. Here are two examples.

EXAMPLE: For a sales training course in a pharmaceutical company, a trainer obtained examples of how area sales managers failed to collect ongoing feedback from account holders who had made recent purchases. The examples were woven into role-playing exercises that successfully engaged participants who previously had disliked the "artificiality" of role playing.

EXAMPLE: Prior to a training program, Head Start teachers were asked to list the most common problem behaviors they faced in their classrooms. The list was utilized in a course worksheet in which participants were asked to evaluate their consistency as classroom managers. The teachers reported that their evaluations were highly revealing because their own lists had been used.

One further reason to conduct assessments is the opportunity it affords to **develop a relationship with participants** prior to meeting them at the training site. Sending a questionnaire to participants, for instance, can be an occasion for writing about yourself and your plans for the upcoming program or for learning about their expectations. Phoning, emailing, or visiting some or all of the participants for an assessment interview can represent a chance to get acquainted in depth. Having some prior contact with participants reduces the feeling of awkwardness when you meet in the session at the start of the program. Here are two examples. If time is short, you could use several of the quick assessment tools available, such as SurveyMonkey, QuestionPro, Zoomerang, SurveyGizmo, or others.

EXAMPLE: A training consultant was asked to conduct a course on organizational change for a management team in an insurance company. When he learned that some members strongly opposed the course, he arranged a meeting prior to the start-up date to gain their trust and interest to participate. The consultant clarified the agenda of the course and responded to the concerns of the group. At the conclusion of the meeting, he obtained not only their agreement to participate but also their commitment to play an active role in planning the course. In the end, he was able to build in content that addressed their needs.

EXAMPLE: A trainer decided to interview some of the participants who would attend her course on performance appraisals. Knowing that management had been unhappy about the quality level of performance appraisals in the organization, the trainer began each interview with both frankness and reassurance by saying, "I have been asked by management to develop a training program to improve the ways performance appraisals are conducted here. I said I wanted to talk to some of the participants first before I planned the program. I'd like to learn straight from the source what actually happens in conducting performance appraisals as they are set up now. That way I might learn more about the problems that are occurring." Word circulated about the interviews and helped to establish greater acceptance of the training program that followed.

To summarize, three major reasons exist for assessing participants prior to the beginning of a training program:

1. It helps to determine the training content.
2. It allows you to obtain case material.
3. It gives you an opportunity to develop a relationship with participants.

WHAT INFORMA- TION SHOULD BE COLLECTED?

As you think about the kinds of information that would be useful to you, consider first asking participants directly ***what are their training needs.*** Going straight to the participants for their input gives them a hand in helping to design their own program. Moreover, involving them in this manner is usually well appreciated.

One simple way to do this for a public workshop is to send out a brief questionnaire similar to the one shown in Figure 1.1. You can attach it to a course registration or confirmation form.

FIGURE 1.1 STRESS MANAGEMENT WORKSHOP PARTICIPANT QUESTIONNAIRE

In order to make your stress management workshop productive for you, please take a few minutes to respond to the following:

1. My current job position is:

2. I have been to a stress management workshop before.

    _____ never   _____ once before   _____ twice or more before

3. I would benefit by a general overview of stress management strategies.

    (no need)   1   2   3   4   5   (strong need)

4. I need to learn more about physical health and stress.

    (no need)   1   2   3   4   5   (strong need)

5. I need to know what stress management resources are available.

    (no need)   1   2   3   4   5   (strong need)

6. I need to know how to manage my emotions more productively.

    (no need)   1   2   3   4   5   (strong need)

FIGURE 1.1 continued

---

7. I need to know how to use relaxation techniques.

(no need)　　1　　2　　3　　4　　5　　(strong need)

8. I need to learn more about developing myself spiritually.

(no need)　　1　　2　　3　　4　　5　　(strong need)

9. What other needs or areas of interest do you have?

10. List three specific questions that you hope this workshop will be able to answer for you:

a. _____

b. _____

c. _____

Please mail this questionnaire in the enclosed envelope before September 25.

Thank you.

For an in-house program, consider sending a pre-course questionnaire similar to the one described in the following case example.

Example: A training department instituted the practice of sending a pre-course participant feedback form to all participants of upcoming courses. It asked three basic questions:

1. What are your expectations of the course you are about to take?

2. Based on the course description, how do you perceive this program helping you in your current position?

3. What additional objectives or needs would you like the course to address?

Such a form usually gains widespread acceptance because it is perceived as a positive desire to meet the needs of company employees.

Besides participants' wishes, many other areas are worth exploring, both with the participants and with others who know them. First and foremost is information concerning the ***nature of the participants' work situations:***

- What are the participants' responsibilities? What does their job entail?
- Whom do they report to or relate to?
- In what aspects of their work will the skills and knowledge you will teach be employed?

If you were asked to conduct a program on meeting management, for example, you would want to know to what extent the participants' work involved team meetings and what those meetings were like. If you were conducting a public workshop on conflict resolution, knowing whether or not most of your participants are usually the victims in conflict situations would make a big difference in your design.

Next in importance is information about the ***knowledge, skills, and attitudes of the participants:***

- How familiar are participants with the content of your training program?
- How much opportunity have they had to practice or utilize skills that have been demonstrated to them previously?
- What are their feelings about the training topic? Do they value its importance?

Suppose you were designing a program on coaching and counseling skills for managers. It would be useful to assess what skills they already have acquired about coaching new employees or what attitudes they have held about the value of counseling troubled employees. Likewise, you would benefit from knowing how many participants in a weight control program have ever seriously exercised or what they fear about being thin.

Finally, it is helpful to find out any ***conditions that will affect participant involvement*** in the training program:

- What kind of support are participants likely to receive in implementing the training they are given?
- Are participants worried about their level of competence relative to that of other participants?

- Do participants feel they have been sent to the program because someone thinks they need to be "fixed"?

- Are participants unaccustomed to the active learning methods you hope to employ?

Assume, for example, that you have been asked to conduct a program for employees with writing deficiencies. Naturally, it would be useful to know if these employees have merely been sent to the program as opposed to having been positively encouraged by their supervisors to improve their skills.

Notice in the two questionnaires shown in Figures 1.2 and 1.3 how several areas of assessment information are tapped.

FIGURE 1.2 HEALTHCARE CUSTOMER SERVICE TRAINING PARTICIPANT QUESTIONNAIRE

Please take a few moments to complete this questionnaire. Your answers will be used to tailor the direction and content of our upcoming customer service training program here at Vital Health System. Thank you in advance for taking the time to respond. Your response will be considered confidential and will not be revealed to anyone other than the training program designers.

1. My work is primarily (check one): clinical _____ non-clinical _____

2. The people I would like to provide better customer service to are (check as many as apply):

    ___ patients   ___ supervisors
    ___ patients' family members   ___ vendors
    ___ doctors   ___ subordinates
    ___ co-workers   ___ visitors
    ___ other _____

3. Indicate the degree of difficulty you have providing excellent customer service in the following situations:

	Easy	Somewhat difficult	Very difficult
on the telephone	____	____	____
providing service to people from other cultures	____	____	____
difficult customers	____	____	____
angry or upset customers	____	____	____
delivering bad news or a "no" answer	____	____	____
when customer wants an apology	____	____	____
when there are a lot of customers	____	____	____
when under stress	____	____	____

FIGURE 1.2 continued
---

4. Describe three skills you would like to learn in this session:

   a.

   b.

   c.

5. Briefly describe a recent challenging situation in which you provided excellent customer service.

6. Briefly describe a recent situation in which you found it difficult to provide your best customer service.

7. Complete the following sentence:

   One of the reasons that make it difficult for me to provide good customer service is

   _____

8. Check the following terms associated with customer service that you are familiar with:

___ escalating the situation	___ service recovery
___ reading intent	___ Press Ganey
___ building rapport	___ expressing empathy
___ "I" messages	___ moments of truth

FIGURE 1.3 BANK TRAINING PARTICIPANT QUESTIONNAIRE

A new account management tool is being implemented at the bank. The tool will impact one of the existing software tools, Business First. Business First is a workflow management tool that is used by the analysts to make a decision on applications for business credit cards. The training session you will attend is designed to help users understand how the new account management tool will impact their daily activities in Business First. Your responses to this brief questionnaire will assist us in maximizing the value of this training.

FIGURE 1.3 continued
---

1. What is your current position? _____

2. From the list below, please circle the tasks that you perform within your role at the bank. If a task is not listed, please state what that task is in the space provided for "Other."

   a. Work apps in queues

   b. Contact customer

   c. App data entry

   d. Decision apps

   e. Assign credit lines

   f. Issue new cards

   g. Manage team of analysts

   h. Determine credit policies

   i. Other: _____

3. Below is a list of terms you may or may not be familiar with. For each term, check the statement that best describes your understanding of the term.

   a. New Account Build

      ☐ Never heard of it! What is it?

      ☐ Heard about it, but not sure what it does!

      ☐ Understand the basics behind the concept.

      ☐ I've got it covered.

   b. Existing Account Check

      ☐ Never heard of it! What is it?

      ☐ Heard about it, but not sure what it does!

      ☐ Understand the basics behind the concept.

      ☐ I've got it covered.

   c. TSYS

      ☐ Never heard of it! What is it?

      ☐ Heard about it, but not sure what it does!

      ☐ Understand the basics behind the concept.

      ☐ I've got it covered.

FIGURE 1.3 continued

---

d. CPS

☐ Never heard of it! What is it?

☐ Heard about it, but not sure what it does!

☐ Understand the basics behind the concept.

☐ I've got it covered.

4. Have you ever participated in the testing of the Business First system?
___ yes   ___ no

5. Rate the performance of the Business First system (i.e., speed, reliability, user friendliness) on the scale below. If needed, please give more detail behind your rating.

___ 1 (excellent)

___ 2

___ 3

___ 4

___ 5 (poor)

What questions or concerns would you like to see addressed in the training session?

HOW CAN INFORMATION BE COLLECTED?

If you had unlimited time and resources, how would you ideally collect information for a training program you were designing? Would you only utilize a questionnaire? Give this question some thought and then compare your ideas to the chart in Figure 1.4. As Figure 1.4 indicates, you can choose among a wide variety of techniques to gather assessment information. In addition, you can easily combine some of them. Here is a case example.

FIGURE 1.4 ADVANTAGES AND DISADVANTAGES OF NINE BASIC NEEDS ASSESSMENT TECHNIQUES

	Advantages	*Disadvantages*
Observation		
• Can be as technical as time-motion studies or as functionally or behaviorally specific as observing a new board member interacting during a meeting.	• Minimizes the interruption of routine work flow or group activity.	• Requires a highly skilled observer with both process and content knowledge (unlike an interviewer who needs, for the most part, only process skill).
• May be as unstructured as walking through an agency's offices on the lookout for evidence of communication barriers.	• Generates in situ data, highly relevant to the situation where response to identified training needs/interests will impact.	• Carries limitations that derive from being able to collect data only within the work setting (the other side of the first advantage listed in the preceding column).
• Can be used normatively to distinguish between effective and ineffective behaviors, organizational structures, and/or process.	• (When combined with a feedback step) provides for important comparison checks between inferences of the observer and the respondent.	• Holds potential for respondents to perceive the observation activity as "spying."
Questionnaires		
• May be in the form of surveys or polls of a random or stratified sample of respondents, or an enumeration of an entire "population."	• Can reach a large number of people in a short time.	• Make little provision for free expression of unanticipated responses.
• Can use a variety of question formats: open-ended, projective, forced-choice, priority-ranking.	• Are relatively inexpensive.	• Require substantial time (and technical skills, especially in survey model) for development of effective instruments.
• Can take alternative forms such as Q-sorts, slip-sorts, or rating scales, either pre-designed or self-generated by respondent(s).	• Give opportunity of expression without fear of embarrassment.	• Are of limited utility in getting at causes of problems or possible solutions.
• May be self-administered (by mail) under controlled or uncontrolled conditions, or may require the presence of an interpreter or assistant.	• Yield data easily summarized and reported.	• Suffer low return rates (mailed), grudging responses, or unintended and/or inappropriate respondents.

FIGURE 1.4 continued

	Advantages	*Disadvantages*

Key Consultation

• Secures information from those persons who, by virtue of their formal or informal standing, are in a good position to know what the training needs of a particular group are: a. board chairman b. related service providers c. members of professional associations d. individuals from the service population • Once identified, data can be gathered from these consultants by using techniques such as interviews, group discussions, questionnaires.	• Is relatively simple and inexpensive to conduct. • Permits input and interaction of a number of individuals, each with his or her own perspectives of the needs of the area, discipline, group, etc. • Establishes and strengthens lines of communication between participants in the process.	• Carries a built-in bias, since it is based on views of those who tend to see training needs from their own individual or organizational perspective. • May result in only a partial picture of training needs due to the typically non-representative nature (in a statistical sense) of a key informant group.

Print Media

• Can include professional journals, legislative news/notes, industry "rags," trade magazines, in-house publications.	• Is an excellent source of information for uncovering and clarifying normative needs. • Provides information that is current, if not forward-looking. • Is readily available and is apt to have already been reviewed by the client group.	• Can be a problem when it comes to the data analysis and synthesis into a useable form (use of clipping service of key consultants can make this type of data more useable).

FIGURE 1.4 continued

	Advantages	*Disadvantages*

Interviews

- Can be formal or casual, structured or unstructured, or somewhere in between.
- May be used with a sample of a particular group (board, staff, committee) or conducted with everyone concerned.
- Can be done in person, by phone, at the work site, or away from it.

- Are adept at revealing feelings, causes of and possible solutions to problems which the client is facing (or anticipates); provide maximum opportunity for the client to represent himself spontaneously on his own terms (especially when conducted in an open-ended, non-directive manner).

- Are usually time-consuming.
- Can be difficult to analyze and quantify results (especially from unstructured formats).
- Unless the interviewer is skilled, the client(s) can easily be made to feel self-conscious.
- Rely for success on a skillful interviewer who can generate data without making client(s) feel self-conscious, suspicious, etc.

Group Discussion

- Resembles face-to-face interview technique, e.g., structured or unstructured, formal or informal, or somewhere in between.
- Can be focused on job (role) analysis, group problem analysis, group goal setting, or any number of group tasks or themes, e.g., "leadership training needs of the board."
- Uses one or several of the familiar group facilitating techniques: brainstorming, nominal group process, force-fields, consensus rankings, organizational mirroring, simulation, and sculpting.

- Permits on-the-spot synthesis of different viewpoints.
- Builds support for the particular service response that is ultimately decided on.
- Decreased client's "dependence response" toward the service provider since data analysis is (or can be) a shared function.
- Helps participants to become better problem analysts, better listeners, etc.

- Is time-consuming (therefore initially expensive) both for the consultant and the agency.
- Can produce data that are difficult to synthesize and quantify (more a problem with the less structured techniques).

FIGURE 1.4 continued

	Advantages	*Disadvantages*

Tests

- Are a hybridized form of questionnaire.
- Can be very functionally oriented (like observations) to test a board, staff, or committee member's proficiency.
- May be used to sample learned ideas and facts.
- Can be administered with or without the presence of an assistant.

- Can be especially helpful in determining whether the cause of a recognized problem is a deficiency in knowledge or skill or, by elimination, attitude.
- Results are easily quantifiable and comparable.

- The availability of a relatively small number of tests that are validated for a specific situation.
- Do not indicate if measured knowledge and skills are actually being used in the on-the-job or "back-home group" situation.

Records, Reports

- Can consist of organizational charts, planning documents, policy manuals, audits, and budget reports.
- Employee records (grievance, turnover, accidents, etc.).
- Includes minutes of meetings, weekly, monthly program reports, memoranda, agency service records, program evaluation studies.

- Provide excellent clues to trouble spots.
- Provide objective evidence of the results of problems within the agency or group.
- Can be collected with a minimum of effort and interruption of work flow since it already exists at the work site.

- Causes of problems or possible solutions often do not show up.
- Carries perspective that generally reflects the past situation rather than the current one (or recent changes).
- Need a skilled data analyst if clear patterns and trends are to emerge from such technical and diffuse raw data.

FIGURE 1.4 continued		
	Advantages	*Disadvantages*

Work Samples

• Are similar to observation but in written form.	• Carry most of the advantages of records and reports data.	• Case study method will take time away from actual work of the organization.
• Can be products generated in the course of the organization's work, e.g., ad layouts, program proposals, market analyses, letters, training designs.	• Are the organization's data (its own output).	• Need specialized content analysts.
• Written responses to a hypothetical but relevant case study provided by the consultant.		• Analyst's assessment of strengths/weaknesses disclosed by samples can be challenged as "too subjective."

Source: Steadham, 1980, pp. 56–61. Copyright 1980 by the American Society for Training and Development, Inc. Reprinted with permission. All rights reserved.

EXAMPLE: The president of a credit union contracted out for a team-building program for his senior management team. In preparation for the program, the trainer requested a copy of the new business plan that the team had recently submitted to its board of directors and a copy of the minutes of the team's weekly meetings in the last two months. He also interviewed the president and the three vice presidents of the credit union. These interviews focused on the problems facing the entire twelve-member team. On the basis of the interviews, the trainer designed a questionnaire. Before all the team members were sent the questionnaire, the interviewees were asked to evaluate and approve the first draft. Several items were reworded to use language that was friendly to the group. Figure 1.5 reproduces the final questionnaire, preceded by the message that accompanied it.

FIGURE 1.5 SENIOR MANAGEMENT EMAILED QUESTIONNAIRE

Dear (Team Member):

I am a team-building consultant who has been asked to conduct a special two-day course with the senior management staff of your credit union.

FIGURE 1.5 continued

As your organization is making a clear commitment to its own professional growth and development, I hope that you will see these two days as a valuable opportunity to communicate with each other without the constraints of daily deadlines and to build relationships with each other that will make you feel cohesive and united in purpose.

We will begin with some activities designed to "warm us up" and help us feel good about working together as a group. Following this, there will be some skill-building exercises to increase your group's effectiveness as a problem-solving team. The third phase of the course (and the longest) will be focused on identifying issues that need to be worked through in order to maximize your future effectiveness as a group.

An excellent way to begin doing some of this work is to collect information through a questionnaire and to feed back that information for group discussion during the course. I would like you to join with your colleagues in filling out the attached questionnaire. Your honest responses will enable the group to gain a clear view of itself.

Your participation will be totally anonymous. My job will be to *summarize* the results and report them to you for your reactions.

Thank you in advance for your cooperation and support. I look forward to working with you.

1. To what extent do you agree or disagree with the following statements?

   a. We avoid conflict among ourselves to keep things peaceful.
      (strongly disagree)   1   2   3   4   5   6   7   (strongly agree)

   b. We are dedicated to the credit union movement.
      (strongly disagree)   1   2   3   4   5   6   7   (strongly agree)

   c. We speak up when we need to; there can be healthy disagreements among us.
      (strongly disagree)   1   2   3   4   5   6   7   (strongly agree)

   d. We don't communicate with each other frequently enough.
      (strongly disagree)   1   2   3   4   5   6   7   (strongly agree)

   e. It's not always clear who's responsible for a certain assignment or problem ("I thought you were going to do it").
      (strongly disagree)   1   2   3   4   5   6   7   (strongly agree)

   f. Others don't understand my operation and its needs.
      (strongly disagree)   1   2   3   4   5   6   7   (strongly agree)

   g. There's little backbiting around here.
      (strongly disagree)   1   2   3   4   5   6   7   (strongly agree)

FIGURE 1.5 continued

---

h. We have a tendency to be unrealistic.
   (strongly disagree)   1   2   3   4   5   6   7   (strongly agree)

i. There are different beliefs among us about the way the credit union
   should conduct its business and relate to members.
   (strongly disagree)   1   2   3   4   5   6   7   (strongly agree)

j. Men and women in our group can work comfortably together.
   (strongly disagree)   1   2   3   4   5   6   7   (strongly agree)

k. We give each other recognition and words of appreciation.
   (strongly disagree)   1   2   3   4   5   6   7   (strongly agree)

l. It's hard to know what others think about the issues and problems
   around here.
   (strongly disagree)   1   2   3   4   5   6   7   (strongly agree)

m. We are well organized, with clearly defined procedures. Things
   run smoothly here.
   (strongly disagree)   1   2   3   4   5   6   7   (strongly agree)

n. Decisions are controlled from the top.
   (strongly disagree)   1   2   3   4   5   6   7   (strongly agree)

2. Because the president holds the key leadership role in this credit
   union, it would be helpful to provide him with some feedback. Please
   comment about the following:
   What are some things you would like the president to

   a. Continue doing?

   b. Stop doing?

   c. Start doing?

3. What suggestions do you have to maximize your teamwork and team
   effectiveness in the future?

As a result of the data obtained from the reports, interviews, and questionnaire, the trainer discovered that two problems significantly affected the effectiveness of this team: (1) a lack of understanding of the needs of each work unit in the credit union and (2) poor team meetings. The standard course on team building offered by the trainer was redesigned in order to give significant attention to these two problem areas.

One additional technique for assessing participants may be considered in addition to those already discussed. If conditions warrant, a trainer can give a ***pre-course assignment*** to participants both to learn about their skills and to obtain case material for the course, as shown in the following example.

EXAMPLE: A pre-course assignment was used in a train-the-trainer program. The confirmation reproduced in Figure 1.6 was emailed to participants. When Part One of the assignment was returned, it was possible to assess how well the participants were able to specify training objectives. Part One was also used as an exercise in the training program: When the portion of the program devoted to the skill of specifying objectives had been completed, participants were asked to rewrite their own statement of objectives. Part Two of the assignment also served to provide course material for the program.

FIGURE 1.6 TRAIN-THE-TRAINER PRE-COURSE ASSIGNMENT

TO: Participant
FROM: Human Resources Department
SUBJECT: Administrative Information and Pre-Course Assignment

We are pleased to confirm your enrollment in the Active Training program that is being conducted at the Federal Plaza Building on June 30 through July 2.

As our organization changes, the ability to train and develop people on the job has become increasingly critical. Our main purpose in this seminar is to help managers and professional staff to effectively and efficiently share their expertise with others.

This seminar is designed to help you improve your effectiveness in any training you may be asked to do. Our goal is to help you with your specific training needs. To ensure that we can accomplish this, please complete Part One of the pre-course.

Assignment by Monday, June 22.

PART I

COMPLETE AND RETURN TO *(trainer)*

AT *(place)* BY *(date)*

Select a topic that you might be asked to teach over a two- to three-hour period.

This topic could be something that you've already taught in a training program or a topic that you can imagine teaching in the future.

What are your objectives for this session? Outline them below.

PART II

COMPLETE AND BRING TO CLASS ON *(date)*

Choose a fifteen-minute segment from the training topic you described in Part One and follow these directions:

- Specify your objectives for this fifteen-minute segment.
- Think about how you would present this fifteen-minute segment.
- Identify the instructional materials, if any, you would use. *Please bring an example of these materials to class.*
- Develop an outline of your presentation.

NOTE: *On the second day of the program, you will be asked to present this material to four or five other participants. In this way, you will get some useful feedback on your presentation style.*

WHAT IF THERE IS NO TIME TO DO A PROPER ASSESSMENT?

The last question to be considered is a practical one. Not all situations are ideal; obstacles to undertaking assessment data collection do arise. With significant lead time, you can utilize many of the techniques outlined here. But you may easily face a situation in which a training program has to be designed and implemented hastily and/or the identity of the participants is largely unknown (this is particularly true for public workshops).

When these problems occur, try not to be discouraged. You will, of necessity, have to design the program by making your best guesses about the nature of the participants and their needs. However, you will still have some ability to obtain quick information and adjust the design accordingly. Here are some recommendations:

1. Phone a contact person who may have some familiarity with the participants and ask that person the basic questions listed at the beginning of this chapter.

2. Phone a few known participants, introduce yourself, and ask them some key questions. Hope that their responses are representative and treat them as a sample of the larger group. Or ask a contact person to set up a phone interview schedule for you.

3. Have any relevant materials (surveys, meeting notes, or records) delivered to you.

4. Contact other trainers who have worked with your training group to get their opinions and impressions.

5. Talk to participants who arrive early on the day of the program and obtain whatever information you can.

6. Design some activities at the beginning of the program that will enable you to make some assessments of the group. (More information about this is given in Chapter 3.)

If you have done some contingent planning in your overall design, it still should be possible to make final adjustments before your session begins.

WORKSHEET

ASSESSING TRAINING NEEDS

Before going on to the next chapter, try your hand at applying the ideas in this chapter. Use this worksheet to outline how you might assess participants for your next training program.

Information Desired: (check as many as desired)

_____ Participants' stated needs

_____ The nature of the participants' work

_____ Participants' knowledge

_____ Participants' skills

_____ Participants' attitudes

_____ Conditions affecting participant involvement

Methods Desired: (check as many as desired)

_____ Observation   _____ Print media   _____ Tests

_____ Questionnaire   _____ Interview   _____ Records, reports

_____ Key consultation _____ Group discussion _____ Work samples

Assessment Outline:

_____

_____

_____

_____

_____

_____

_____

_____

_____

_____

_____

_____

_____

◆   ◆   ◆

Chapter Two

Developing Active Training Objectives

After assessing participants, you are in a position to start planning your training program. At this stage, it is not enough to simply list the topics you intend to cover. An active training program is constructed in terms of the achievement of objectives. *The critical question, therefore, is not what topics to cover but what you want participants to value, understand, or do with those topics.* A clear sense of where you want to go and what you are trying to accomplish is the single most important ingredient for designing active training programs.

Determining training objectives may take long-term thinking up front, but it is worth it. Objectives are the pillars of your program, not constraints. The single best reason to work hard on developing training objectives is that objectives drive your training design. When you are designing a training program, you are figuring out what steps will lead to the accomplishment of your objectives. If you are not clear about your objectives, you might overlook some of the learning experiences that your participants require. Here is a case in point.

EXAMPLE: A trainer's assessment revealed that a group of real estate sales learners knew little about the closing process in the sale of properties. Consequently, the trainer decided to cover this topic in his real estate course. He did a good job of explaining how a closing is done, but afterward participants still seemed hazy about how to conduct a closing themselves. Wanting to improve the situation, he decided to ask experienced sales personnel to identify the specific on-the-job skills the learners would need to possess when dealing with closings. Their responses enabled him to develop a clear set of objectives for the next time he taught the course. Specifically, he concluded that learners needed to be able to

- Describe the closing cost payments for which the buyer would be responsible.
- Clearly and concisely answer typical customer questions about closing costs.
- Estimate closing cost payments for different types of properties.

With these defined, the program was redesigned to include experiences that not only taught the closing process but also tested the group's understanding of the process and allowed ample opportunities to practice situations in which this knowledge would be applied on the job.

When you set training objectives, you also wind up setting appropriate limits on how much material you will cover. Active trainers keep their content level moderate because they are serious about achieving their objectives. They realize that covering too much material is a sure way to prevent real learning from taking place.

Clearly stated objectives also provide participants with a list of what is expected of them. Knowing what they are being held accountable for gives participants direction and responsibility. They can then be active partners in your program rather than mere attendees.

SETTING LEARNING GOALS

Once you have decided on the basic subject matter for a training program, begin your planning by setting general learning goals. Learning-goal statements articulate the basic purpose and outcomes you want to achieve. As you develop learning goals for your training program, keep in mind that some types of learning differ from others.

Three major types of learning are easily remembered as "ABC":

1. Affective learning
2. Behavioral learning
3. Cognitive learning

Affective learning includes the fostering of attitudes, feelings, and preferences. For example, you may want participants to value a certain situation, procedure, or product. Or you may wish them to become more aware of their feelings and reactions to certain issues and new ideas. Here are some examples of affective learning:

- First-line supervisors in an engineering company explore their feelings about managing the work of employees who were previously their coworkers.

- Bank managers examine the extent to which their orientation was inward-looking or customer-focused.

- New hires share reactions to their first weeks on the job, including feelings about corporate culture, new procedures, and relations with coworkers.

Behavioral learning includes the development of competence in the actual performance of procedures, operations, methods, and techniques. For example, you may want participants to practice skills you have demonstrated and receive feedback on their performance. Here are examples of behavioral learning:

- Participants attending new-employee orientation learned how to complete payroll time cards.

- Research and development personnel practiced creative thinking techniques by applying them to problems back on the job.

- Staff nurses at a hospital practiced ways to effectively prepare preoperative patients who were about to undergo surgery.

Cognitive learning includes the acquisition of information and concepts related to course content. You may want participants not only to comprehend the subject matter but also to analyze it and apply it to new situations. Here are some examples of cognitive learning:

- Participants in a training program called "The Law and the Workplace" learned the legal definition of sexual harassment and applied it to issues in their jobs.

- Spouses of alcoholics learned to identify common characteristics of codependency, such as people pleasing, workaholism, and perfectionism.

- Managers with responsibility for hiring learned to identify unlawful questions that should not be asked in an interview.

Although it is possible to design your training program with only one of these types of learning in mind, a design that incorporates all three is more likely to result in lasting change. Even a relatively short program can include affective, behavioral, and cognitive learning goals, as represented in these two examples.

EXAMPLE: A trainer accepted an assignment to teach managers how to use a new purchasing system. She decided that her overall learning goals were to have participants do the following:

- Value the benefits of the new system (affective learning)
- Complete and process the forms (behavioral learning)
- Determine the correct forms to use (cognitive learning)

EXAMPLE: For a course on understanding team dynamics, the trainer chose to devote one session to the task and maintenance roles members need to play in teams. He designed the session so that participants would be able to:

- Identify people's current and future preferences for task or maintenance roles in a team (affective learning)
- Utilize new task and maintenance behaviors when facilitating a team meeting (behavioral learning)
- Differentiate between task and maintenance behaviors when they are exhibited by colleagues at a team meeting (cognitive learning)

Of course, your training program may be a response to a specific organizational problem. In this instance, you can focus on the kind of learning goal that is dictated by the problem it is addressing:

1. *Cognitive* goals are the priority when there is a lack of knowledge. This is often referred to as a "don't know" situation.
2. *Behavioral* goals are the priority when there is a lack of skill. This is often referred to as a "can't do" situation.
3. *Affective* goals are the priority when there is a lack of desire or fear about using new knowledge or skills. This is often referred to as a "won't do" situation.

SELECTING OBJECTIVES

Once you have established a set of learning goals, the next step is to break those goals down into specific training objectives (or outcomes). These should represent the concrete accomplishments to be attained in the training. Each learning goal will have one or more objectives that, when met, will identify accomplishment of that goal. Here is a case example.

EXAMPLE: A trainer in a term lending seminar for bankers set for himself the *cognitive* learning goal that participants would become familiar with the key business and legal considerations in structuring a term lending agreement that would meet both the bank's and the customers' needs. The results he wanted to achieve included the ability to analyze complex corporate organizations and financial statements and to understand how complex credit facilities are structured. The training objectives he selected were that, at the completion of the seminar, participants would be able to:

- Identify the key credit risks in a range of complex lending situations

- Analyze the corporate structure of an organization with multiple subsidiaries, with emphasis on the appropriate lending entity

- Identify key management issues for at least three companies seeking term lending facilities

For the *behavioral* learning goal of applying term lending strategies on the job, the results he wanted to achieve included the drafting of a term lending agreement for review by a more experienced bank officer. The objectives he developed were that, at the completion of the seminar, participants would be able to:

- Draft a proposed structure for term credits for the three companies previously analyzed

- Draft terms for each of the credits and discuss them with the appropriate bank attorneys

- Monitor at least two ongoing term credit facilities and write waivers and amendments as appropriate

Finally, the trainer wanted to include the *affective* learning goal that participants would value the interests of both the borrower and the lender in a term loan. The objectives developed were that, at the completion of the seminar, participants would be able to:

- Identify their personal feelings about business risk and protection

- Support the goals of each party for a term lending agreement, unless the goals were mutually exclusive

Sometimes trainers have too many objectives crammed into one program. To avoid this, be careful to distinguish between objectives that are nice to obtain and those that are necessary. For example, it may be critical for insurance claims adjusters to know how to access medical reference books in their office when evaluating injury claims. It would be "nice" but not critical, however, to teach them common prefixes and suffixes in medical terminology. Likewise, there is little point in setting objectives that can be achieved before participants ever come to the training program. For example, the learning of factual information such as the features and benefits of new products and services can be accomplished by having participants complete a virtual pre-course or a reading assignment. By expecting them to acquire *knowledge* before a training program, you can select higher-order objectives that involve *application* (using information), *analysis* (dissembling information), *synthesis* (putting information together), and *evaluation* (judging the value of information).

Whether something is required training or not can depend on a thorough analysis of the tasks involved in a job. Consider eight criteria for including a task in a training course (see Figure 2.1). Think about how you would apply these criteria to a task area you teach, such as performance appraisals or project management.

FIGURE 2.1 CRITERIA FOR SELECTING A JOB TASK FOR TRAINING

1. The percentage of job incumbents who actually perform the task

2. The percentage of total work time that job incumbents spend on the task

3. How critical the task is

4. The amount of delay that can be tolerated between the time when the need for performance of the task becomes evident and the time when actual performance must begin

5. The frequency with which the task is performed

6. The difficulty or complexity of the task

7. The probability of deficient performance of the task by job incumbents

8. How soon the task must be performed after a person is assigned to a job that involves it

---

Finally, the selection of training objectives may also hinge on one's understanding of adult learning needs. For example, adult learners tend to be less enthralled by survey courses. They prefer single-concept or single-theory courses (Zemke and Zemke 2001). Adult learners also want to see the immediate value of the skills and knowledge they are taught. They require information on the significance and application of the training topic (Vella 1994). Furthermore, adult learners like to build on prior experience. They expect the opportunity to relate what you teach them to what they already know or have thought about (Knowles et al. 2005).

SPECIFYING OBJECTIVES

When you have selected your objectives, state them in a form that will make them effective tools for managing, monitoring, and evaluating the training. Typically, training objectives use a format such as "By the completion of the program, participants will be able to…" (the specific objectives would then be listed).

This written format will give you specific criteria for determining whether the course design is appropriate. For example, if your objective is that participants will be able to utilize a skill in a job-related situation, you might ask if sufficient time to practice that skill has been built into the course.

When training objectives are more technical in nature, some trainers make it a practice to state not only what participants should be able to do after training but also under what *conditions* and according to what *standards* this will happen. Conditions include such things as the availability of informational aids or an allowance for performance simplifications. Standards consist of the level of performance being sought in terms of perfection, time utilization, output, and so forth. Here are two examples.

EXAMPLE: At the end of this training session, employees will be able to process lockbox items at a rate of five hundred per hour with no more than two errors per 1,000 items.

EXAMPLE: When practicing the splicing of cables, participants will complete five splicings in a thirty-minute period according to code.

If objectives are in the right format, the development of training evaluations can be very straightforward. In fact, evaluations can relate specifically to previously stated objectives. A comparison of the written objectives to the participants' experiences provides a direct means of evaluating the success of your training program.

You should be careful, however, to avoid overspecifying your training objectives, particularly in nontechnical training programs.

When teaching management skills, for instance, being overly precise about objectives can lead to mechanistic training. No one wants managers to do everything precisely "by the book," with little room to exercise their personal style and their own sense of the right way to do things. Often, your job is not to train but to educate—to expose participants to new ways of thinking, feeling, and acting and allow them to integrate these ways into their being. You may be advocating a five-step procedure for counseling troubled employees, but your participants may willingly accept and adopt only some of the steps. Or they may decide that they need to figure out an entirely different first step to make the procedure work for them. The better you educate participants concerning your subject matter, the less likely they are to leave the program as mindless clones.

EXPRESSING OBJECTIVES

With the previous caution in mind, it is still important that the training objectives are written in a style that is easy to understand and to the point. Avoid commonly misinterpreted terms such as those in Figure 2.2. Additionally, use specific action verbs to assist both the group members and the sponsor of your training program to evaluate your program. Figure 2.3 lists action verbs that are frequently used when writing training objectives.

FIGURE 2.2 TIPS FOR WRITING OBJECTIVES

Skill	*Commonly Misinterpreted Terms*	*Behavior Terms*
Knowledge	To know, learn	To write, define, repeat, name, list
Comprehension	To understand, appreciate	To restate, discuss, describe, explain, review, translate, locate
Application	To show, apply a thorough knowledge of	To operate, illustrate, use, employ, sketch
Analysis	To analyze	To differentiate between, appraise, calculate, test, compare, contrast, solve, criticize
Synthesis	To establish creativity	To compose, propose, plan, design, manage, collect, construct, organize, prepare
Evaluation	To show good judgment	To evaluate, rate, select, estimate, measure

---

FIGURE 2.3 EXAMPLES OF ACTION VERBS USED FOR WRITING TRAINING OBJECTIVES

Administer	Consolidate	Expedite	Proceed
Adopt	Consult	Formulate	Process
Advise	Control	Furnish	Promote
Analyze	Coordinate	Implement	Propose
Anticipate	Correlate	Improve	Provide
Appraise	Correspond	Initiate	Recommend
Approve	Delegate	Inspect	Report
Arrange	Design	Instruct	Represent
Assemble	Determine	Interpret	Research
Assign	Develop	Investigate	Resolve
Assist	Devise	Issue	Review
Assume	Direct	Maintain	Revise
Assure	Discuss	Monitor	Schedule
Authorize	Dispose	Negotiate	Secure
Calculate	Disseminate	Notify	Select
Circulate	Distribute	Obtain	Sign
Clear	Draft	Operate	Specify
Collaborate	Endorse	Participate	Stimulate
Collect	Establish	Perform	Submit
Compile	Estimate	Place	Supervise
Concur	Evaluate	Plan	Train
Conduct	Execute	Practice	Transcribe
Confer	Exercise	Prepare	Verify

COMMUNI-CATING TRAINING OBJECTIVES TO OTHERS

Communicating your objectives effectively to others is an important skill to develop. You may submit your training plans to management for approval only to discover that they are confused by your language or put off by the format of your objectives. In addition, participants can feel overwhelmed by a laundry list of objectives like those sometimes presented in course descriptions or by language that is laden with jargon. Figure 2.4 contains such an example. Organize objectives into a clearer, easier-to-read list such as the example in Figure 2.5.

FIGURE 2.4 MANAGEMENT SKILLS: TRAINING OBJECTIVES

When you complete this course, you will be able to

- Define and identify what affects motivation
- Discuss the impact of leadership style on motivation
- Identify your leadership style
- Identify and determine different leadership strategies
- Explain the impact of effective communication on motivation and leadership
- Demonstrate effective verbal and nonverbal communication skills
- Use positive reinforcement and coaching skills
- Give corrective or negative feedback to keep motivation intact and maximize workers' productivity
- Use the performance appraisal process effectively
- Recognize the benefits of teamwork and win-win situations
- Describe the difference between compromise and collaboration
- Assess the impact of your style on team development
- Remove barriers to teamwork and overcome resistance to change
- Develop a strategy to promote and build teams
- Discuss ways to maximize individual workers' learning
- Identify common pitfalls made in on-the-job training and ways to avoid them
- Systematically plan, implement, and follow up with on-the-job training skills
- Explain your role in customer service and the overall company image
- Use effective communication skills with customers to build relationships and establish a rapport
- Demonstrate effective conflict resolution techniques
- Develop personal action plans for improvement

FIGURE 2.5 SHELTER PRODUCTS: TRAINING OBJECTIVES

At the end of this course, you will be able to

A. **Define the following mortgage terms:**
   1. Mortgage
   2. Condominium
   3. Co-op and co-op loan
   4. Second mortgage
   5. Equity source account
   6. Refinancing
   7. Bridge loan
   8. Real estate loan

B. **Perform calculations**
   1. Demonstrate use of an amortization table
   2. Show how you determine monthly payments of principal and interest for fixed- and adjustable-rate mortgage loans
   3. Explain origination fees and the annual percentage rate

C. **Mortgage finance**
   1. Explain the role of the secondary market for mortgage funds
   2. Identify FNMA requirements and their relationship to the NYBD RAAC

WORKSHEET

DEVELOPING ACTIVE TRAINING OBJECTIVES

Try your hand at specifying objectives. Take the content of a program you are presently conducting or hope to teach in the near future and state the objectives you have for the program on the worksheet below.

Upon completion of this [module/course], participants will be able to:

_____

_____

_____

_____

_____

_____

_____

_____

_____

_____

_____

_____

_____

_____

_____

_____

_____

_____

_____

_____

_____

_____

_____

_____

_____

◆　◆　◆

Chapter Three

Creating Opening Exercises

*O*nce you have gathered information about the needs of your intended participants and selected your training objectives, you can start planning your program. Opening exercises are an important element in the beginning of an active training program. This is true for both classroom and online instructor-led training sessions. They can sometimes be considered as the "appetizers" to the full meal: They allow participants to get a taste of what is to follow. Although some trainers choose to begin a course with only a short introduction, including at least one opening exercise in your design is a first step that has many benefits.

WHAT OPENING EXERCISES ACCOMPLISH

Many people assume that opening activities are only social in nature. If participants are strangers to each other, something has to be done to allow them to introduce themselves to each other. For this reason, probably the most popular icebreaker in the training world is to pair participants, have them interview each other, and then have them introduce their partner to the large group. Imagine how many times people have experienced this ritual! There are many more creative and compelling icebreakers and a much wider view of their function.

In the first moments of an active training program, three goals are equally important, even if the program is short or an assessment has preceded the course:

1. ***Team building***—helping participants to become acquainted with each other and creating a spirit of cooperation and interdependence

2. ***On-the-spot assessment***—learning about the attitudes, knowledge, and experience of the participants

3. ***Immediate learning involvement***—creating initial interest in the training topic

All three of these goals, accomplished singly or in combination, help to develop a training environment that engages the participants, promotes their willingness to take part in some active learning, and creates positive training norms. You can take as little as five minutes or as much as two hours on opening activities (depending on the overall length of your program); it will be time well spent.

Team Building

Team-building exercises foster positive group attitudes by asking participants to learn each other's names and to get to know each other. If the members have already met, opening exercises can help them to become reacquainted after a period of separation. Either way, an opening design that stresses team building can develop a feeling of spirit and pride among the members of your program.

There are numerous getting-acquainted exercises that give participants an opportunity to introduce themselves to the other members of the group in an interesting and nonthreatening manner. An excellent example is Name Bingo, the instructions for which appear in Figure 3.1.

FIGURE 3.1 INSTRUCTIONS FOR NAME BINGO

---

1. Participants mill around the room and meet each other.

2. Each time a participant exchanges names with someone, she or he writes the new name anywhere on a Bingo form.

3. After all participants have met, each one places an O in any unused box.

4. The trainer then places a copy of everyone's name in a hat.

5. The hat is passed around the group, one participant at a time. Each participant picks a name out of the hat. Everyone places an X on the box containing the name picked.

6. Whenever any player obtains 5 Xs in a row (horizontally, vertically, or diagonally), he or she yells "Bingo!" (Eventually, everyone will get Bingo several times.)

FIGURE 3.1 continued

---

7. As their names are picked, participants should introduce themselves to the group and share three facts about themselves.

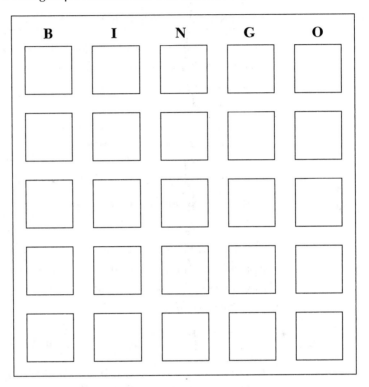

Note: Use a three-by-three format if the group includes fewer than ten people or a four-by-four format if the group numbers between ten and sixteen.

Almost all opening exercises can be varied to produce different effects. For example, Name Bingo can be modified to increase self-disclosure. Besides names, participants can be asked to obtain and record on the Bingo form one fact about each person they meet. *Each time participants are asked for a fact about themselves, they are required to share one that is different from those given to other participants.* In step 7, all the participants share the many facts they have learned about the person whose name is picked. This change lengthens the exercise, however, so it's best to use it only when the group is small.

A fun way to do group building once participants have become acquainted is a takeoff on the game show "To Tell the Truth" (see Figure 3.2 for instructions).

FIGURE 3.2 INSTRUCTIONS FOR TO TELL THE TRUTH

1. Ask each participant to write down (legibly!) on a card three personal facts not previously shared with the group.

2. Mix up the cards and distribute a card to each participant. (Be sure no one receives his or her own card.)

3. Have each participant read the card she or he has been dealt, then ask for three guesses as to whose card was read. Prior to the guesses, request that participants not reveal their identity even if it is guessed.

4. Ask, "Will the real bearer of this card please stand up?"

5. Allow for surprise or self-congratulatory applause.

A more self-disclosing yet fun-filled way to accomplish the same purpose is Predictions, a guessing game based on first impressions. Participants are formed into small groups to do the activity, which is described in Figure 3.3.

FIGURE 3.3 PREDICTIONS

Your job is to predict how each person in your group would answer the following questions. (Try to be as specific as possible. Don't be afraid of bold guesses!)

When you have finished your predictions, the participants should respond to the questions themselves.

1. Where did you grow up?

2. What were you like as a child? A student?

3. Were your parents strict or lenient?

4. What type of music do you enjoy?

5. What are some of your favorite leisure activities?

6. How many hours do you usually sleep nightly?

Note: Other questions can be added or substituted.

Other team-building activities are especially appropriate for a group where members already know each other well. Often, they involve some way for the group to produce something they can take pride in. One example that can be used in a longer training program is called TV Commercial (see Figure 3.4).

FIGURE 3.4 TV COMMERCIAL INSTRUCTIONS

---

1. Divide participants into teams of no more than six members.

2. Ask teams to create a thirty-second TV commercial that advertises their team, their organization, their common job, or the importance of the training topic.

3. The commercial should contain a slogan (for example, "Just Do It") and visuals.

4. Explain that the general concept and an outline of the commercial are sufficient. However, if teams want to act out their commercials, let them.

5. Before each team begins planning its commercial, discuss the characteristics of currently well-known commercials to stimulate creativity (for example, the use of a well-known personality, humor, or a comparison to the competition).

6. Ask each team to present its ideas. Praise everyone's creativity.

Each of these activities could be adapted to your virtual classroom, but let's consider a couple of ideas to build your team that are specifically designed for a virtual classroom. A great way to build the virtual team is to use YouTube Introductions (see Figure 3.5) or Twitter Introductions (see Figure 3.6).

FIGURE 3.5 YOUTUBE INTRODUCTIONS

---

1. Video yourself as you talk to your online participants for about five minutes. Decide if your message will be to welcome them, clarify objectives, assign details, excite them about the topic, or anything else. Make your message positive and motivating.

2. Create a login to the website YouTube and upload your video. YouTube will generate a hyperlink to your posted video.

3. Email the link to participants and invite your participants to record video clips to introduce themselves.

4. During the introductions at the start of your session, be sure to have a way to include anyone who was unable to create a video clip as an introduction.

FIGURE 3.6 TWITTER INTRODUCTIONS

---

1. Have a whiteboard with a grid where you have input the name of each participant in one square.

2. Ask each participant to introduce themselves in 140 characters or less. They can write a sentence or a group of descriptive words.

3. Comment on the diversity and when possible how the descriptions relate to the content of the session.

Yet another way to promote group cohesion is to invite participants to set ground rules that provide agreements about how they will interact and work with each other. One way to accomplish this is to provide a list of several possible ground rules. Ask participants to select three from the list. Tabulate the results and take note of the rules most often selected. This can be done in a physical or a virtual classroom.

The following items might be suitable for your list depending on whether it is a virtual session or not:

- Respect confidentiality.
- Ensure everyone participates when working in small groups.
- Start on time.
- Let others finish what they are saying without being interrupted.
- Speak for yourself.
- Be brief and to the point.
- Use appropriate language.
- Be prepared for the session.
- Avoid distractions.
- Ask questions.
- Give everyone a chance to speak.
- Build on each other's ideas before criticizing them.

On-the-Spot Assessment

On-the-spot assessment exercises ask participants to do such things as:

- Share their learning goals or expectations
- Raise questions or concerns they may have about the course
- Relate their knowledge and experience to the course topics

- List the successes and problems they have experienced that are relevant to the course
- Explore their opinions and attitudes about the course topic

Such exercises elicit information that will help you to gauge the expertise of the group while giving participants a sense of immediate participation. Often, you can request the information you want in a spontaneous manner by asking ***general questions*** in the opening minutes of the training program—for example, "What motivated you to be here today?" or "Do you have any concerns about today's session or what you may be asked to do?" Or you can ask ***training-specific questions*** such as these used in a time management seminar: "Who uses a 'to-do' list on a daily basis?" You can use the raised hand tool in a virtual setting. "How does it help you to organize your day?" Responses can be shared verbally in a physical classroom or written in a virtual classroom.

Structured exercises can also be used to gain on-the-spot assessment information, as the following examples illustrate.

EXAMPLE: Managers participating in a mandatory workshop on new corrective action policies were asked to discuss the following questions with their seat partner:

1. From your experience, what constitutes a "problem behavior"?

2. How do you feel when you have to confront a problem employee?

3. What actions have you taken in the past to discipline employees?

After each question, the trainer asked two or three participants to share their answers with the whole group. As group members had an opportunity to explore their own perspectives on handling problem situations before learning new corrective action procedures, the trainer gained valuable information about the training group.

EXAMPLE: Family therapy trainees were asked to form trios. Each trio was asked to generate two questions, one concerning the theory of family therapy and the other concerning the practice of family therapy. The questions had to relate to topics the participants hoped to learn about during the training program. Some of the questions that emerged were these:

- (Theoretical) What is the role of interpretation in family therapy?
- (Practical) Do you have to see the entire family to do family therapy properly?

- (Theoretical) Are the various models of family therapy really different from each other?

- (Practical) Is a "fifty-minute" hour enough for most family sessions?

The trainer gained in two ways from hearing these questions. She not only learned some of the issues that participants wanted to discuss but also found out about their knowledge regarding program content and their expectations regarding its level of sophistication.

Another design to consider, outlined in Figure 3.7, focuses on the concerns participants might bring to a training session. These questions could be adapted for use in a chatroom in a virtual learning setting.

FIGURE 3.7 CONCERNS OF A TRAINING GROUP

1. Hand out a blank index card to each participant.

2. Ask the participants to write down any concerns they have about the nature of the present training program (names should be withheld). These concerns might include the following:

   - How difficult or time-consuming the training may be

   - How they can participate freely and comfortably

   - How they will function in small learning groups

   - How available the trainer will be

   - What access there will be to reading materials

   - What the time schedule for the course will be

3. Request participants to pass the card clockwise around the group. Each time a participant receives a card, she or he should read it and place a checkmark on the card if it contains a statement that is also of concern to the reader.

4. By the time all of the participants have gotten back their own cards, each person will have reviewed the concerns of the entire group. At this point, hold an open discussion of the concerns that have emerged.

Variation: Instead of holding a discussion, identify the top four concerns in the group by establishing which cards contain the most checks. Break the class into four groups and invite each group to elaborate on the concern written on one of the four index cards. Ask each group to summarize its discussions for the whole class.

Immediate Learning Involvement

Immediate learning involvement exercises ask participants to respond to initial questions about the course content, to try out learning activities related to the course content without previous instruction, or to view presentations or demonstrations that give an initial description of skills to be learned within the program. These activities help to introduce the course in a dramatic, active manner that draws the participants into the training program right from the beginning of the session.

One of the simplest ways to involve participants for this purpose is to display an interesting proverb or slogan related to the training topic and then ask each participant to introduce herself or himself and share reactions to the statement. (Divide into small groups if the total group size is too large.) Here is a sample of sayings that could be used for well-known topics:

- Why put off until tomorrow what you can do today? (time management)
- It's not what you say but how you say it. (communication)
- You can't sell a product until you understand how it works. (sales)
- We cannot fully understand the beginning of anything until we understand the end. (planning)
- Nobody washes a rented car. (employee empowerment)
- A company is known by the people it keeps. (customer service)
- There is no "I" in TEAM. (team building)
- Yesterday's home runs don't win tomorrow's ball games. (product improvement)
- Managers do things right; leaders do the right things. (leadership)
- The only person who likes change is a wet baby. (organizational change)

Another simple immediate involvement technique is called Active Knowledge Sharing (see Figure 3.8). This is a great way to draw participants immediately into the subject matter of your course. It would work with any group and with any topic.

FIGURE 3.8　ACTIVE KNOWLEDGE SHARING

1. Provide a list of questions pertaining to the subject matter you will be teaching. You could include some or all of the following categories:

   - Terms to define (for example, "What does diversification mean?")

   - Multiple-choice questions concerning facts, concepts, procedures, policies, and so on (for example, "Being a team player does NOT involve (a) patience; (b) collaboration; (c) sharing the credit; and (d) constant fun.")

   - People to identify who are important to the subject matter (for example, "Who is Jim Collins?")

   - Questions concerning actions one could take in certain situations (for example, "How would you deal with an employee who is persistently late?")

   - Incomplete sentences (for example, "A _____ identifies the basic categories of tasks you can perform with a computer application.")

2. Ask participants to answer the questions as well as they can.

3. Then, invite them to mill around the room, finding others who can answer questions they do not know how to answer. Encourage participants to help each other. Or invite participants to compare answers with a partner or small team.

4. Reconvene the full group and review the answers. Fill in answers unknown to any of the participants.

Finally, you can create an immediate learning-involvement exercise that is tailored to introduce your particular training topic. Naturally, the development of a customized exercise requires greater effort than the simpler techniques described earlier, but the return on your investment of time will be rewarded many times over. Here are some examples.

EXAMPLE: A trainer began a program on multiple intelligence by asking participants: "What do Albert Einstein, Michael Jordan, and Mother Theresa have in common?" After participants responded with their thoughts, the trainer pointed out that all three are "geniuses." While Einstein is usually seen as the epitome of genius, there are several ways in which very intelligent people express their genius. Einstein is an example of logical-mathematical intelligence, Michael Jordan is an example of physical intelligence, and Mother Theresa is an example of interpersonal intelligence.

EXAMPLE: Participants in a course on conflict resolution were given a sheet that listed, in scrambled fashion, fourteen methods of handling conflict, ten of which might be considered "negative" methods and four of which might be considered "positive." They were asked to circle the five methods they personally used most often and underline the five methods used most often by other people in their personal and/or professional lives. The selections were then tabulated across the full group, and significant discrepancies were observed. Typically, the participants saw themselves as users of positive methods more often than they perceived others doing so. The trainer then pointed out the human tendency to project negative attitudes on others and asked participants to discuss how this tendency affects people's behaviors in conflict situations.

In a virtual classroom, participants are often asked to be online ten minutes prior to starting the session. You could get participants involved before the session begins in a number of ways. Jo Lynn Feinstein shares ideas with us in Webinar Warmups (see Figure 3.9). This is a great way to draw participants immediately into the subject matter of your course. It would work with any group and with any topic.

FIGURE 3.9 WEBINAR WARMUPS: WHAT TO DO BEFORE THE WEBINAR BEGINS

- Show a continuous loop series of brain teasers.

- Show a brief video clip that illustrates a concept from your program.

- Post a discussion question, and show instructions on how to use the chat feature.

- Post two or three survey questions, and show instructions on how to "vote." Remember to show the survey results when you begin the webinar.

- Post the whiteboard with a standard quadrant grid and show instructions on how to use the arrow feature. Pose a question and let participants use the arrow feature to display their answer. Example: How long have you been designing learning?

Over 10 years	6 to 10 year
1 to 5 years	New and eager to learn

FIGURE 3.9 continued

- Show a series of cartoons related to your topic.
- Show a series of cartoons related to business, from that industry if your audience all comes from the same industry.
- Show a Fast Draw story depicting a concept from your program.
- Show a series of slides reviewing the foundational concepts that precede your program.
- Show a series of interesting or surprising facts, a la "Did you know...?"

Multipurpose Exercises

While it is possible to design one of each kind of exercise as part of your course introduction, too much time spent on opening exercises may require you to skimp on the meat of the training program. The best approach is to design one opening exercise that simultaneously accomplishes ***team building, on-the-spot assessment,*** and ***immediate learning involvement.*** An example is an opening exercise called Rotating Trio Exchange, described in Figure 3.10. This is an in-depth way for participants to get acquainted and become immediately involved in the course topic. At the same time, valuable assessment information is obtained.

FIGURE 3.10 ROTATING TRIO EXCHANGE

Participants are asked to discuss within trios a variety of questions that help them to get to know each other; learn about their attitudes, knowledge, and experience; and begin discussion of the course content. For example, a group of managers could be divided into groups of three and asked such questions as "How have you been managed by others?" "What advice would you give yourself to be more effective as a manager?" and "What do you want to learn from this training program?"

Similar questions could be developed for other subject-matter areas. In a course on stress management, participants could be asked questions such as "What are some of the causes of stress in your job? At home?" or "How do you currently try to deal with stress in your life?" With each question posed by the trainer, new groups are formed by rotating two members, thereby increasing the number of participants who become acquainted with each other.

Another opening exercise that both fosters group building and provides assessment information is based upon a scavenger hunt. Participants receive a set of questions that must be answered with the names of other group members. Use a wide variety of questions that touch upon both personal information and course content. (This activity is extremely flexible, because you can easily adapt the questions to fit any type of group.) You might want to offer a token prize to the participant who finishes the scavenger hunt first. When a winner has been declared, reassemble the participants and survey the entire group about each of the items. Promote short discussions of some items. A sample human scavenger hunt for a team-building workshop is given in Figure 3.11.

FIGURE 3.11 HUMAN SCAVENGER HUNT

Read the following items. Then, for each item, find someone in the group who fits the description. Write his or her first name in the space after the item. You may not use any person's name more than once.

Find someone . . .

1. Who has the same first initial as you

2. Who thinks that teams often waste time

3. Who meets in teams more than three hours a week

4. Who was born in the same month as you

5. Who likes to do things alone

6. Who has had prior training in team problem-solving tools

7. Who thinks that an effective team usually has a fair amount of conflict

---

If you have time, it is also possible to sequence together opening exercises that flow well with each other and promote team building, on-the-spot assessment, and immediate learning involvement. Figure 3.12 contains the opening sequence of a training program on coaching and counseling skills. Notice how all three goals are accomplished.

**FIGURE 3.12 OPENING SEQUENCE FOR COACHING
AND COUNSELING TRAINING PROGRAM**

---

1. Overview of the Program

   a. Welcome participants and briefly explain the distinction between coaching and counseling. (As a coach, the manager identifies a need among employees for instruction and direction, usually directly related to their current work assignments. A coaching relationship is indicated when employees are open to advice and show little defensiveness. As a counselor, the manager identifies a problem that is interfering with the work performance of her or his employees. A manager needs to switch from a coaching to a counseling mode when employees are not as open to her or his input.)

   b. Indicate the importance both coaching and counseling play in a manager's work and the sensitivity a manager must have in knowing when to use each.

   c. Share these objectives:

   • To understand the value of coaching and counseling in a manager's work

   • To know when to coach and when to counsel

   • To examine how one's personality affects the coaching or counseling role

   • To develop basic competence in applying coaching and counseling skills

2. Quartet Exchange

   a. Form quartets and ask them to discuss the following question: "How have you been coached and counseled by managers in your career? Which approaches were effective and which were ineffective?"

   b. Invite four participants to share with the full group a personal example of a manager, two sharing examples of an effective manager, and two sharing examples of an ineffective one.

   c. Form new quartets and ask them to identify specific examples in which coaching and counseling have taken place or might take place in their work as managers.

   d. Obtain one example from each participant and record it on newsprint. Retain the list as a data bank of examples that can be used in later designs.

FIGURE 3.12 continued

e. Form new quartets one more time and ask them to respond to the following question: "What are some of your strengths and weaknesses when coaching and counseling employees?" Suggest that each person in the group take a turn sharing his or her response.

3. The Difference Between a Coach and a Counselor

   a. Refer to the newsprint list that was made previously and identify some situations that clearly call for coaching, some that call for counseling, and some that may involve both.

   b. Give out a handout that defines coaching to half the group and a handout that defines counseling to the other half. Have each participant read over her or his definition. Pair participants with different handouts and ask them to explain their contents to each other.

4. Initial Questions About Coaching and Counseling

   a. Ask participants to state on an index card one question they have about how to be an effective coach and counselor.

   b. Pass the index cards around the group in a clockwise direction so that each person gets to read each index card.

   c. Invite participants to place a check on any card that expresses a question that is important to them.

   d. Identify the questions that received the most votes and respond to each by (1) giving an immediate, but brief, answer; (2) postponing the question to a later, more appropriate time in the program; or (3) noting that the program will not be able to address the question (promise a personal response, if possible).

Source: Silberman, 1992, pp. 21–22.

WHAT TO KEEP IN MIND WHEN CREATING OPENING EXERCISES

As you design your active training program, take the time to consider carefully what initial objectives you wish to accomplish in the opening moments of your session. Your goals might include any combination of team-building, assessment, or involvement exercises. In addition, you should be aware of other considerations as they relate to the particular group you will be training:

   1. *Level of threat.* Is the group that you will be training open to new ideas and activities or do you anticipate hesitation and reservations

from the group members as you begin your session? Opening with an exercise that exposes participants' lack of knowledge or skill can be risky; group members may not yet be ready to reveal their limitations. Alternatively, an activity that asks participants to comment on something familiar to them eases them into the course content.

2. ***Appropriateness to group norms.*** A group of executive managers may initially be less accepting of playing games than would a group of students. Health care professionals and therapists might feel more comfortable sharing their feelings in a Rotating Trio Exchange exercise (see Figure 3.10) than would a group of research scientists. You are setting the stage for the entire course as you plan your opening activity; consider your audience and design appropriately.

3. ***Relevance to training content.*** Unless you are interested in a simple exchange of names, an initial design offers an excellent opportunity for participants to begin learning course material. Adapt one of the icebreakers suggested here to reflect the material you are planning to teach in your course. The closer your exercise ties into the course content, the easier a transition you will be able to make to your next design.

These design considerations have relevance for every aspect of your training program but are especially important in the opening stages. A successful opening exercise sets the stage for a successful program; likewise, one that seems threatening, silly, or unrelated to the rest of your course can create an awkward atmosphere that will be difficult for you to overcome.

TEN WAYS TO OPEN AN ACTIVE ONLINE VIRTUAL TRAINING SESSION

An engaging virtual training session begins from the moment participants join in. Set the stage for interactivity right from the start. Online classes experience high truancy rates as a course progresses. You can prevent this by ensuring you start strong. In typical face-to-face classes, trainers often spend the first minutes asking participants to share something about themselves. This practice is just as important as reviewing the course agenda and should be maintained in the online setting as well. As the first assignment, have participants submit a post to the group outlining their interests as related to the course and outside the course as well. Cindy Huggett, CPLP, shares these ideas from her experience to start strong by implementing an active online virtual training session.

1. Invite learners to join the session ten minutes early, so they are ready to begin at the start time and to mitigate any technical issues.

2. Be prepared early so that you can greet each learner by name when they join in to make them feel immediately welcome.

3. Engage learners with an activity, such as a poll question, as soon as they connect. Use some of the ideas earlier in this chapter to get them involved.

4. Post a rolling slide show to inform learners about administrative items (so you don't need to spend time reviewing logistics at the start).

5. Help learners get comfortable with the platform tools one at a time by inviting them to click and type on screen.

6. Play upbeat music to set an engaging tone.

7. Turn on your webcam to say hello, and invite participants to do the same (even if you don't plan to use it throughout the session).

8. Set expectations by letting learners know that this will be an interactive session. Ask learners to remove surrounding distractions in their workspace, and to "raise their hand" once they have done this step.

9. Take the temperature of the group. Ask each person to indicate if they are able to be fully engaged, or if something is blocking their full involvement. This helps people see how serious you are about their NOT multitasking.

10. Invite learners to connect with each other via chat, to form relationships and help them realize they are in a "room" with others.

TEN WAYS TO OBTAIN PARTICIPATION

No matter how creatively you design your opening exercises, they may still fall flat if the training group is reluctant to participate or if certain participants dominate. A wide range of methods can be used to obtain active participation in the opening phase of a training program. If you use a few of them on a consistent basis, you will avoid the phenomenon of hearing from the same participants all the time. Here are ten possibilities, one or many of which likely will suit the opening exercise you have in mind. You can also use these methods when designing activities for other portions of an active training program.

1. ***Open discussion.*** Ask a question and open it up to the entire group without any further structuring.

   Use open discussion when you are certain that several participants want to participate. Its voluntary quality is also appealing. Don't overuse this method. If you do, you will limit participants to those who are comfortable about raising their hand. If you have a very participative group and are worried that the discussion might be too lengthy, say beforehand, "I'd like to ask four or five participants to share…" If you are worried that few people will volunteer, say, "How many of you can tell us…?" rather than "Who can tell us…?"

2. ***Response cards.*** Pass out index cards and request anonymous answers to your questions.

   Use response cards to save time, to provide anonymity for personally threatening self-disclosures, or to make it easier for shy people to contribute. The need to state yourself concisely on a card is another advantage of this method. Say, "For this discussion, I would like you to write your thoughts first before we talk together any further." Have the index cards passed around the group or have them returned to you to be read at a later point. Be careful to make your questions clear and encourage brief, legible responses. In a virtual setting you could do this before the session.

3. ***Polling.*** Verbally poll all participants or provide a questionnaire that is filled out and tallied on the spot.

   Use polling to obtain data quickly and in a quantifiable form. Pose questions that call for a clear-cut answer such as "I agree" or "That's true." Ask participants to raise their hand when the responses they agree with are given. In place of raising their hand, you can ask them to hold up response cards that represent their choice (for example, a yellow card might indicate "false") or place a color-coded dot on a designated area of a large form such as a chart. If you use a questionnaire, make it short and easy to tally immediately. In a virtual classroom use your polling tools.

4. ***Subgroup discussions.*** Form participants into subgroups of three or more to share and record information.

   Use subgroup discussions when you have sufficient time to process questions and issues. This is one of the key methods for obtaining everyone's participation. You can assign people to subgroups randomly (for example, by counting off) or purposively (for example, by forming an all-woman group). Pose a question for discussion or give the subgroup a task or assignment to complete. It is often helpful to designate group roles such as facilitator, timekeeper, recorder, or presenter and to obtain volunteers or assign members to fill them. Make sure that participants are in face-to-face contact with each other. Try to separate subgroups so that they do not disturb each other. This is a good way to use the breakout session feature for virtual classrooms.

5. ***Partners.*** Form participants into pairs and instruct them to work on tasks or discuss key questions.

Use partners when you want to involve everybody but do not have enough time for small-group discussion. A pair is a good group configuration for developing a long-term supportive relationship and/or for working on complex activities that would not lend themselves to larger group configurations. Pair up participants either by physical proximity or by a wish to put certain participants together. Often, it is not necessary to move chairs to create pair activities. You can ask pairs to do many things, such as reading and discussing a short written document together, developing or responding to a question, or comparing their results to those of some activity they performed previously on an independent basis. Give instructions such as "Read this handout together and discuss it. Come up with examples or applications of what you are reading," "Create a question you both have about this topic," "Discuss together your response to the following question," or "Compare your results on this survey. How are you alike or different?"

6. ***Go-arounds.*** Go around the group and obtain short responses to key questions.

Use this method when you want to obtain something quickly from each participant. Sentence stems (for example, "One thing that makes a manager effective is…") are useful in conducting go-arounds. Invite participants to "pass" when they wish. Avoid repetition, if you wish, by asking each participant for a new contribution to the process. If the group is large, create a smaller go-around group by obtaining short responses from one side of the room, from people who are wearing glasses, or from some other smaller sample.

7. **Games.** Use popular games or quiz game formats to elicit participants' ideas or knowledge.

Use games to stimulate energy and involvement. Virtually any game can be adapted for training purposes, including basketball, Bingo, darts, Jeopardy, poker, Family Feud, Pictionary, Wheel of Fortune, bowling, Scrabble, soccer, and crossword puzzles. Be sure that the game requires everyone's participation and make the instructions crystal clear.

8. **Calling on the next speaker**. Ask participants to raise their hand when they want to share their views and ask the present speaker in the group, not the trainer, to call on the next speaker.

Say, "For this discussion, I would like you to call on each other rather than having me select who is to speak next. When you have finished speaking, look around to see whose hand is raised and call on someone." (Do not allow participants to call on people who have not indicated a desire to participate.) Use calling on the next speaker when you are sure that there is a lot of interest in the discussion or activity and you wish to promote participant interaction. When you wish to resume as moderator, inform the group that you are changing back to the regular format.

9. **Panels.** Invite a small number of participants to present their views in front of the entire group.

Use panels when time permits to have a focused, serious response to your questions. Rotate panelists to increase participation. An informal panel can be created by asking for the views of a designated number of participants who remain in their seats. Serve as panel moderator or invite a participant to perform this role.

10. **Fishbowls.** Ask a portion of the group to form a discussion circle and have the remaining participants form a listening circle around them.

Use a fishbowl to help bring focus to large-group discussions. Although it is time-consuming, this is the best method for combining the virtues of large-and small-group discussion. Bring new groups into the inner circle to continue the discussion. You can do this by obtaining new volunteers or assigning participants to be discussants. As a variation of concentric circles, you can have participants remain seated at a table and invite different tables or parts of a table to be the discussants as the others listen.

You can combine some of these ten methods of obtaining participation. For example, you might pose a question, form partners to discuss it, and then obtain whole-group reaction through methods such as open discussion, calling on the next speaker, and panels. By inserting the partner exchange first, you will have more people ready to participate in the whole-group setting. Or begin with response cards, followed by a go-around or subgroups.

WORKSHEET

CREATING OPENING EXERCISES

This worksheet can help you to plan an opening exercise for your next training program. Modify one of the sample exercises from this chapter or go ahead and create your own.

Goals Desired: (check as many as desired)

_____ Team building

_____ On-the-spot assessment

_____ Immediate learning involvement

Method Selected: (check as many as desired)

_____ Open discussion   _____ Go-arounds

_____ Response cards   _____ Games

_____ Polling   _____ Calling on the next speaker

_____ Subgroup discussions   _____ Panels

_____ Partners   _____ Fishbowls

Activity Outline:

_____

_____

_____

_____

_____

_____

_____

_____

_____

_____

_____

_____

_____

◆ ◆ ◆

Chapter Four

Preparing Brain-Friendly Presentations

As you move from designing the opening exercises to the more central portion of your training program, you will almost certainly decide to present some of the information you wish to cover in a presentation-type format. Presenting or lecturing is the most efficient and lowest-cost method of transmitting information in a classroom setting and is useful for conveying information to a large group, especially when you need to get across general knowledge. It is a standard tool that remains in use in most training environments.

If you are committed to active training, however, you face a potential problem: *Presentations put participants in a position of sustained, passive listening.* This is even true when tools such as PowerPoint presentations are used to visually highlight key points. As we noted in Part One of this book, learning cannot occur simply by listening and seeing. It requires the person's own mental processing to take place. Therefore, presenting by itself will never lead to real learning.

Nonetheless, a presentation still can hold an important place in an active training program if you work to involve participants and maximize understanding and retention through participative techniques (Thiagarajan 2005). To accomplish these ends, a presentation has to be as carefully designed as any other training activity.

FIVE WAYS TO GAIN YOUR AUDIENCE'S INTEREST

The first design element you should consider if you want a presentation to be effective is a method to grab hold of your listeners' attention. Instead of diving right into your course content, try building your participants' interest and involvement in the subject matter. These five

75

techniques (with examples) will help you to do just that. Although the five techniques were originally developed for presentations in a physical classroom, trainers in virtual classrooms face the same issues—if not worse, since they are unable to make eye contact with participants to ensure that they are connecting to the content. Virtual trainers need to use these types of techniques more often and on shorter intervals to maintain their participants' interest and keep them actively involved.

Introductory Exercise

Begin with a game or fun-filled activity that dramatically introduces the main points of the presentation.

EXAMPLE: A presentation on the merits of one-way versus two-way communication was about to begin. Before plunging in, the trainer utilized the short activity in Figure 4.1 to build interest in the presentation. You can do this in a virtual training. You do not need to have participants close their eyes. At the end of your instructions, have them turn on their webcams and hold up the sheet as you call on each one.

FIGURE 4.1 PAPER-TEARING EXERCISE

Time Allocation: Five minutes

Materials: Blank 8-by-11-inch sheets of paper for each participant

Instructions:

1. Tell the participants the following: "We are going to play a game that will show us some important things about communication. Pick up your sheet of paper and hold it in front of you. Now close your eyes and follow the directions I will give you—and no peeking!"

2. Give the following directions, carrying them out yourself with your own sheet of paper and pausing after each instruction to give the group time to comply:

   "The first thing I want you to do is to fold your sheet of paper in half."

   "Now tear off the upper right-hand corner."

   "Fold it in half again and tear off the upper left-hand corner of the sheet."

   "Fold it in half again. Now tear off the lower right-hand corner of the sheet."

FIGURE 4.1 continued
---

3. After the tearing is complete, say something like "Now you can open your eyes, and let's see what you have. If I did a good job of communicating and you did a good job of listening, all of our sheets should look the same!" Hold your sheet up for them to see. It is highly unlikely that any sheet will match yours exactly. There will also be a variety of shapes among the participants.

4. Observe the different shapes. There will probably be much laughter.

5. Ask the group why no one's paper matched yours. You will probably get responses like "You didn't let us ask questions!" or "Your directions could be interpreted in different ways." Then lead into a presentation on the need for two-way communication in the workplace.

EXAMPLE: A trainer was about to give a presentation about the ways in which people in organizations feel stuck because they believe they lack the resources to obtain the results expected of them. Before the presentation, the trainer gave participants six toothpicks each and challenged them to create four triangles with the toothpicks. After several frustrating minutes, the participants complained that the result couldn't be obtained because there weren't enough toothpicks. The trainer then showed the participants that they did indeed have "enough resources." The solution lies in making a three-dimensional pyramid with the six toothpicks, thereby creating three standing triangles and one base triangle. After the exercise, the trainer began his presentation about the importance of creative problem solving in organizations. Be a creative virtual trainer and ask participants to have six toothpicks at their desks for the virtual classroom. You will not only be able to use this activity, but will create curiosity and interest before the session. Want to be really creative? Video someone completing this exercise. Use a tight close-up shot. When it comes time to demonstrate the solution, play the video in a superfast mode.

Leadoff Story or Interesting Visual

Begin with a work-related anecdote, fictional story, cartoon, or graphic that focuses the audience's attention on the subject matter of your presentation.

Example: A trainer accepted an assignment to deliver time management training to a group of hospital administrators. Instead of jumping into a presentation on organization and time wasters, she began her presentation with the well-known leadoff story recounted in Figure 4.2.

FIGURE 4.2 A STORY ABOUT TIME MANAGEMENT

The utility of planning the day's work is seen clearly in a well-known story concerning Charles Schwab. When he was president of Bethlehem Steel, he presented Ivy Lee, a consultant, with an unusual challenge. "Show me a way to get more things done with my time," he said, "and I'll pay you any fee within reason."

Handing Schwab a sheet of paper, Lee said, "Write down the most important tasks you have to do tomorrow and number them in order of importance. When you arrive in the morning, begin at once on No. 1 and stay on it till it's completed.

Recheck your priorities; then begin with No. 2. If any task takes all day, never mind. Stick with it as long as it's the most important one. If you don't finish them all, you probably couldn't do so with any other method, and without some system you'd probably not even decide which one was most important. Make this a habit every working day. When it works for you, give it to your team. Try it as long as you like. Then send me your check for what you think it's worth."

Some weeks later Schwab sent Lee a check for $25,000 with a note saying that the lesson was the most profitable he had ever learned. In five years, this plan was largely responsible for turning Bethlehem Steel Corporation into the biggest independent steel producer in the world. Schwab's friends asked him later about the payment of so high a fee for such a simple idea. Schwab responded by asking, "What ideas are not basically simple?"

He reminded them that, for the first time, not only he but his entire team were getting first things done first. On reflection Schwab allowed that perhaps the expenditure was the most valuable investment Bethlehem Steel had made all year.

Source: Excerpted by permission of the publisher from *The Time Trap* © 1990 Alec MacKenzie. Published by AMACOM, a division of the American Management Association. www.amanet.org. All rights reserved.

Example: During a course on measurement and testing, a trainer was about to present on four ways that psychological tests are validated (predictive validity, concurrent validity, construct validity, and content validity). Before the start of his presentation, he displayed a list of the vocabulary words on the Wechsler Adult Intelligence Scale. He then asked participants if they thought that the use of such vocabulary words was a valid way to test intelligence. After receiving a variety of opinions (mostly dissenting), he proceeded to explain how test developers make positive claims about the validity of using vocabulary words to test intelligence and how these procedures can be used for all psychological tests.

Initial Case Problem

Present a short problem around which the presentation will be structured.

EXAMPLE: Figure 4.3 outlines a brief case problem that was used to introduce a presentation given to claims adjusters on what constitutes a work-related injury.

FIGURE 4.3 CASE PROBLEM 1: CLAIMS ADJUSTMENT

Sarah Secretary drives to work each day. Her route takes her past the post office. Each day she stops and picks up the mail for the office, and on her way home each afternoon she drops off the outgoing mail. One day, on her way home, she is involved in a two-car accident and is injured.

Is it compensable? As I discuss the factors defining a work-related injury, try to answer this question for yourself.

EXAMPLE: The case problem in Figure 4.4 was used to introduce a presentation on résumé writing.

FIGURE 4.4 CASE PROBLEM 2: RÉSUMÉ WRITING

Joan has been an employee of a national pharmaceutical company for the last seven years. She began her work at the company as a secretary in the human resources department and after four years moved into an entry-level position as a benefits administrator. Her job responsibilities included answering employees' benefit questions, handling the enrollment of new employees into one of the company's medical plans, and researching any problems that employees had as they filed insurance claims with the medical plan providers.

FIGURE 4.4 continued

Yesterday Joan found out that her job had been eliminated. All responsibility for benefits administration will be handled out of corporate headquarters in New York. Joan and three other coworkers have been told that they will be let go at the end of the month. Once they have left the company, they will each receive three months of job severance pay.

Joan is terrified of looking for a new job. She enjoyed working at the company very much and hates to think of starting all over again somewhere else. Moreover, she has not written a résumé since the last time she had to look for a new job. The old résumé identified only her skills as a secretary, yet Joan is certain that she would like to continue her career in benefits and not return to a secretarial position.

What advice could you give Joan as she writes her new résumé? As you learn tips on résumé writing, think through how Joan can best present her last seven years of work at the pharmaceutical company.

Test Questions

Ask participants a question related to the presentation topic (even if they have little prior knowledge), so that they will be motivated to listen to your presentation for the answers.

EXAMPLE: Most people might think that the purchase of a co-op is financed by a mortgage; in fact, co-ops are financed with loans, because co-op owners do not actually own their apartments but, rather, own shares in a corporation. Thus, the lender does not hold title to the property and cannot repossess an apartment in the event of foreclosure. A one-dollar mortgage is a way for a bank to establish title when a home equity loan is taken on a co-op. Such a loan is generally a second mortgage, so this device gives the lender some security.

Before presenting this information in a presentation on the nature of co-op loans in a course for loan officers, the trainer asked this simple question: "Why would anyone want a one-dollar mortgage?" He invited several responses by urging participants to speculate. During this time, he did not convey the correct answer. Then he proceeded with his presentation, explaining to participants that at the end of the presentation the answer to the question would be clear.

EXAMPLE: A trainer was preparing a presentation on techniques for managing meetings effectively. Concerned that participants would find the presentation boring, she decided to introduce it with a true-false test (see Figure 4.5). Instead of going over the answers immediately, she promised participants that the correct answers would become evident during her presentation. The group was all ears.

FIGURE 4.5 MEETINGS QUESTIONNAIRE

True or false?

_____ 1. Preparing an agenda in advance tends to promote meeting efficiency.

_____ 2. Distributing an agenda to members in advance generally does not affect the efficiency of meetings.

_____ 3. Starting meetings on time is inconsiderate to latecomers; wait until everyone is present before starting the meeting.

_____ 4. Begin to wind meetings down five to ten minutes before the meeting is scheduled to end.

_____ 5. Brief meetings (ten minutes or shorter) can be efficiently held standing.

_____ 6. Experts consider the ideal meeting length to be two to two-and-a-half hours.

_____ 7. Most experts advise holding meetings even if the agenda does not justify the expenditure of time and money.

_____ 8. Reading something out loud at a meeting when a printed version has been distributed is generally considered to be a waste of time.

_____ 9. Meetings are the most efficient forums for making general announcements.

_____ 10. Don't hold a large meeting to deal with a problem that affects only a few people.

Preview of Content

Give highlights or "coming attractions" of the presentation in an enthusiastic manner to entice interest and involvement.

EXAMPLE: A trainer was about to give a lengthy presentation on a new automated purchasing system. To build interest in the presentation, he stated: "You have been asked to come here today for an explanation of our new automated contract writing system. Before I get into details about how the system operates, I want each one of you to realize that, when you leave this room today, you will know how to use the system effectively. You will no longer need to copy-and-paste approved templates and check them to ensure everything is accurate. You will also know how to use the system to effectively monitor your contracts progress through finance. You will save anywhere from two to eight hours every week."

EXAMPLE: A trainer introduced a presentation on the history of leadership theory with the following remarks: "For the next twenty minutes, we are going to explore how our thinking about the nature of leadership has changed dramatically over the last thirty-five years. In that span of time, we have gone from rather simple notions of what makes a good leader to highly complicated models of leadership behavior. You be the judge! Are we any better off today than we were back in the eighties? My opinion is that we are better off but I don't know if you'll be convinced."

These few remarks immediately hooked the group's active attention to what might have been a presentation that met with resistance because of its theoretical nature. Both examples could be easily implemented in your physical or virtual classroom.

FIVE WAYS TO MAXIMIZE UNDER-STANDING AND RETENTION

After engaging the interest of your audience with one or more of these five interest-building techniques, it is time to begin the actual presentation. As you design your presentation, remember that your instructional goal is to maximize the participants' understanding and retention of the subject matter. Ultimately, the participants will learn more if they can focus their attention on the subject matter and make the ideas relevant to them. Five ways to maximize understanding and retention follow; try to use some or all of them as you present to your virtual or physical participants.

Opening Summary

At the beginning of the presentation, state (or summarize in writing) the presentation's major points and conclusions to help participants organize their listening.

EXAMPLE: A trainer began a presentation on the Project Evaluation and Review Technique (PERT) with the following opening summary: "I'm going to give you a thumbnail sketch of PERT before we look at it in detail. PERT was developed by the Department of the Navy for the Polaris missile. It is useful in the *planning, scheduling,* and *monitoring and control* aspects of project management. In the planning phase, it requires you to list the tasks entailed by the project, calculate the gross requirements for resources, and make time and cost estimates. In the scheduling phase, it involves laying out the tasks in a time sequence and detailing scheduling or resource requirements. In the monitoring and control phase, it entails reviewing the schedule and actual performance; revising the schedule, if necessary; and assessing the likelihood of jeopardy and cost escalation. PERT can be employed in such applications as building construction, installation of a computer system, or end-of-month closing of accounting records. Now let's take a closer look at the process and examine when and how it works."

Headlines

Reduce the major points in the presentation to headlines that act as verbal subheadings or memory aids.

EXAMPLE: A trainer was giving a presentation on supervisory styles. She decided to use these three catchy terms to describe the alternatives that are open to supervisors. Whether in a physical or virtual classroom you can add drama with a little color and animation.

Tell & Sell. In this mode, the supervisor explains to employees what is expected of them and why their cooperation is needed.

Tell & Listen. In this mode, the supervisor also initially explains to employees what is expected and then asks for (and listens to) their feedback to her or his requests.

Listen & Tell. In this mode, the supervisor asks the employees to comment on the work they are doing, listens to their responses, and then tells them his or her reactions to their work performance.

EXAMPLE: To become a better active listener, a trainer asked participants to consider the acronym PROPOSAL found in Figure 4.6.

FIGURE 4.6 AN ACTIVE LISTENING ACRONYM

P *Probe for understanding.* As a listener, your role is to understand what the speaker is saying and meaning. This may require you to ask questions, dig for deeper understanding.

R *Reflect.* One of the best ways to make sure you are understanding the speaker is to reflect back to that person what you have heard. Opening phrases like "So what I'm hearing is **...**" or "Is this what you mean?" are only two of many ways to begin reflective statements.

O *One thing at a time.* When you are listening, LISTEN. Ignore distractions around you. Don't shuffle papers or mentally plan your response. You have plenty to do just listening.

P *Pause.* You do not have to respond to the speaker's comments immediately. When you allow yourself a momentary silence, you free your mind to form your response during that silence.

O *Observe nonverbal behavior.* Much of what's being said is not being "said." To truly understand, you must pay attention to body language, gestures, facial expressions, vocal inflections, and so on. These clues will really help you understand the speaker's message.

S *Summarize.* To make sure you are comprehending the speaker's message, summarize his or her comments. It ensures that you do understand the speaker; and the speaker will appreciate that you are checking your understanding!

A *Acknowledge.* Acknowledge the message. This doesn't mean you must agree. It simply means that they know you are really hearing the message. Acknowledging the sender is just as important as acknowledging the message.

L *Let the speaker finish.* Interrupting is a waste of time! You frustrate the speaker and sacrifice a complete understanding of the message. Let the speaker finish; then pause to reflect and respond as appropriate.

Source: Eikenberry, 2004, p. 167. Used with permission.

Examples

As much as possible, provide real-life illustrations of the ideas in the presentation.

EXAMPLE: In a course on alcoholism and the family, the trainer explained that family members may not be the cause of a parent's alcoholism but may play a role in keeping the problem alive. He then gave the following example of enabling an alcoholic.

Consider the family of George, a retired mechanical engineer and an alcoholic. George began as a social drinker and eventually stepped over the invisible line into alcoholism. His wife, Joann, a registered nurse, played a key role in enabling George to remain an alcoholic. By taking on many of George's responsibilities, including budgeting, providing additional income, and handling the physical maintenance of the home, Joann was able to ensure that the household ran smoothly. By doing this, of course, she kept George from having to confront his alcoholism. George's eldest children, Bill and Cathy, also contributed to the enabling process. Successes outside the family, both of them projected the appearance of "having it together," but in truth they were often depressed. A younger sister, Laura, did her share by becoming a difficult teenager, refocusing family anger away from her father to her. All the members of the family adopted three rules that helped to maintain the status quo: (1) keep negative feelings to yourself, (2) don't talk about Dad's drinking with other family members, and (3) don't let outsiders know what happens in the family.

EXAMPLE: In a course called "Selling to Your Client's Style," the trainer was teaching the personality types described in the Myers-Briggs Type Indicator (MBTI), a widely used instrument to help people understand their personal style and the style of others with whom they work. She was discussing the differences between a "Thinker" (T) type and a "Feeler" (F) type and illustrated the distinction by the following example: "A prospect you are selling to who is a T will probably speak in a concise fashion, will appear to be firm and tough-minded, likes to argue, and is focused on the bottom line. To be effective with a T, don't ramble, be logical, and address objections head-on. A prospect who is an F, on the other hand, will appear personable and friendly, takes time to get to know you, seems to like harmony, and is more interested in process than outcome. It's best to spend time getting to know such a person, to be friendly and warm, to be affirming, and to understand that the prospect may have difficulty being critical and may not reveal her or his true feelings about your product or service."

Analogies

If possible, create a comparison between your material and the knowledge or experience the participants already have.

EXAMPLE: A trainer is discussing adult learning needs. She likens the human mind to a computer and points out that people cannot acquire knowledge if:

Their *computers* are turned off.

They don't have the right applications.

They are not allowed to *process* the information.

They don't have a chance to *save* the information.

Many well-known concepts are effectively explained by way of analogy. Here are a few:

- Another person cannot adjust his or her behavior to meet your needs unless you provide sufficient feedback. You are like a *thermostat* and the other person is like a *heating or cooling unit*. A thermostat reflects the temperature in a room for the heating or cooling unit. When the temperature is too hot or too cold, the heating or cooling unit can adjust its behavior by relying upon the thermostat for feedback that indicates when to do so.

- A database will hold and organize information for you like an *office file cabinet*. Your information is stored in files like the *folders* in your office file cabinet.

- When your selling style is very different from your client's, think of your client as *an AM receiver and you are sending* radio waves on an *FM transmitter*.

- A body's ability to contain stress is much like a *rain barrel* that overflows when the water reaches the top. We all have rain barrels to contain our stress. As they begin to fill, we start to experience stress-related symptoms. When they reach the point of overflowing, we may have serious illnesses.

Visual Backup

Use flip charts, PowerPoint slides, or brief handouts so that participants can see as well as hear what you are saying.

EXAMPLE: To explain the concept of "win-win" negotiation, a trainer shows the cartoon sequence in Figure 4.7.

FIGURE 4.7 LOSE/LOSE BECOMES WIN/WIN

Source: D.W. Johnson and F.P. Johnson, *Joining Together: Group Theory and Group Skills*, 4th ed. (Needham Heights, MA: Allyn & Bacon, 1991), p. 317. Used with permission.

EXAMPLE: An effective way to conceptualize the control of upper levels of management in some organizations is to compare their decision-making power to a window shade. Initiative at lower levels of management is often inhibited when the shade is drawn too far down. It is even worse when the window shade is drawn differently every day. In this instance, initiative is further inhibited because middle managers and supervisors are continually confused about where their areas of responsibility lie. This model is illustrated in Figure 4.8.

FIGURE 4.8 THE WINDOW SHADE MODEL OF POWER

FIVE WAYS TO INVOLVE PARTICIPANTS DURING A PRESENTATION

No matter how scintillating your presentation is, the participants are still placed in a passive role as they listen to a presentation. Fortunately, steps can be taken to enlist group participation right during the presentation. Following are five suggestions.

Listening Role

Assign participants the responsibility of actively listening to the presentation.

At the end, they should be able to produce points they agree or disagree with, questions to clarify the presentation, a summary of its contents, or quiz questions for other participants. Assignments can be given to the group as a whole, to teams, or to specific individuals.

EXAMPLE: A business writing trainer was about to give a presentation on six strategies for organizing and communicating information (definition, classification, example, process analysis, comparison and contrast, and cause and effect). The participants were asked to listen carefully to the description of each strategy so that at the end of the presentation they would be able to provide a summary to their seat partners. You can easily do this in an online chatroom.

EXAMPLE: A trainer was about to give what might ordinarily be a boring presentation on statistics concerning the current job market, turnover rates, and the cost of replacing an employee. She instead distributed a list of questions for participants to answer as she presented on the changing job market. By directing participants to search for information covered in the presentation, the trainer was able to actively capture her audience's attention. In a virtual setting you will want to ask participants to download and print the questions before your session.

Guided Note Taking

Provide instructions or a form indicating how participants should take notes during the presentation.

Stop at intervals for the participants to write reactions or ideas that go beyond what you have presented.

EXAMPLE: In a project management seminar, the trainer was lecturing about the cost management process, including the financial planning of the project and the subsequent collection, organization, and analysis of actual cost data to attain the project's cost objective. Participants had a worksheet in their seminar binder with the following terms: *input, process, output,* and *feedback*. After the trainer discussed each element in the process, participants were asked to recall his remarks in the appropriate section of the worksheet and write down any questions they had. In a virtual setting you could ask participants to list questions in the chat room as they come to mind. If someone is there to assist you, the person could coordinate questions, sort through duplicates, and organize the questions for an efficient Q&A.

EXAMPLE: For a training session on delegation, the instructor distributed a handout entitled "The Dos and Don'ts of Delegation." The handout format was a T-chart, with two columns labeled "Do Delegate" and "Don't Delegate."

As the presentation was given, participants could make notes on the chart. When completed by the participants, it would look like this:

Do Delegate	*Don't Delegate*
All routine or sporadic clerical duties	An emergency or short-term task where there is no time to explain or train
Minor decisions	Morale problems
Routine questions	Assignments from your boss that he or she expects you to do
Minor staffing problems	
Anything your subordinates are expected to do when you're not there	A job no one else in the unit is qualified to do
	Hiring, firing, or disciplinary matters

Spot Challenge

Interrupt the presentation periodically and challenge participants to give examples of the concepts presented thus far or answer spot-quiz questions.

This technique works well online. In a virtual classroom introduce a process called, "Tag! You're it!" Start with a roster with all participants' names, locations, emails, and cell phone numbers. Alert everyone that they will be called upon randomly to answer questions, make a comment, and provide a point of learning. This helps with the tendency to zone out during a session.

EXAMPLE: Before a presentation on hiring interviews, a trainer explained to her audience that she would stop periodically to obtain audience responses. She proceeded to discuss criteria that determine questions that are *clearly legal, not illegal but ill advised,* and *clearly illegal.* The trainer utilized a transcript of a hiring interview that contained all three types of questions. Participants were challenged to identify which questions belonged in each category.

EXAMPLE: A trainer was lecturing on the rights of developmentally disabled adults living in community living arrangements. After each section of the presentation, he gave a multiple-choice quiz to participants to test their understanding of the presentation material. Before continuing the presentation, he reviewed the answers to each quiz question.

Synergetic Learning

Provide different information to different participants.

Allow them to compare notes and briefly teach each other. To save time in a virtual setting, pair participants up using the breakout session feature at the beginning of your session and tell them they will work in pairs throughout the session. If participant do not know each other, or do not know each other well, prepare a slide with the paired assignments ahead of time that includes names, titles, locations, and photos of each participant.

EXAMPLE: In a course on group process, the trainer divided the training group in half. One group was sent to another room to read information about the *maintenance* roles performed in effective groups. During this time, the other group heard a presentation on the *task* roles performed in effective groups. Then the "maintenance" group returned to hear a presentation designed to reinforce what they had read. At the same time, the "task" group was sent out to read information that reinforced the presentation they had just heard. Members from each group were then paired up to teach each other the material they had just learned.

EXAMPLE: In a course on business insurance, accountants were learning about "loss exposures" and their impact on business assets and income and capital. One-half of the group was given the following chart and was asked to study it with a learning partner so that each of them could share the examples it contains with a participant in the other half of the group.

Types of Loss Exposure

1. Sudden, often violent occurrences that all businesses are exposed to daily, such as fire, flood, wind, vandalism, weight of snow or ice, or frozen pipes

2. Exposure of premises, operations, product liability, directors' and officers' losses, professional liability loss, and so on

3. Employee dishonesty, injury of employees, and computer losses

4. Fines, closures, prosecution, added costs in construction, and taxes

Meanwhile, the trainer gave the other half of the group a brief on the four categories of loss exposures (without examples):

1. External

2. Legal

3. Internal

4. Governmental

Participants from each half of the group were paired up. They told each other what they had learned and, together, attempted to sort the examples into the four categories. The full group was then reconvened and reviewed what they had learned synergistically.

Illuminating Exercise

During the presentation, intersperse a brief activity that illuminates the information, ideas, and skills being presented.

EXAMPLE: A trainer gave a brief presentation summarizing the problems managers face today, including low productivity, poor quality of service, high stress, and low morale. The trainer also noted that traditional management solutions tend to use an approach that, like the mythological Hydra, often generates two new heads for every one solved. A different approach is needed, which she called "creating the ideal." At this point, the trainer interrupted the presentation with an exercise. She asked each participant to find a partner of approximately equal weight and strength. One of the pair was asked to hold out his or her arm horizontally and to resist the partner's attempts to bend it. Most arms were easily bent. The trainer then requested the individual to imagine his or her arm as a steel rod before the partner attempted to bend it and to sustain the vision in the process. In most pairs, arms remained straight despite increased effort from the partners. The presenter then continued: "Better results are obtained with less effort. The key is what one focuses on. In the first case, the individual tried to achieve contradictory results: keeping his or her arm straight and resisting having it bent. In the second case, he or she focused solely on the desired result." The trainer then presented four key elements that go into making a visionary approach to problem solving work. This demonstration could also be shown in a video and virtual participants could be encouraged to try it out after the session.

EXAMPLE: A team-building instructor utilized an exercise called the "team machine" to help participants understand several points about teamwork. His instructions to participants are reproduced in Figure 4.9.

FIGURE 4.9 THE TEAM MACHINE INSTRUCTIONS

- Lift your right hand and move it as if you are clapping. Listen to the sound of one hand clapping.

- Raise your left hand and clap with both hands. If your task is to clap, wouldn't you want to use all of your available resources?

- This is an example of how the human system operates on an individual level.

- Each person has several parts and the parts work together to get things done.

- There are other types of systems. Imagine a six-cylinder car—a well-timed, synchronized machine. Each cylinder fires in sequence so the system can function.

- Imagine this automobile running on only four or five cylinders. What would happen to the power? Or what if you put the plug wires on haphazardly?

- Organizational teams are just like individuals and automobiles. The teams work best when they use all of their resources, when there is a plan and they have a coordinated system for getting things done.

- Let's experiment. Watch me as I stand here making a motion and a sound with my voice. Let's pretend we're making a human machine, a well-timed machine. (The facilitator chooses the first participant.)

- Please come up here. (The facilitator points to a place with a large space.)

- Now I would like you to make a unique sound with your voice, place one hand out in front of you, and make a motion with your body. Good.

(The facilitator asks the remaining individuals to come up one at a time and arrange themselves in a circle.)

To each member say:

- Make a different sound, a different motion, and use one hand to connect to the person in front of you.

FIGURE 4.9 continued

After completing the circle, say:

- Continue making your interesting sounds and motions. Notice how you take turns, how you bob and weave or wax and wane.

Here are some things to think about:

- Have we somehow woven ourselves into a pattern in which we all contribute our vocal and motor skills?
- Is the sum more than the parts?
- Are we synchronized?
- Is there a group system here, something bigger and more complex than each individual?
- Now we have a system for doing things. This is the hallmark of an effective team.

Source: This exercise was developed by Jeffrey D. Kindler. Used with permission.

FIVE WAYS TO REINFORCE PRESEN-TATIONS

When a presentation is completed, the conventional behavior is to wrap it up with a recap of the major points and a question-and-answer period. Although these conventions have merit and should not be overlooked in your planning, there are some more exciting and active ways to debrief and reinforce what has been presented. Consider these five methods.

Press Conference

Invite participants to prepare questions that are submitted to the trainer for her or his response.
   Use this same technique in a physical or virtual classroom.

   EXAMPLE: At the conclusion of a presentation on "reserving factors" in an accident claim, participants were formed into quartets. Each quartet was asked to pose a question to the trainer that would help to clarify the presentation. Participants were urged to bring up hypothetical cases to incorporate into their questions.

EXAMPLE: During a seminar on a new statistical software package, the trainer gave participants three questions that emerged from the material she had just covered. Participants were asked to vote for one question to be answered by the trainer before she continued with the seminar. By doing this, the trainer helped the participants to review what they had learned throughout the day.

Participant Review

Ask participants to review the contents of the presentation with each other (in any group configuration) and commit the major points to memory, or give them a self-scoring review test.

EXAMPLE: A trainer gave a presentation on six "job-centered motivators," which Herzberg believes have long-term effects on employees' attitudes:

1. Achievement
2. Recognition for achievement
3. The work itself
4. Responsibility
5. Growth
6. Advancement

When he finished, he asked participants to put away their notes and write down the six motivators from memory, providing an example of each. He then allowed participants to check their answers against their notes. This is a great activity for a virtual classroom.

EXAMPLE: After a presentation on virtual learning, the trainer gave eighteen participants one card each that contained either a word or its description. Each participant had to find the mate to his or her card. Figure 4.10 provides a list of these words and their descriptions.

FIGURE 4.10 VIRTUAL LEARNING WORD MATCH

- *Asynchronous:* Anytime, anyplace access to education or training materials
- *Authoring Tools:* Software for creating graphics, multimedia presentations, text files, and other resources to produce learning materials

---

FIGURE 4.10 continued

- *Bridge:* Device designed to interconnect three or more telephone lines to link multiple locations for audio teleconferencing

- *Chat:* Real-time text conversation between users over the Internet

- *Cookie:* Information stored on a user's computer after visiting a website; tracks data about the user

- *Groupware:* Software that supports online group collaboration for email communications, shared files, and online chats

- *Interactive Technology:* Technology that permits two-way participation

- *Podcast:* A series of digital-media files that are distributed over the Internet using syndication feeds for playback on portable media players and computers

- *Whiteboard:* A virtual classroom application that allows documents and content materials to be posted on the screen for all participants to see in real time

---

Group Processing

Ask participants to reflect on the presentation's implications for them.

Utilize any group format you feel will maximize the quality of the processing.

EXAMPLE: A training group had just heard a presentation on five steps to effective team facilitation. They were asked to break into small groups to discuss the following two questions:

1. "Which ideas were new for you and which were not?"

2. "Which ideas do you think apply to your team?"

EXAMPLE: A trainer completed a presentation on ten key points to remember when conducting a hiring interview:

1. Build rapport

2. Describe job and organization to candidate

3. Be aware of your body language

4. Review candidate's résumé

5. Ask as much as possible about candidate's past behavior

6. Allow for silence

7. Maintain control

8. Seek contrary evidence

9. Answer candidate's questions

10. Make important notes during the interview

She then asked participants to discuss the following questions with a seat partner:

- Which of these behaviors come easily to you? Which are difficult?

- Which do you want to practice more?

- What would help you to remember these key points the next time you conduct an interview?

Post-Presentation Case Problem

Pose a case problem for participants to solve based on the information given in the presentation.

EXAMPLE: In a training program on mortgage product sales, the trainer gave a presentation on the ingredients of a mortgage commitment. When the presentation was completed, the following short case problem was presented to participants:

A customer has received a good-faith estimate but is not sure that this represents a mortgage commitment. The customer is confused and makes an appointment with you for an explanation.

In trios, participants were asked what they would explain to the customer.

EXAMPLE: At the conclusion of a presentation on bank products, the participants were formed into two groups and given the following case problem:

A customer's daughter was just accepted at a college with very high tuition. Unfortunately, she does not qualify for a federally guaranteed loan. She has come to you for alternatives. What would you recommend?

After small-group discussion, individuals from each group were matched with each other to compare notes on the case problem.

Experiential Activity

Design an activity that dramatically summarizes or illustrates the presentation you have given.

Utilize any of the experiential learning approaches that are presented in Chapter 6 (role playing, games and simulations, observation, mental imagery, writing tasks, and action learning projects).

EXAMPLE: A trainer gave a presentation on family systems to drug and alcohol counselors who were learning to use a family treatment approach in their work. In particular, the presentation examined issues of proximity in families: how some family members are closely connected and how others become disengaged. At the conclusion, he asked participants to join him in forming a circle and holding hands. He then released himself from the hand of the person to his right and began to lead the person to his left (and consequently all the other participants who were connected to her) over and under the clasped hands of the other participants. The net result was a human knot, with some participants facing others and some facing no one. In addition, some participants emerged in comfortable body positions while others were in awkward positions. With the knot of participants entangled, the trainer (who managed to end up in a comfortable position facing several other participants) began a discussion of a recent controversial film. The discussion ensued for several minutes, with some participants contributing easily and others with little desire to become involved. The knot was then untangled and participants returned to their seats. The trainer asked the group to discuss their experiences in the knot and to relate them to the presentation he had just presented. This is a dramatic demonstration of the varied degrees of involvement and detachment within a group or human system.

EXAMPLE: A trainer had just finished a presentation entitled "How Brain Dominance Affects Teaching and Learning Style." She wanted to reinforce the presentation with a demonstration showing that if we only teach from our preferred mode, frustration will result for both teacher and student. She asked participants to pair off and asked each pair to decide who would be the student and who would be the teacher. "Students" then were asked to write out their responses to this question: "What are the first two steps you would like your teacher to take in order to help you learn how to drive a car most effectively?" "Teachers" were asked to respond in writing to a comparable question: "What are the first two steps you would take in order to teach someone how to drive a car most effectively?" Each pair was then asked to compare responses and discuss any discrepancies and/or similarities between the steps proposed by the "teacher" and the steps desired by the "student." Pairs were also asked to compare their scores on the Hermann Brain Dominance Inventory (Hermann 1995), which had been previously completed and profiled for each participant, and to try to draw some conclusions about the impact of their learning style on their approach to teaching.

AN EXAMPLE OF A WELL-DESIGNED PRESEN-TATION

When putting together a well-designed presentation, respect the four-part sequence that has been described in this chapter. Always begin with a strategy to build interest. Once the audience is mentally involved, provide the information you wish to impart, using the ways described here to maximize understanding. During this period of time, stop once or several times and obtain audience participation. When the presentation has been completed, reinforce what you have taught with the strategies just discussed. Here is an example of this flow.

EXAMPLE: You are going to a presentation on situational leadership styles, a model developed by Ken Blanchard (1997). According to this leadership model, the preferred style of a leader is dependent on the characteristics of the people she or he is leading. The styles are referred to as directing, coaching, supporting, and delegating.

1. To build interest in the presentation, you might use the following test question:

   What characteristics of the people you lead might determine when you could adopt one of the following styles: *directing, coaching, supporting*, and *delegating?*

   Obtain several responses and remain accepting of participants' answers. Do not reveal the "correct" answers.

2. Provide a handout that contains the following:

Style	Situation	Description
Directing		
Coaching		
Supporting		
Delegating		

Explain the situation factors and general description of each style. For example, you would tell the audience that "low-maturity" people (those who are unable and unwilling to take responsibility and are lacking in competence or confidence) function best with directive leaders who provide clear supervision: defining roles, setting goals, and organizing work assignments. As you discuss each style, invite participants to take notes on the handout (in a virtual setting they will have downloaded the handout). Be sure to provide good examples for each style and use the analogy of parenting children as they grow into adolescence. Use a graphic icon on your slides to accompany the presentation of each style, such as a whistle for a coach or a bridge for a supportive leader.

3. Divide the audience into four groups (place them in a breakout in a virtual classroom) and give each group one of the following assignments after you have presented each style:

Questioners: Ask a question about this style.

Agreers: Explain why you agree that this is the best style in this situation.

Naysayers: Explain why you disagree that this is the best style in this situation.

Example givers: Give a work-related situation in which this style makes sense.

Call on each team to question, agree, and so forth.

4. Give participants several case situations. Ask them to identify which style fits each situation. Follow this activity with a role-playing activity in which the participants are asked to portray each style. In a virtual classroom ask for volunteers with whom you role play. Discuss their reactions to the role play, exploring their comfort in being able to shift gears in each situation. Hold a press conference in which you are asked final questions about the model.

WORKSHEET

PREPARING BRAIN-FRIENDLY PRESENTATIONS

Use this worksheet to assist you in the design of a well-organized presentation that will initiate participants' interest in your subject matter, retain that interest throughout the presentation, enlist direct participation, and reinforce what has been presented.

Interest-Building Strategies:
(*check as many as desired*)

_____ Introductory exercise

_____ Leadoff story or interesting visual

_____ Initial case problem

_____ Test question

_____ Preview of content

Notes on techniques:

_____

_____

_____

_____

_____

Understanding- and Retention-Maximizing Techniques:
(*check as many as desired*)

_____ Opening summary

_____ Headlines

_____ Examples

_____ Analogies

_____ Visual backup

Notes on techniques:

_____

_____

_____

_____

_____

WORKSHEET continued

Participant Involvement:
(*check as many as desired*)

_____ Listening role

_____ Guided note taking

_____ Spot challenge

_____ Synergetic learning

_____ Illuminating exercise

Notes on techniques:

_____

_____

_____

_____

_____

Lecture Reinforcing:
(*check as many as desired*)

_____ Press conference

_____ Group processing

_____ Post-lecture case problem

_____ Participant review

_____ Experiential activity

Notes on techniques:

_____

_____

_____

_____

_____

_____

◆   ◆   ◆

Chapter Five

Finding Alternative Methods to Presenting

While a well-designed presentation can be an effective training method, overreliance on presenting usually leads to boredom, lack of involvement, or limited learning for the participants. A different method can often take the place of a presentation entirely. A presentation can also be reinforced by utilizing another method. In this chapter, we will examine eight alternatives to presentations that you can use even if your participants have little prior knowledge of the subject being taught. These methods are:

1. Demonstration
2. Case study
3. Guided teaching
4. Group inquiry
5. Information search
6. Study group
7. Jigsaw learning
8. Learning tournament

DEMON-STRATION

Instead of talking about a concept, procedure, or set of facts, you may be able to walk through a demonstration of the information in action. Involving participants in the demonstration, if possible, is important so that they can actually hear, see, and touch the relevant learning materials. The advantage of a demonstration is that it adds showing to merely telling. Here are two examples.

EXAMPLE: On the third afternoon of a five-day course on family process, a trainer began a module on family permeability—how a family relates to the outside world. He began by explaining that no family is self-sufficient; all need the stimulation and support of others. However, a family needs to rely on itself as well, since always turning to outsiders, he suggested, robs a family of its integrity. At this point, the trainer thought about continuing his presentation, raising specific issues families face in considering how open they want to be. Fearing that he had already presented too much in the afternoon session, he decided instead to invite one of the participants to be interviewed about her family. By discussing a number of specific questions with the participant (for example, "How much time do you spend with family and with friends?" "Are the religious and sex education of your children left up to professionals?" "Do you tell others about any problems occurring in the family?" "How much contact does the family have with people of other races, religions, or cultures?"), the trainer provided a stunning demonstration of how a family negotiates issues of permeability.

EXAMPLE: In a course on communication, a trainer was about to present a model by group psychologist Jack Gibb on defensive versus non-defensive communication. According to Gibb, people become defensive when others are evaluative, controlling, strategizing, neutral, superior, and overly certain. They become less defensive when others are descriptive, problem-oriented, spontaneous, empathetic, egalitarian, and provisional. Rather than defining and illustrating each of these twelve qualities, the trainer chose instead to create a live demonstration. She enlisted four participants to hold a discussion on the value of annual performance appraisals. The twelve categories were prominently displayed on flip-chart paper off to the side of the discussion group. As the trainer heard an example of one of the communication categories emerging from the group discussion, she pointed to the category being demonstrated. In ten minutes, all the defensive communication categories had been illustrated, but few of the non-defensive ones. To demonstrate the remaining non-defensive behaviors, the trainer joined the discussion group and showed how the communication of one member could induce lowered defensiveness in others. She then encouraged others to try out the newly demonstrated behaviors.

Here are some procedural guidelines for conducting creative demonstrations:

1. Choose a concept (or a set of related concepts) or a procedure that can be illustrated by demonstration. Some examples include:

   - An office requisition procedure

   - A project management planning tool

   - A feedback loop

   - A hidden agenda in a team meeting

2. Use any of the following methods:

   - Have some participants come to the front of the room and ask them to physically simulate aspects of the concept or procedure.

   - Create large cards that name the parts of a procedure or concept. Give out cards to some participants. Place the participants with cards in such a way that they are correctly sequenced.

   - Develop a role play in which the participants dramatize the material you are teaching.

   - Using volunteer participants, walk through a procedure that involves several people.

   - Set up a dramatization ahead of time with several participants in an online course.

3. Discuss the learning drama that you have created. Make whatever teaching points you want.

CASE STUDY   A case study is like a written demonstration. You are providing an account of a real or fictitious situation, including sufficient detail to make it possible for groups to analyze the problems involved. You can also embed information in a case study that is normally given in presentation. The major benefit of a case study is that abstract information is presented concretely. Notice in the two case examples that follow how participants learn what the trainers want to teach without the trainers having to give it to them in a presentation.

EXAMPLE: In a course on stress management, the trainer normally used a presentation format to present five behavior characteristics that contribute to stress and five ways to reduce it. She decided instead to give out the case example in Figure 5.1 and to ask the participants, working in breakout rooms, to identify those characteristics and stress management strategies. The answers were written on whiteboards and shared once time was up. To the trainer's delight, the participants hit on every one of the points that she had planned to cover in the presentation.

FIGURE 5.1 CASE STUDY: STRESS FOR SUCCESS

A CASE STUDY

Sally: Mary, Hello! How are you? I have been thinking about you a lot lately. We never get together anymore and I miss you. This morning I put you right at the top of my to-do list and made calling you a number-one priority.

Mary: Thanks for calling, Sally. I've been so-so. Frankly, I've been a little depressed and so tired lately. I never seem to get everything done. Between the house, my job, the kids, and my family, there just aren't enough hours in the day. I've been getting up an hour earlier to catch up, and I'm still behind. I feel like such a failure.

Sally: I am so glad I called today. We need to talk more than I imagined. I can't wait to share some of the exciting new things that I've learned that have made my life so much easier. From the sound of your voice, I think some of these things will help you. I feel it is important that we stay in touch. We need to take care of ourselves. That includes keeping our special friendship going. Can we make a date for a nice lunch for one day this week? We'll plan to go somewhere special. We deserve to treat ourselves. That is one of the new things I've learned to do. I've made a list of all the things I find pleasurable and I pick at least one and do it every day.

Mary: You must be better organized than I am. I just don't have time to do something pleasurable for myself. I'm such a mess.

Sally: Mary, it doesn't have to take a lot of time. It can be something as simple as buying a candy bar you like and eating it. Or taking a bubble bath after the kids are in bed.

Mary: Sally, don't you feel guilty doing that?

Sally: No. Now when can we go to lunch?

Mary: I don't know when I can do it. I drop all the kids off at school at 8 AM on my way to my part-time job; I'm trying to keep my hand in at the law office while the kids are small. I'd feel guilty wasting all that education, just sitting home. Then, I have to pick up Johnny at 12:45 every day from kindergarten. I drop him off at my mother's while I go to the office for a few hours to do John's billing and accounting. He depends on me, so he can go to lunch with some of his business friends. He's so busy this time of year. I have an evening meeting at least two nights a week

---

FIGURE 5.1 continued

---

because I'm running the scouting bazaar this month. They couldn't find anyone else to do it. The kids were going to be so disappointed. I just couldn't say no when they asked me.

Sally: Mary, stop a minute. Take a deep breath. You are running a mile a minute. No wonder you are exhausted and overburdened. If you can't say no to all those other requests, I must insist that you not say no to me. This lunch is going to be a most important one for you. I am going to teach you how to say "no." It can change your life. It has mine.

Mary: But, how can I possibly make time? I don't have anyone to help me. I do everything for everyone. Everyone depends on me.

Sally: That is another thing we are going to talk about. For now, I have a suggestion, so that we can get this plan started. First, does your mother drive?

Mary: Yes, but I hate to ask her for help. She has her hands full with Dad. I try to help her as much as I can.

Sally: Mary, please listen! Just try my suggestion. What do you have to lose? First, talk to John about our luncheon date. Ask him which day would be most convenient for him to stay in the office for lunch. If necessary, negotiate another time to do the billing for that day. Then, call your mother and ask her if she can pick up Johnny at school at 12:45 and take him home with her on that day. Of course, you will have to make a to-do list of all the things that you have committed to this week that you can't delegate, reschedule, or cancel before you know which day will be best for you.

Mary: I don't know, Sally. I hate to ask people to do my jobs.

Sally: Mary, why are they your jobs? One of the things I've learned is that I can delegate some of my jobs to other people at work and at home. It isn't necessary for me to do everything myself. It wasn't easy at first. Everyone was used to me doing all the jobs. I had to practice how to delegate, that is, giving some of the less important jobs to other people to do. I had to practice just saying "No!" The hard part was figuring out what was important to me and what wasn't. That is another part of changing this hectic merry-go-round life. I really had to look at all the roles I play in my life. Are they all necessary? What does being a "Mommy" mean? What does being a wife mean? I've started redefining my roles and it has worked wonderfully well. I'll tell you exactly how to go about it when we meet for lunch. I'll call you tomorrow morning to set up a definite date. Can't wait to see you. Bye.

Source: This case study was written by Charlotte B. Milligan, Training Director, American Business Management Publications, Inc., Philadelphia, PA. Reprinted with permission.

Finding a case study that exactly fits the bill can be a daunting task. (See Jean Barbazette's *Instant Case Studies* (2004) to start you off.) Or you may decide to write a case that is especially geared to your training program. Here are some suggestions for writing your own cases:

- Identify the issues, concepts, or principles you want to teach.

- Brainstorm situations (real-life, thinly disguised, or highly fictional) that illustrate the concepts or principles.

- Choose one situation that seems the most promising and develop the characters, the events, the background data, and the actions taken.

- Write a first draft of the case and ask someone else to read it without any further information from you. Obtain feedback about its clarity and interest level.

- Rewrite the case and develop discussion questions. Think about adding graphic aids such as charts and photographs or including segments on audio or video elements.

You might also decide to introduce some tension and conflict into a case study. Four kinds of these cases are *gateway, challenge, performance management*, and *role play* (Stringer 1999). A *gateway* case introduces an entire course or module. It contains a broad array of problems and challenges that will show up throughout the program. A *challenge* case creates competition among two or more teams. It contains a situation in which a team must make the right decisions to succeed. A *performance management* case asks participants to figure out how to complete a work-related task or negotiate a work-related problem. A *role play* case involves participants as characters in a situation that must be handled effectively.

You might also consider the value of having participants create their own case studies. Here is a procedure you can follow to do this:

1. Divide the group into pairs or trios. Invite them to develop a case study that the remainder of the group can analyze and discuss.

2. Indicate that the purpose of a case study is to learn about a topic by examining a concrete situation or example that reflects that topic. Give some of these examples:

   - A transcript of a performance review can be analyzed to study how to appraise employees effectively.

   - An account of how a company set up a succession-planning program can be used to study promotion policies.

- A dialogue between a manager and an employee can be examined to learn how to provide positive reinforcement.

- The steps taken by management in a company undergoing a merger can be studied to learn about organizational change.

3. Provide adequate time for the pairs or trios to develop a short case situation or example (one hundred to two hundred words long) that poses an issue to be discussed or a problem to be solved that is relevant to the subject matter of the session. Give these suggestions:

- Use either a real situation or example or an invented one for the case study.

- Make the material subtle and challenging; don't be obvious about what's right or wrong.

- Allow for different points of view.

4. When the case studies are complete, have the groups present them to the large group. Allow a member of the group to lead the case discussion.

GUIDED TEACHING

Instead of a presentation, ask a series of questions to tap the knowledge of the group or obtain their hypotheses or conclusions. Record their ideas, if possible, and compare them to the presentation points you have in mind. The guided teaching method is a nice break from straight lecturing and allows you to learn what participants already know and understand before making your own instructional points. Because it utilizes a Socratic teaching technique, this method encourages self-discovery. Here are two examples.

EXAMPLE: In a basic management skills course, the trainer wanted to broaden participants' thinking about motivation. He displayed the following question on a PowerPoint slide: "Why does an employee quit?" Numerous and varied responses were given: insufficient money, limited opportunity, lack of recognition or appreciation, conflicts with the supervisor, desire for a career change, and so on. Participants were then asked to categorize their answers into like groups. By interspersing his own ideas, probing, and prompting, the trainer guided the group into identifying three categories: employee factors such as career change, management factors such as conflicts and recognition, and organizational or system factors such as reward systems and culture.

EXAMPLE: While training nurses to develop a plan for teaching patients to prepare for surgery, a trainer decided to refrain from lecturing and instead to use a guided teaching approach. She began by asking the participants what they would want to know before they begin preparing the patient (the patient's fears and concerns, understanding of the surgery, and so on). She then led the group into identifying any deviations in anatomy and physiology and the corrective effects of surgery to be addressed in the teaching plan. From issues of anatomy and physiology, the trainer moved to what elements of the preoperative waiting period the group felt were important to include in the plan (for example, diagnostic studies or dietary and activity restrictions). This discussion flowed into an examination of the components of the postoperative period (recovery room, pain management, exercises, and so on) that needed to be presented. Whenever possible, the trainer asked other questions based on participants' responses (for example, "Yes, mentioning the equipment that the patient can expect to see surrounding him or her postoperatively is an important item. What would you say if you were unsure what equipment would be used?").

Here are some procedural guidelines for using a guided teaching approach:

1. Pose a question or a series of questions that stimulate the thinking of participants. Ask questions that have several possible answers, such as "How can you tell how intelligent someone is?"

2. Give participants some time in pairs or subgroups to consider their responses.

3. Record the ideas of participants. If possible, sort their responses into separate lists that correspond to different categories or concepts you are trying to teach. In the sample question in item 1, you might list ideas such as the ability to solve difficult puzzles or rebuild an engine under the category of motoric intelligence.

4. Present the major learning points you want to teach. Have participants figure out how their responses fit into these points. Note ideas that add to the learning points of your lesson.

GROUP INQUIRY

Instead of asking questions, the trainer can challenge participants to devise their own questions to further their understanding of a topic.

If participants have little prior knowledge of the material, they should be presented with relevant instructional materials first (for example, work examples or handouts) to arouse their curiosity and interest and to stimulate questions. Posing a problem that the group must solve might also encourage questions. Allow sufficient time for the group to form some questions, then field the questions one at a time or as a whole group. This method allows you to gear teaching to participants' needs. This works well in a virtual setting when participants have downloaded the content.

Notice how participants' questions are sparked in these two examples.

EXAMPLE: For a course entitled "New Drug Development," the trainer handed out a chart that described what occurs during preclinical and clinical testing of a new drug. Participants were placed in small groups and asked to study the chart and circle any terms or symbols they did not understand. Since the chart was somewhat ambiguous, many items were circled. For example, participants wanted to know the difference between a Phase I, Phase II, and Phase III study and what was meant by "long-term" animal testing. After providing answers to these questions, the trainer asked the participants to study the chart further and develop "why" and "how" questions, such as "Why is animal testing continued after human testing begins?" and "How does the Food and Drug Administration monitor a drug after it has been approved?" Because of the lively questioning, participants were highly engaged and left the session with a good understanding of drug-testing procedures.

EXAMPLE: For a course entitled "Cross-Cultural Issues for an International Assignment," the trainer emailed descriptions of a series of interactions between Indonesians and Americans. One such incident is described in Figure 5.2.

FIGURE 5.2 THE QUIET PARTICIPANT

Machmud, a native of Indonesia, had recently been promoted to a position of authority and was asked to represent his company's and Indonesia's needs at the head office in Butte, Montana.

His relationships with his fellow workers seemed cordial but rather formal from his perspective. He was invited to attend many policy and planning sessions with other company officials, where he often sat, rather quietly, as others generated ideas and engaged in conversation.

FIGURE 5.2 continued

The time finally came when the direction the company was to take in Indonesia was to be discussed. A meeting was called, which Machmud was invited to attend. As the meeting was drawing to a close after almost two hours of discussion, Machmud, almost apologetically, offered his first contribution to the meeting. Almost immediately, John Stewart, a local vice president, said, "Why did you wait so long to contribute? We needed your comments all along." Machmud felt that John Stewart's reply was harsh.

Source: Brislin, 1986. Reprinted by permission of Sage Publications.

Rather than explaining the specific cultural differences involved in each incident, the trainer invited the group to ask him questions, based on the descriptions, about Indonesians, their behavior, and their culture. Some of their questions were immediately relevant to understanding the assigned incidents, while other questions were helpful in understanding a wide range of events that the participants might experience when working with Indonesians. It was unlikely that the group would have developed as many insightful questions without the stimulus of the critical incidents.

Here are some procedural guidelines for using group inquiry:

1. Distribute to participants an instructional handout of your own choosing. (You may use a PowerPoint slide or page in a text instead of a handout.) Key to your choice of handouts is the need to stimulate readers' questions. A handout that provides broad information but lacks details or explanatory backup is ideal. The goal is to evoke curiosity. An interesting chart or diagram that illustrates some knowledge is a good choice. A text that's open to interpretation is another good choice. You may also find presentations on YouTube or one of the many TedTalks that could stimulate interest.

2. Ask participants to study the content with a partner or small group. If online, request that all participants read or review the material before the session and place them in a breakout room. Request that each group make as much sense of the written material or the video as possible and identify what they do not understand by placing questions next to the information they do not understand

or listing it on a whiteboard online. Encourage the participants to insert as many question marks as they wish (or have them highlight what they question). If time permits, combine small groups and allow time for the participants to help one another.

3. Reconvene the group and field participants' questions. In essence, you are teaching through your answers to participants' questions rather than through a preset lesson. Or, if you wish, listen to all the questions together and then teach preset content, making special efforts to respond to the questions the participants posed.

4. If you feel that participants will be lost trying to study the material entirely on their own, provide some information that orients them or gives them the basic knowledge they need to be able to inquire on their own. Then proceed with participant self-study and questioning.

5. In a virtual classroom, be sure to email these materials to participants before the session, along with what will be expected of them.

INFORMATION SEARCH   This method is like an open-book test. Hand out worksheets containing questions about the topic. Have the group search for the information, which you would normally cover in a presentation on the Internet or in source materials you have provided. This is especially important if there are resources they should be familiar with as a result of your session, such as documents, reference guides, corporate artifacts, and work-related equipment. In some cases you may develop customized worksheets. The search can be performed by small teams or individuals. You can even set up a friendly competition to encourage full participation. Notice how an information search method serves to liven up dry material in the following two examples. In a virtual setting participants could search for the information prior to the start and then you can ask them to share it during the webinar.

Example: For a mortgage product sales and marketing program, a trainer devised a worksheet containing fill-in-the-blank items, true-false items, and a matching test. (See Figure 5.3 for some sample questions.) Participants were organized into teams and told to gather information from a variety of sources found in the training room. Each team also needed someone with a calculator feature on a Smartphone. When a team completed all items to the satisfaction of all team members, it brought the results to the trainer for scoring. Teams were given points on how quickly they finished. A penalty of sixty seconds per incorrect answer was assessed before the final results were tallied.

FIGURE 5.3 INFORMATION SEARCH

Your mortgage applicant has indicated that a deposit of $10,000 has been made. What follow-up steps must be taken to account for this earnest money?

To be eligible for a mortgage from our bank, second homes must be family- and owner-occupied.

True _____   False _____

In the space to the left of each number, write the letter corresponding to the correct definition.

_____ 1. Principal   A. A conveyance of interest in real property as security for payment of a debt

_____ 2. Amortization   B. The amount of the loan outstanding at a particular point

_____ 3. Mortgage   C. The process of paying down principal through the life of the loan

---

EXAMPLE: A typical new employee orientation program is a dump of information about the organization participants are entering. Instead, a trainer divided participants into small groups and distributed some company literature to each member. The participants were challenged to be the first group that successfully found answers to the following questions:

- In what year was the company founded?
- Where is the company's home office?
- Who is the current CEO?
- What was the company's net profit last year?

- How many employees work for the company?
- What are the company's major products?

Here are some procedural guidelines for using information search:

1. Create a group of questions that can be answered by searching for information that can be found in resource material you have made available for participants. The resource material can include

   - Websites, or other computer-accessed information
   - Organizational documents, such as a strategic plan or a marketing plan
   - A textbook or other reference guides
   - Magazine or journal articles
   - Online videos
   - Course materials or specially-prepared handouts
   - Maps or diagrams
   - Corporate manuals, employee handbooks
   - Artifacts
   - Work-related equipment

2. Hand out the questions about the topic.

3. Have participants search for information in small teams. Consider setting up a competition to encourage participation.

4. Review the answers as a large group. Expand upon the answers to enlarge the scope of learning.

STUDY GROUP

Ask participants to read a short, well-formatted handout covering presentation material and then place them in small groups to clarify its contents. A study group is an excellent way to cover new material without lecturing. Here are examples.

EXAMPLE: Sales representatives were given a handout explaining a SPIN sales call sequence: *situation* questions, *problem* questions, *implication* questions, and *need-payoff* questions. They were placed in study groups and asked to review the handout found in Figure 5.4.

Following this, they were challenged to develop a model sales call that illustrated the use of these four types of questions.

FIGURE 5.4 SPIN QUESTIONS

Successful salespeople ask a lot of questions, but they're definitely not asked at random. A successful sales call follows a distinct pattern that research psychologist Neil Rackham calls the SPIN sequence.

A SPIN sales call follows this sequence:

1. ***Situation questions.*** At the start of a call, ask data-gathering questions such as "How long have you had your present equipment?" or "Could you tell me about your company's growth plans?"

2. ***Problem questions.*** After the buyer's situation has been established, ask questions to uncover problems, such as "Is this operation difficult to perform?" or "Are you worried about the quality you get from your old machine?" These questions explore difficulties and dissatisfaction in areas where the seller's product can help. Inexperienced people don't ask enough problem questions.

3. ***Implication questions.*** These questions take a customer's problem and explore its effects or consequences. This helps the customer understand a problem's seriousness or urgency. For example, you might ask, "How will this problem affect your future profitability?" or "What effect does this reject rate have on customer satisfaction?"

4. ***Need-payoff questions.*** These questions get the customer to tell you the benefits your solution could offer. Typical questions are "Would it be useful to speed this operation by 10 percent?" or "If we could improve the quality of this operation, how would that help you?" Need-payoff questions have a strong relationship to sales success. Rackham has found that top performers ask more than ten times as many of these questions per call as do average performers!

Source: Trifiletti and Alexandri, 2004, p. 335. Used by permission.

EXAMPLE: In a course on team development, a trainer gave participants a handout that charted the differences between effective and ineffective teams along eight dimensions. He then formed study groups and asked participants to take turns reading aloud each of the eight sets of statements on the chart (for example, "Controversy and conflict are seen as positive keys to members' involvement" versus "Controversy and conflict are ignored, denied, avoided, or suppressed"). After reading the statements, each reader was told to ask other group members the following questions:

"Do you want the statements clarified?"

"How do you interpret the statements?"

"Can you give an example from your experience that is related to the statements?"

"Do you agree with the statements?"

The groups were then reassembled, and participants discussed the chart as a whole using a fishbowl format.

Here are some procedural guidelines for using a study group:

1. Give participants a short, well-formatted handout covering presentation material, a brief text, or an interesting chart or diagram. Ask them to read it silently. A study group works best when the material is moderately challenging or open to widespread interpretation.

2. Form subgroups and give them a quiet space to conduct their study session.

3. Provide clear instructions that guide participants to study and explicate the material carefully. Include directions such as these:

   - Clarify the contents.

   - Create examples, illustrations, or applications of the information or ideas.

   - Identify points that are confusing or that you disagree with.

   - Argue with the text; develop an opposing point of view.

   - Assess how well you understand the material.

4. Assign jobs to group members such as facilitator, timekeeper, recorder, or spokesperson.

5. Reconvene the total group and do one or more of the following:

   - Review the material together.

   - Quiz participants.

   - Obtain questions.

- Ask participants to assess how well they understand the material.
- Provide an application exercise for participants to solve.

JIGSAW LEARNING

Jigsaw learning is a variation of a study group. Rather than asking each group to study the same information, you can give different information to different groups and then form study groups composed of representatives of each of the initial groups. It is an exciting alternative whenever the material to be learned can be segmented or "chunked" and when no one segment must be taught before the others. Each participant learns something that, when combined with the material learned by the others, forms a coherent body of knowledge or skill.

Notice how jigsaw learning was employed in the following examples.

EXAMPLE: In a program on succession planning, a trainer formed five groups, with five members in each group. A member from each group selected a component of succession planning by picking one from a hat. The five components were: *replacement charts, critical-position profile, high-potential profile*, and *individual-potential assessment*. Each group received handouts on the component it had picked; these were read and discussed within the group. Then five new groups were formed, each containing one representative from the initial study groups. In these groups, each member explained her or his component to the others. By taking part in this process, every participant was responsible for teaching some of the information to other participants.

EXAMPLE: In an online course on sexual harassment prevention, a trainer divided participants into six study groups and emailed each group material on one of six legal factors that help to decide what constitutes sexual harassment:

1. Quid pro quo harassment
2. Unwelcome behavior
3. Isolated occurrences
4. Hostile environment
5. Prior romantic involvement
6. Ordinary reasonable person

Groups were asked to study the material and to convene one conference call prior to the online course. During the online session jigsaw groups were formed, assigned a breakout room, and given the following six questions to discuss:

1. If a woman has tolerated repeated requests for a date by her boss, does she still have grounds for claiming sexual harassment?

2. Does there have to be a repetitive series of incidents to claim sexual harassment?

3. Does the fact that the victim suffered no mental anguish affect her claim?

4. Whose standards determine how offensive an act is—men's or women's?

5. What is the clearest violation of the law?

6. Can you allege that someone you previously dated sexually harassed you?

The trainer pointed out that all the required information to answer these questions had been acquired by someone in the jigsaw group. The participants were then instructed to share their knowledge to answer the six questions.

Here are some procedural guidelines for using jigsaw learning:

1. Choose learning material that can be broken into parts. A part segment can be as short as one sentence or as long as several pages. (If the material is lengthy, ask participants to read their assignment before the session.) Examples include

   • A multipoint handout (for example, "Ten Strategies for Forming Teams")

   • A text that has different sections or subheadings

   • A list of definitions

   • A group of magazine-length articles or other kinds of short reading material

2. Count the number of learning segments and the number of participants. In an equitable manner, give out different assignments to different groups of participants. For example, imagine a group of twelve participants. Assume that you can divide the learning materials into three segments or "chunks." You might then be able to

form quartets, assigning each group either segment 1, 2, or 3. You would then ask each quartet or "study group" to read, discuss, and learn the material assigned to it.

3. After the study period, form jigsaw learning groups. Such groups contain a representative of each of the other study group. In the example just given, the members of each quartet could count off the numbers 1, 2, 3, and 4, then form jigsaw learning groups of participants with the same number. The result would be four trios. Each trio would consist of one person who had studied segment 1, one who had studied segment 2, and one who had studied segment 3. The diagram in Figure 5.5 displays this sequence.

FIGURE 5.5   JIGSAW LEARNING EXAMPLE

Total Group Explanation

Study Groups

Jigsaw Learning Groups

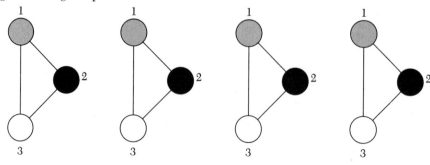

4. Ask the members of the jigsaw groups to teach each other what they have learned or give the groups a set of questions that depend on the varied knowledge of their members.

5. Reconvene the full group for review and any questions remaining to ensure accurate understanding.

In many instances, the number of participants cannot be divided evenly into the number of learning segments and adjustments have to be made (for example, uneven groups). The easiest format for jigsaw learning involves learning partners. Combine the learning material into two segments, assigning one segment to one member of a pair and the other segment to his or her partner. For example, in a seven-point handout, one person can be assigned points 1–4 and the partner can be assigned points 5–7. You can easily create "study buddies" with the same assignment. Then have the original pair teach each other what they have studied.

LEARNING TOURNAMENT   This technique combines a study group and team competition. It can be used to promote the learning of a wide variety of facts and concepts, especially if the information is dry. If you use this approach, provide participants with learning material that you would normally cover in a presentation. Give them time to read and study the material with the knowledge that they will be tested on its contents. Form teams to review the information and test each other. Then give a short quiz on the material to each participant, review (and elaborate on) the answers, and provide instructions on how to score the results and obtain a team average score. To achieve the feeling of a tournament, repeat this process a few times so that teams can rise or fall in their standings relative to each other.

Here are two examples of using learning tournaments.

EXAMPLE: In a session on human resource management, the trainer distributed information about the Americans with Disabilities Act and asked teams to study the facts it contained. In the first round of the learning tournament, every participant took a true-false test. The participants were given five statements:

1. Any new building over two stories high must have an elevator.

2. Organizations with under seventy-five employees are exempt from compliance.

3. Physical requirements for a job may be listed in the job description.

4. The cost of retraining a newly disabled employee is completely assumed by the employer.

5. The term "reasonable accommodations" is clearly defined by government regulations.

After the answers were reviewed by the trainer, the participants totaled their individual scores to obtain a team score. Round 1 was now over and each team returned to study the information further to prepare for round 2 of the tournament. At that time, an additional set of true-false statements was asked of the participants.

EXAMPLE: A trainer decided to use a learning tournament to motivate the learning of "Ten Ways to Obtain Participation," described in Chapter 3. Participants were placed into teams of four members each and given ten minutes to study the material. They were then given the following fill-in-the-blank statements:

- This is a way to obtain participation by asking participants to write instead of speak.

  _____ _____ (response card)

- These are useful in conducting a "go-around."

  _____ _____ (sentence stems)

- This technique is a timesaver when you want small-group discussion but do not have enough time.

  _____ (partners)

- This technique is best when you want to promote participant-to-participant interaction.

  ____ ____ ____ ____ ____ (call on the next speaker)

Here are some procedural guidelines for using a learning tournament:

1. Divide participants into teams with two to eight members. Make sure the teams have equal numbers. (If this cannot be achieved, you will have to average each team's score.)

2. Provide the teams with material to study together.

3. Develop several questions that test comprehension and/or recall of the learning material. Use formats that make self-scoring easy, such as multiple-choice, fill-in-the-blank, true-false, and terms to define.

4. Give a portion of the questions to participants. Refer to this as "round 1" of the learning tournament. Each participant must answer the questions individually.

5. After the questions have been given, provide the answers and ask the participants to count the number they answered correctly. Then have them pool their score with the scores of every other member of their team to obtain a team score. Announce the score of each team.

6. Ask the teams to study again for the second round of the tournament. Then ask more test questions as part of round 2. Have teams once again pool their scores and add them to their round 1 score.

7. You can have as many rounds as you would like, but be sure to allow the team to have a study session between each one.

8. Optionally you may wish to use an online service to provide you with content such as Sporcle, a trivia quiz website on which users have a set time limit to name all the items within a given subject, or Quizlet, an online learning tool with over thirty-five million user-generated flashcard sets.

APPLYING THE ALTERNATIVES TO A COMMON TOPIC

In order to help you consider how the eight alternatives might be applied to a common topic, take a look at the email in Figure 5.6. If you received such an email, how would you respond? Some suggestions follow.

FIGURE 5.6 EMAIL MESSAGE

TO: John Trainer, Assistant Vice President
FROM: Philip Doe, Senior Vice President
Subject: Training

I have noticed that some of the people in our current credit training class still have a poor understanding of some basic accounting principles. I think we should start with the difference between a balance sheet and an income statement.

FIGURE 5.6 continued

Here are some points to stress:

- The balance sheet provides a capsule view of the financial status of an enterprise at a particular date. It helps external users to assess the financial relationship of the assets, liabilities, and owner's equity. Trainees should understand:

  The difference between current and long-term assets

  The difference between current and long-term liabilities

  The difference between liabilities and owner's equity as a claim against assets

  The difference between capital stock and retained earnings

  How to use the previous year's financial information for comparison purposes

- The income statement provides a measure of the success of an enterprise over a specific period of time. It shows the major sources of revenues generated and the expenses associated with these revenues. The income statement helps external users to evaluate the earnings potential of the company.

  Trainees should understand:

  What gross margin measures and how it is derived

  How operating income is determined

  How the bottom line is arrived

  How to compute earnings per share

I know I don't have to tell you how important it is for future credit analysts to have a clear understanding of these two key financial statements. I know that this material is being taught now, but it's not sinking in. Maybe it's the method. Can you think of any better alternatives to just lecturing on this material? Let's brainstorm.

I'd like to see your ideas.

---

1. **Demonstration.** Illustrate the preparation of both an income statement and a balance sheet by walking through the process in a hypothetical situation. Involve participants in some of the steps, such as separating the income statement accounts from the balance sheet accounts and performing the basic calculations.

2. ***Case study.*** Prepare a written case description of an owner of a business who is seeking help in preparing an income statement and a balance sheet for the year ending December 31. Describe in detail the data provided by the owner and how this information was organized by the accountant in order to prepare the two statements. Have the participants complete the income statement and balance sheet; then hold a discussion to review the two processes and how they differ.

3. ***Guided teaching.*** Provide the participants with a list of account balances of a real or fictitious company. Ask them to select accounts that should be reported on the income statement and accounts that would appear on the balance sheet. If no one in the group knows the answers, encourage speculation. Present the correct lists. Ask the participants if they can figure out the basis for the two lists (for example, revenue and expense accounts belong on the income statement, while accounts showing the company's financial position belong on the balance sheet). After the group understands the basis for separating the accounts, discuss a proper format for preparing the income statement and the balance sheet. Ask as many questions as you can to push the participants into their own inferences and deductions.

4. ***Group inquiry.*** Provide examples of an income statement and a balance sheet for a company. Ask participants to study the examples in order to figure out how the two processes differ. Volunteer no further information, but encourage participants to ask you as many questions as they like. Using their own powers of inquiry and discovery, participants should be able to understand the concept being taught.

5. ***Information search.*** Create quiz questions on the difference between a balance sheet and an income statement. Give out a short reading assignment that effectively describes and illustrates the two processes and have the participants, individually or in small teams, search the material for answers to the questions in the quiz.

6. ***Study group.*** Give participants the reading assignment described in the previous suggestion; then form small groups so that they can clarify with each other the contents of the reading assignment. Reconvene the full group and answer any questions. Make *brief* presentation points where necessary.

7. *Jigsaw learning.* Pair up participants. Give one member of the pair information about a balance sheet and the other member information about an income statement. Ask them to teach each other what they have read and to figure out the difference between the two.

8. *Learning tournament.* Form teams and give them reading material about balance sheets and income statements. Stop their study session and quiz them on the difference between the two. Compare the scores of each team. Have the teams return to study the reading material; then quiz them again about the details of balance sheets and income statements.

Now consider a very different challenge. Imagine that you want participants to have a solid grasp of the twelve ways to improve meetings listed in Figure 5.7. What alternatives to lecturing would you select to teach this material? Compare your thoughts with the suggestions that follow.

FIGURE 5.7 TWELVE WAYS TO IMPROVE YOUR MEETINGS

1. Send out agendas in advance.

2. Be prepared with supporting facts and opinions.

3. Select problems that can be managed and solved.

4. Don't waste time. Stick to the issues at hand.

5. Agree on a definition of the problem before moving to solutions.

6. Allow adequate time for each problem-solving step.

7. Encourage positive confrontation.

8. Focus on the issues, not the people.

9. Take turns chairing long meetings.

10. Vary the pace of the meeting between reporting and discussion.

11. Rank alternative solutions before deciding on the best ones.

12. Determine a date on which to check on implementation of the decision.

---

1. *Demonstration.* Illustrate the twelve ways to improve your meetings by simulating a meeting with your participants. Use such topics as summer party planning or monthly budget evaluations. Give participants a checklist (such as a copy of the twelve suggestions) to guide their observations of your techniques.

2. ***Case study.*** Hand out a case description of two meetings held one week apart: an ineffective one and one that was productive from beginning to end. Ask participants to figure out how the improvement might have been achieved.

3. ***Guided teaching.*** Put up on the wall two sheets of flip-chart paper that are blank except for the titles "Good Meetings" and "Bad Meetings." Ask participants to recall their own experiences in meetings, and volunteer suggestions as to what made the meetings positive or negative. List suggestions on the charts; then compare them to the presentation points you have in mind.

4. ***Group inquiry.*** Hand out a copy of the twelve ways to improve meetings. Divide the participants into small groups. Ask each group to come up with three questions that they would like you to answer concerning the information on the handout. Answer the questions in a large-group format.

5. ***Information search.*** Provide brief examples of the twelve ways to improve meetings without identifying which example illustrates which suggestion. Have pairs work together to match examples to the suggestions on the list. Ask the pairs to find examples on the Internet of good and/or poor meeting examples.

6. ***Study group.*** Divide participants into small groups and ask each group to study the twelve ways to improve meetings, clarifying each point and discussing their opinions of its worth.

7. ***Jigsaw learning.*** Divide the twelve points into three sets of four each. Divide participants into trios and give one set to each member to read. Reconvene the trios and give each trio the task of using its members' respective information to improve the effectiveness of a meeting in which none of the twelve ways are present.

8. ***Learning tournament.*** Create teams of two and give members the list in Figure 5.7. Tell each pair that they have two minutes to memorize the list. Give teammates one minute to test each other. Then ask each team to write down the twelve ideas from memory. The team with the highest number recalled wins the tournament.

Now consider a topic from your own training situation. How could you avoid lecturing about it? As you think about this, remember that the methods can also be combined. For example, group inquiry can almost always follow one of the other alternatives. Used in this way, it serves as a way to debrief the training activity. Likewise, a study group can precede many of the other methods in order to provide a knowledge base for later application.

WORKSHEET

FINDING ALTERNATIVE METHODS TO PRESENTING

Use the following worksheet to design an alternative to the presentation you selected in Chapter 4.

Topic: (check one)

_____ Demonstration

_____ Case study

_____ Guided teaching

_____ Group inquiry

_____ Information search

_____ Study group

_____ Jigsaw learning

_____ Learning tournament

Design Outline:

_____

_____

_____

_____

_____

_____

_____

_____

_____

_____

_____

_____

_____

_____

_____

_____

_____

◆   ◆   ◆

Chapter Six

Using Experiential Learning Approaches

Active training promotes learning by doing. As indicated, even a presentation has to be designed to involve the participation of the learner and, at times, it can be replaced by one of several methods that facilitate more direct acquisition of information. Still other methods place an even greater premium on active, participatory learning.

Experiential learning not only enhances the understanding of concepts but is also the gateway to skill development. Whenever you want participants to develop skills (e.g., creating spreadsheets, operating equipment, interviewing job candidates), it's imperative to go beyond showing them how to do it. They must do it themselves, not just once but often, at first with your guidance and then on their own.

Experiential learning approaches are particularly suited for affective and behavioral training goals. They help participants become aware of their feelings and reactions to certain issues and new ideas. In addition, they allow participants to practice and refine new skills and procedures. In this chapter, we will examine and illustrate six major experiential learning approaches:

1. Role playing

2. Games and simulations

3. Observation

4. Mental imagery

5. Writing tasks

6. Action learning

ROLE PLAYING

Role playing is a staple in any active trainer's repertoire. It is the best-known way to help participants both experience certain feelings and practice certain skills. Let's say, for example, that your training objective is to have participants get in touch with their feelings about confronting others (something many supervisors and, indeed, people in general avoid). You can set up a dramatic situation in which participants are required to confront someone else and then discuss the feelings generated by the role-playing experience. In addition, you can design a role-playing exercise to enable participants to practice constructive methods of confrontation.

Scripting

You have many choices when designing role-playing exercises. One set of choices has to do with the *scripting* of the drama. Scripting is concerned with the development of roles and the situation in which the drama is placed. Here are six options:

1. ***Improvisation***. Participants can be given a general scenario and asked to fill in the details themselves. This approach promotes spontaneity and the opportunity to gear the scenario to one's own work experience. Because the situation is not clearly outlined, however, participants may have difficulty creating details on their own.

   EXAMPLE: "Let's imagine that you are at a restaurant and your order is overcooked. Let's have Mary be that customer and request that the order be redone. What if Frank is the waiter and he gives the customer a hard time? Mary, you will try to persuade the waiter to redo the order. I'd like to see you both use all the skills we've been practicing so far."

2. ***Prescribed roles***. Participants can be given a well-prepared set of instructions that state the facts about the roles they are portraying and how they are to behave. This approach gives you the most control over the script, so the dramatic tension you want to create is easily obtainable. However, participants may not identify with the roles and situation you have developed or they may get lost if the scenario is too complex.

   EXAMPLE: "You are an accountant for an insurance company. You have been with the company since your graduation from college three years ago. You really like the company, feel you are doing well, and are looking forward to a promotion. You like your work except for writing letters, emails, and notes on your accounting reports. You've never admitted it to anyone, but you've always had difficulty in English. Your manager has just called you in. You're afraid it might be about your writing. You'll admit your deficiency only if your manager seems genuinely interested and concerned; otherwise, you will make up excuses."

3. *Semi-prescribed roles*. Participants can be given information about the situation and the characters to be portrayed but not told how to handle the situation. By not prescribing how characters are to behave, this approach provides greater latitude for the participants. Some of them, however, may create a scenario different from what the trainer intended.

EXAMPLE: "You are a recently appointed supervisor of a support engineering group that has overall responsibility for maintaining and improving test equipment hardware and software at its repair centers. There are twenty engineers, differing widely in age and experience with the company. Each engineer is responsible for a specific list of test equipment. Up until now, staff members have not been called upon to work on test equipment that is not on their designated lists. This has meant that when one of them is sick or on vacation or has a priority assignment, it is difficult for anyone else to take up the slack.

"You have decided to assemble a small team within the group to develop Support Test Equipment Protocols (STEPs) that will provide the information necessary to support the various pieces of test equipment. With these STEPs, you will be able to establish a rotation system within the group. The people you have invited to be on the team include two senior project engineers and two hardware and software technicians.

"This is the first meeting of the group. Begin the meeting."

4. *Replay of life*. Participants can portray themselves in situations they have actually faced. This approach has the advantage of bringing the most realism to the drama. However, it can be difficult to re-create the actual situation and the role play may then flounder.

EXAMPLE: "I'd like each of you to think about the last time you gave a performance appraisal. Tell your role-playing partner what generally happened and reenact the situation, the first time keeping to the approach you took when you actually gave the appraisal and the second time altering your approach to include the suggestions I have demonstrated."

5. *Participant-prepared skits*. Participants can be asked to develop a role-playing vignette of their own. This approach provides them with time to create a role play and gives them a chance to rehearse before a final performance. Participants will respond especially well to this approach if they are invited to address their real-life problems and incorporate them into the skits. However, some of the spontaneity of the previous options is lost.

> **EXAMPLE:** "I'd like you and your partner to take the three management styles we've just discussed and create a skit that shows a manager using each of the styles while giving project instructions to an employee. Base your skit on your own experiences. Take about ten minutes to prepare your skits. When you're ready, let me know and we will take a look at what you've come up with."

6. *Dramatic readings*. Participants can be given a previously prepared script to act out. This approach creates the least anxiety of any of the previous options and allows the least skill practice.

> **EXAMPLE:** "Here is a script of an exit interview. It demonstrates very effectively some of the problems and some of the solutions we've been examining. In your pairs, one will be the interviewer and the other will be the employee who is leaving the company. Read your parts aloud to get a feel for the tension and relief experienced in the situation."

Of course, a trainer has the option of combining these scripted choices. For example, participants could be asked to read a script and then act out the same drama without the script in front of them. Or they could be allowed to prepare their own scenario, followed by a trainer-prepared scenario. Mixing scripting options in this manner helps to minimize the disadvantages of any single option.

What about Virtual Role Plays?

Scripted role plays work best in a virtual classroom setting. Create a slide that sets up the activity. For example, "Scripted Role Play: How to Address a Hijacked Presentation." Explain that you need two volunteers and show a second slide that says, "Two volunteers needed. Click 'Raise Hand' to volunteer." Select the first two people who raise their hands and assign the two roles: the presenter and the person who is hijacking the presentation. Unmute the audio for the two volunteers. Show the next slide on which a script is written and ask the volunteers to read it aloud. The script should be labeled for the "presenter's" text and the "hijacker's" text. Generally the exchange will be no more than six to eight exchanges. You can demonstrate a "wrong way" first, pause for comments from the rest of the group, and then demonstrate the "right way" with an additional slide and more script. Note that without the visual clues and body language that are present in a physical classroom, it's difficult to carry out a traditional role play. Scripting a role play provides a place to start and often they will continue on with additional comments of their own.

Staging

Another set of choices has to do with *staging*. Staging is concerned with the format you use for the role play, regardless of the content. Here are five options:

1. **Informal role playing**. The role play can evolve informally from a group discussion. An informal format reduces the stage fright often experienced with role playing.

   EXAMPLE: A participant says, "I can't get any cooperation from my boss." Wanting to understand the situation better, you spontaneously respond, "In order for me to have a clearer picture of what usually transpires between you and your boss, let me pretend to be your boss and you ask me for something you need from me. I'll respond the way I think your boss typically does, but if I'm off base, let me know. We don't have to set this up in any formal way. Stay seated where you are and just start off the conversation."

2. **Stage-front role playing**. One pair, trio, or the like can role-play in front of the group, which will observe and offer feedback. Staging a single-group role play focuses everyone on a single drama for later discussion and feedback and allows for maximum coaching and feedback by the trainer. Often, stage-front role plays are the most anxiety-producing for the participants chosen. In addition, the rest of the participants are relegated to an observer role.

EXAMPLE: "I need three volunteers who will portray for the rest of us a family discussing the college choices of their child, who is a high school junior. Would someone agree to be the father, someone the mother, and someone the student?"

3. *Simultaneous role playing*. All participants can be formed into pairs for a two-person drama or trios for a three-person drama, and simultaneously undertake their role plays. A multiple-group format reduces anxiety and allows everyone to participate. However, the trainer may have difficulty monitoring the dramas that unfold and the level of performance demonstrated by participants.

EXAMPLE: "I'd like you to pair up with the person seated next to you and turn your chairs around to face each other. You should move away from the other pairs so that you have some privacy. One of you needs to volunteer first to be the client; the other will be the salesperson. Each of you will then get to practice how to close a sale."

4. *Rotational role playing*. Actors in front of the group can be rotated, usually by interrupting the role play in progress and replacing one or more of the actors. Although this option involves a single-group drama, several participants can still be included. This approach is less demanding than a nonrotating stage-front drama.

EXAMPLE: "I'd like to set up a scene in which an irate customer is calling to complain that her claim check has not yet arrived and the claims adjuster somehow needs to remain courteous under great pressure. This time we'll do something a little different. After every thirty seconds of the conversation, I'll tap out the role players, and their parts will be picked up by the next person in line."

5. *Repeated role playing*. Regardless of the staging option chosen, the role play can be reenacted. This is always a good idea when you want participants to have a second chance after the initial feedback.

EXAMPLE: "Now that you've had a chance to try out this problem situation once, I'd like you to try it a second time. This time make any changes you'd like that will improve upon your performance. Think of it as a dress rehearsal before going out to the real world and actually doing it. Good luck!"

Once again, there are many ways to combine these staging options. For example, simultaneous role playing can be followed by a stage-front format. Or rotational role playing can precede the use of different actors. Also consider the numerous choices generated by combining different scripting and staging approaches. In fact, with six of each, you have thirty-six different options. To introduce role playing to a reluctant group, for example, you can divide participants into pairs (simultaneous staging) and give them a prepared script to read (dramatic readings). To refine skill development later on, you might try the use of different actors to stage a semi-prescribed role play.

Processing

You have six choices for *processing* the role play. Processing pertains to reflective discussion or debriefing of the role play or to giving performance feedback to the role players.

1. **Designated observers**. One or more observers can be added to each role-playing group and given specific instructions about what to observe and how to give feedback. (If you are using a single, stage-front role play, choose specific participants to be feedback observers.) Peer feedback is a two-edged sword. Participants are less threatened by it but, at the same time, they may not value it as much as the trainer's feedback.

     EXAMPLE: "In your trio, each of you will take a turn observing the other two. When a role play is finished, share with the actors the nonverbal behaviors you saw that didn't seem to match what was being said."

2. **Self-assessment**. The role players themselves can discuss their reactions to the experience. Ask open-ended questions first so that the role players are free to make observations on their own. Ask more pointed questions later on, probing gently about feelings, intentions, and reactions.

     EXAMPLE: "Take a few minutes as a group and share how you felt about the role play. When did you feel effective and when did you feel that others were effective? What felt uncomfortable? What would you like to do better the next time?"

3. **Open audience discussion and feedback**. Invite the group as a whole to give their reactions and feedback to a role play. You can avoid a free-for-all feedback session by providing guidelines such

as asking the audience to give positive feedback first or focusing on specific events rather than global impressions. Try to obtain several points of view because different observers notice different things.

> **EXAMPLE:** "Now that we've seen how Brad handled the customer's complaint, I'd like you first to comment on the good points and then to suggest how Brad could do things differently."

4. ***Subgroup discussion and feedback***. Assign a small group from the audience to each one of the role players and ask the members to discuss what they saw happening. This technique is especially effective after the format of use of different actors. Ask the subgroup members to use the time not only to give feedback but also to obtain the actor's self-assessment.

> **EXAMPLE:** "Since we had three characters in this role play, I will ask the audience to count off by threes. The 'ones' will go off with Joan and discuss her reactions to the role play and the reactions they had to her performance. The 'twos' will go off with Don and do the same. The 'threes' will go off with Lee."

5. ***Trainer observations***. You can give your reactions to the role play for everyone to hear. Because your feedback is often held in high regard, be careful to preserve the self-esteem of the role players and "own" the feedback by saying such phrases as "It seemed to me…" or "I'm not sure how others saw this, but I…"

> **EXAMPLE:** "I'm really impressed by the number of techniques you wove into your performance. I especially liked the way you handled Pat's resistance. Your empathy really disarmed him. You might consider, for fine-tuning purposes, pausing a little more to emphasize what you're saying. Is this feedback helpful?"

6. ***Benchmark comparison***. The role players and observers can compare the performance to an ideal script. Be sure, however, to give participants the opportunity to disagree with the "ideal."

> **EXAMPLE:** "Let's take a look at a textbook example of this sales presentation. Look over this script and find things in it that you wish you had done. But also identify what you don't like. We'll get back together in fifteen minutes, after you've had a chance to read the script and discuss it with your seat partners."

Video Feedback

In addition to the processing options mentioned, you can arrange for *video feedback*. Recommend that each person record themselves on their own phone. Be prepared with an alternative if someone does not have a phone available. Here are some guidelines when facilitating video feedback.

Prior to the Recording

- Give learners adequate time to prepare for recording so that they perform well enough to have a positive learning experience.
- Establish small groups of four or five participants and assign a place well away from the other small groups.
- Lighten the mood so that the performance is as natural and relaxed as possible.
- Consider leaving the room of the video recording session initially to encourage learners to experiment and record each other briefly. Do this to help them become less camera-conscious.

During the Recording

- Don't make teaching points when participants are recording. Hold off until later.
- Do make notes of what the learner is doing well and what needs to be improved. Start to think about what parts of the recording you may want to review carefully with the learner. (If using professional equipment, you may want to keep a running time notation system so that you can easily locate critical parts later on.)

After the Recording

- Give learners uninterrupted time to review their own recordings. You may ask a general questions such as, "So how did that go for you?"
- If you placed them in small groups, use these peer support groups that observed other's performance and recording. Have the members give feedback to each other.
- Develop a written checklist of specific behaviors that learners can look for in analyzing their recordings.
- If possible, review parts of the recording with each learner. Use effective feedback techniques, such as being descriptive, being

specific, focusing on dos rather than don'ts, and obtaining learners' reactions to your feedback. Invite learners to problem-solve as much as possible instead of giving your own advice first.

Active Skill Development

The classic way to teach a skill is to do a "show and tell" demonstration before asking participants to try it themselves. A more "active" approach is to demonstrate a skill, but with little or no explanation. Instead of telling participants what you are doing, you are asking them to observe carefully the demonstration and tell you what you did. This strategy encourages participants to be mentally alert.

Decide on a skill you want participants to learn. Ask the participants to watch you perform the skill. Just do it, with little or no explanation or commentary about what and why you are doing what you do. (Telling the participants what you are doing will lessen their mental alertness.) Give the participants a visual glimpse of the "big picture" (or the entire skill if it involves several steps). Do not expect retention. At this point, you are merely establishing readiness for learning. Then, form the participants into pairs. Demonstrate the first part of the skill, with little or no explanation or commentary. *Ask pairs to discuss with each other what they observed you doing.* Obtain a volunteer to explain what you did. If the participants have difficulty following the procedure, demonstrate again. Acknowledge correct observations. Have the pairs practice with each other the first part of the skill. When it is mastered, proceed with a silent demonstration of the remaining steps, following each part with paired practice. At the end, have participants perform the entire sequence from the beginning to end.

If you have the opportunity to teach one participant a skill, you can also use the "show but not tell" approach, but be sure to make the participant comfortable by asking questions such as: "What did you see me do?" "What else did I do?" "Would you like me to show you again?"

Once participants can perform a skill on their own with your assistance, challenge them to redo the skill all by themselves (from beginning to end if it involves more than one step). If you have given them any learning aid that shows them what to do, ask them to put the aid away and try the skill without it.

This is an ideal time to pair up participants as "practice partners." Invite participants to demonstrate to their partner how to perform the skill in question. Using practice pairs, participants feel challenged but not threatened by having to perform under the watchful eye of the trainer or of the entire group.

You can also invite participants who can perform a skill to serve as peer tutors for participants who are still struggling. Be sure that the tutor does not seek to show off rather than assist. Remind tutors that the participants they are helping must be able to do the skill by themselves. Merely showing fellow participants what to do or correcting their performance will not get the job done.

You might also up the challenge by requiring participants to perform a skill after a period of time has intervened and the skill might be forgotten. For example, after helping participants in a business writing session to apply one grammatical rule, you might go on and help them learn several other rules. The challenge you can provide is to have them use a rule they learned a while back without any reminders from you.

GAMES AND SIMULATIONS

Some trainers are hesitant to use games and simulations in their programs, fearing that participants will find them too contrived or will dismiss them as mere entertainment. And, certainly, like any other training method, games and simulations are not without risk. Used in the wrong way at the wrong time, they may do little good. Used appropriately, however, they can be an enjoyable and effective way to advance training objectives.

One of the advantages of games and simulations is the extent to which they encourage participants to confront their own attitudes and values. An excellent example is the Prisoner's Dilemma Game. This well-known game is set up in such a way that participants make a choice, often without realizing it, to compete rather than to cooperate. The effects of the choice become evident as the game proceeds. It's a terrific way to help participants become aware of their competitiveness. Many other games perform similar self-revelatory functions.

Games and simulations can also help participants grasp the total course content. An advantage of using a game at the beginning section of a program is that it can give participants a chance to experience the whole before discussing the parts. For example, starting a cross-cultural training program with a simulation game such as Bafa Bafa is a great way to prepare people being transferred abroad for the frustrations, joys, and insights that come from contact with a foreign culture. In Bafa Bafa, participants are separated into two groups. Each group becomes a culture and is instructed in the culture's values and traditions. The two groups then exchange "ambassadors," who observe the other group and return to report on what they have learned about its culture. After consultation time, a different set of ambassadors is exchanged with the charge of interacting with the culture being visited. The game provides an excellent chance to help participants focus on what they consider normal, how they act within their own inner circle, and how they interact with strangers. They usually spend an hour playing the game and then up to five hours discussing how stereotypes are formed and perpetuated.

Games and simulations can also help test the behavioral style and performance of participants. Playing a game at the beginning of a course allows the trainer to identify the styles and skills that already exist and those that need to be strengthened. Playing a game at the end of the course enables the trainer to assess the instructional experience. Take, for example, a simulation exercise called Desert Survival. Players are told that their plane has crashed in the desert, that their only priority is to survive, and that only certain items are available to them. In the first part of the game, players must decide how to survive individually. Then the game is replayed, with groups working toward team consensus. A trainer could include this simulation exercise at the beginning of a course on team building to assess how well teams work toward consensus. Near the end of the course, a similar exercise, such as Winter Survival, could be employed to measure progress in teamwork.

Finally, games and simulations can be used to create performance challenges for participants. For example, in a game called "Go to Market," participants receive roles in a fictional company that is bringing a product to market and must figure out how to avoid certain management pitfalls in order to beat a competitor with a similar product to market. In another example using a supply-chain simulation, participants are put in charge of a cell phone company. They must select a model of cell phone to produce and suppliers to manufacture them, forecast demand, and react to news and events affecting the cell phone marketplace. At the end of the simulation, participants face the financial results of their decisions and a performance review by the company's board of directors.

When designing games and simulations, there are several things to keep in mind.

The game or simulation needs to be relevant to the participants.

EXAMPLE: A module on project-planning methods began with a game called Sixty-Four Squares. On a PowerPoint slide the trainer drew a large square and divided it into sixty-four smaller squares (see Figure 6.1). The trainer then selected a square and wrote its letter and number on a piece of paper, without revealing its contents to the group. The participants were challenged to find the "secret square" by asking only six questions. The questions were to be answered by a yes or no. Calling out questions without a plan, it took the group twelve questions to find the secret square. The trainer then commented that the most efficient path to the answer involves a binary approach in which each question reduces the number of eligible squares by 50 percent. For example, if participants had asked whether the secret square

---

FIGURE 6.1 SIXTY-FOUR SQUARES

	1	2	3	4	5	6	7	8
A								
B								
C								
D								
E								
F								
G								
H								

was in rows 1 to 4, they could have ascertained which half of the matrix the square was in. The trainer pointed out that there is also a critical path to follow when it comes to managing a project; the challenge is to find it. All the participants were impressed by the experience, in large part because the game drove home a lesson that was highly relevant to their work situations.

The easiest way to create games and simulations is to mimic the format and characteristics of well-known ones.

EXAMPLE: Technical information is often dry stuff to learn. Television quiz programs can be easily adapted for training groups. Probably the most widely copied ones are "Jeopardy," "Wheel of Fortune," and "Family Feud." Games such as crossword puzzles, bingo, and card games often work, too. You may wish to use applications such as Quizlet or Sporcle to create games for your topics. A clerical staff trainer, for instance, divided participants into teams and gave them an opportunity to teach each other as much information as possible. Then team members were pitted against members of other teams in a head-to-head individual competition of "Trivial Pursuit," using questions from the information the participants had just learned. Thus, both cooperative and competitive methods were used in a gaming approach to learning technical information.

Fun-like, contrived games can be followed by more serious, less contrived ones.

EXAMPLE: The trainer of a course on creative thinking designed for the marketing team of a large training vendor wanted participants to learn and value team brainstorming. He began with a zany exercise in which the team was asked to brainstorm as many uses for dirty undershirts as it could think of. Afterward, the team was asked to select their two most original ideas. The team had a ball, easily generating several ideas and quickly choosing their two best. Next, the team was given an exercise in which they were to generate new ways to market their training services. As each idea surfaced, the only response allowed was to ask a question to clarify each contribution.

The trainer noted that it would be impossible in this brainstorming assignment to select the best ideas as quickly as in the previous one. Instead of a process in which individuals argued for the ideas they thought were best, the team was asked to first develop a set of criteria by which to judge the proposals and to then evaluate each one against the criteria the team had developed. The last step was either to choose the best marketing plans from the original list or somehow to combine the best ideas. Nonetheless, the first exercise had served the purpose of warming the team up and setting the stage for the second and more important exercise.

Instructions for games and simulations need to be carefully thought out.

EXAMPLE: A simulation called "Instant Aging" is designed to sensitize participants to sensory deprivation and the normal process of aging. Participants were given eyeglasses smeared with Vaseline, dried peas to put in their shoes, cotton for both ears, and latex gloves for their hands. They were then asked to take out a pencil and paper and write down their name, address, telephone number, any medication currently being taken, and any known allergies. Next, they were told to take a walk outside the training room, opening the door and finding their way around. The simulation involved a number of directions concerning the order of applying the props, the specific details of the tasks the participants were asked to perform, and the manner in which they were to take turns assisting each other. When all goes well, this experience has a tremendous impact on the participants.

Games and simulations almost always need to be discussed afterward for the experience to be an effective teacher.

EXAMPLE: Talking about what has just happened is important not only to bring the learning into focus but also to take advantage of peer pressure toward positive change. In the middle of a week-long course for new managers at a manufacturing company, the trainer placed a box of Tinker-Toys® in front of the participants, who were seated in pairs. One member of each pair was to assume the role of a supervisor while the other was to be his or her employee. The supervisor's job was to assign the employee the task of building a four-sided object with "something hanging in the middle," and to instruct the employee to accomplish the task in only a few minutes. After the allotted time, each supervisor was asked to seek feedback from the employee about the supervisor's assignment methods and general leadership style. This exchange set the stage for a discussion about appropriate supervisory behavior and direction giving. Many participants enjoyed the experience and felt that they would remember the point of it back on the job. A few participants complained, however, that the exercise was merely a game and that it indicated little about their real work situation. The trainer admitted that the exercise was contrived but then asked others how they found that it applied to their company. Many examples streamed forth from the group and a lively discussion ensued. The resisters, impressed by their peers' insights, were won over.

OBSERVATION Watching others without directly participating can be an effective way to experience learning. Although it is worthwhile for participants actually to practice something, observation by itself can play an important part in a training design. The key is for the observation experience to be active rather than passive. A virtual classroom has a couple of options. A written activity can be submitted to other team members and critiqued. A video can also be recorded and uploaded for "observation" and feedback from the group. If Video Teleconferencing (VTC) is available, many of the options offered can work well in a virtual setting. VTC is a communication technology that permits users at two or more different locations to interact by creating a face-to-face meeting environment. VTC systems transmit bi-directional audio, video, and data streams during the session.

Designing

There are several ways to design observation activities so that participants are actively involved.

Provide aids to help participants attend to and retain pertinent aspects of a demonstration they are watching.

When modeling how to conduct an exit interview, for example, make sure the participants take notice of its critical features by giving an overview of the demonstration and providing a visual display of a few key terms to describe the specific behaviors to be modeled. It may even be helpful to point to these descriptions as they are being enacted. After the demonstration is over, you can help participants retain the observation points by asking them to recall them from memory. You may even want to challenge them to write out an imaginary exit interview that includes all the steps. A pocket-sized card summarizing the features of an exit interview can also be given to the participants for future use as a job aid. Job aids are beneficial to physical and virtual classroom participants.

When participants are observing a role play or group exercise, provide easy-to-use observation forms containing suggestions, questions, and checklists.

Having concrete guidelines helps participants to get the most out of the observation experience. Give them a chance to study the form before the actual observation. You may even want to provide a brief practice exercise. In addition, you can assign specific participants to observe specific behaviors. For example, while some are observing the verbal techniques employed in a sales presentation, others can watch the body language of the presenter.

Provide key questions to help observers focus their attention.

When you find observation forms too specific for your purposes, a few questions can still help to guide observers. For example, observation of group process can be enriched by asking observers to consider (1) who they are most aware of, (2) what that person is doing, (3) what her or his impact is on the group, and (4) how others are reacting to the person.

Expect observers to give constructive feedback in order to challenge them to observe carefully and apply what they have previously learned.

In a longer training program, for instance, you can include several opportunities for observers to provide feedback to each other. At first, these exchanges should be kept short and focused on the positive behaviors displayed. As trust develops in the group, the feedback can be more extensive and more critical. Giving this responsibility to participants pushes them to review what they have been taught and to use it as the basis for their feedback.

Be aware that observers can have strong vicarious experiences if what they are observing has personal impact.

Watching role plays that hit home, for example, often produces a kind of Greek chorus effect. Observers are moved to comment when they can readily identify with the role players. You can facilitate matters by asking observers to disclose the feelings they experienced while watching the drama and to lend emotional support to the role players. Vicarious participation can also be catalyzed by interviews or experiential exercises.

Formatting

Three formats are commonly used in the design of observation activities.

1. The simplest format is to use observers as the audience watching a demonstration, video, role play, and the like "on stage."

   EXAMPLE: Participants in a course on employee discipline watched a video that showed how a supervisor of an accounts payable department confronted one of his bookkeepers.

The bookkeeper had been thirty to forty-five minutes late for work at least seven times in the last three weeks, had come back late from lunch on five occasions, and had made personal calls several times. Prior to the video presentation, the participants were given the observation checklist reproduced in Figure 6.2 for their review. When the video had ended, the participants wrote their responses on the checklist and compared notes with their seat partner. They then reassembled to poll the results of their collective observations.

FIGURE 6.2 OBSERVATION CHECKLIST

---

1. What did the manager do to let the employee know he was listening?

   Maintained good eye contact _____

   Nodded head _____

   Leaned forward _____

   Rephrased well _____

   Other (explain) _____

2. Jot down an example or examples of the manager rephrasing what the employee has told him (for example, "So, let me make sure I understand . . .").

3. Did you notice the manager using any specific rephrasing techniques?

   Verbatim repeating _____

   Paraphrasing _____

   Partial restating _____

4. In general, do you think the manager fully understood the employee's emotion?

   Addressed it directly _____

   Ignored it _____

   Danced around the edges _____

   Other (explain) _____

5. Overall, do you think the manager fully understood the employee's viewpoint before responding? What else might you have asked or clarified?

---

2. Observers can also be assigned to small groups to provide feedback after the small group performs.

   EXAMPLE: On the morning of a three-day course for novice trainers, fifteen participants were divided into three groups. Each participant then gave a ten-minute presentation he or she had prepared the night before; the other four members acted as a training audience. After the presentation, audience observers gave the presenter feedback on (1) things that were done well, (2) skills and techniques used that were previously demonstrated in the course, and (3) suggestions for improvement. Later in the day, participants were asked to reconvene in the same groups. One participant at a time was asked to leave the group for a short time. These people were told, upon their return, to deliver the opening segment of the presentation they had given in the morning. The rest of the members of each group were instructed to select one member each who would act as a troublemaker when the person returned to give the presentation. Other members would then observe and give feedback on how the presenter handled the troublemaker. Finally, observers were asked to identify with the feelings of the beleaguered lecturer.

3. Finally, participants can be arranged in a fishbowl format, where observers form a circle around the individuals they are observing.

   EXAMPLE: Employees of a major defense contractor were taking a course on work team effectiveness. Midway through the course, after learning several work team skills, participants were divided into two equal-sized groups. The members of group A sat around a long conference table, and a member of group B sat directly behind each one of them. Group A was asked to hold a meeting for the purpose of targeting "the most important changes your work teams should make in the way they operate." The group B members were to observe the task and maintenance behaviors of the person in group A seated directly in front of them. After ten minutes, the meeting was interrupted by the trainer, who asked the group B observers to meet with their group A observees and give them feedback. Then, group B was asked to sit at the conference table and conduct the same meeting with group A observing. Again, after ten minutes, a feedback round occurred. This back-and-forth process was repeated two more times, with the net effect that each group had thirty minutes to complete its task and to watch another group undertake the same task. In addition, each participant received feedback three times.

MENTAL IMAGERY

Mental imagery is the ability to visualize an object, person, place, or action that is not actually present. Trainers can design six kinds of imagery experiences:

1. **Visual imagery**—for example, seeing various colored shapes like a golden triangle, a violet circle

2. **Tactile imagery**—for example, shaking someone's hand, feeling its surface and temperature

3. **Olfactory imagery**—for example, smelling the clean mountain air in a pine forest

4. **Kinesthetic imagery**—for example, driving a car, sensing each turn of the wheel

5. **Taste imagery**—for example, attending to the taste and texture of a favorite food

6. **Auditory imagery**—for example, listening to the sound of a voice calling one's name

Being able to design activities that help participants visualize adds a powerful component to your experiential learning repertoire. Although it can be utilized to help participants retain cognitive information, imagery has special value as a way to help them mentally rehearse putting skills into action and to bring feelings and events into focus.

Mental imagery exercises can be used to replace role playing. Since they are internal, they cause less anxiety to participants who are shy about performing before other people. Skills such as speaking before a group or acting assertively, for example, can be practiced successfully through mental imagery, although a minimal amount of role-playing practice must be interspersed with it.

Mental imagery exercises also stimulate discussion. Often it is hard to get a discussion on a particular topic off the ground without a boost. When participants are guided to visualize a real or fantasized experience, thoughts and feelings relevant to a particular topic can be activated. For example, in a workshop on interfaith relations, participants were asked to imagine walking invisibly into the homes of people of different religious faiths and watching how they celebrate different holidays. A discussion followed on the norms of different groups. It was a lively and honest exploration of religious differences.

Guidelines

When conducting mental imagery exercises, certain guidelines are important.

1. *Help participants clear their minds by encouraging them to relax*. Use background music, dimmed lights, and breathing exercises to achieve results.

2. *Conduct warm-up exercises to open the mind's eye*. Ask participants, with their eyes closed, to try to visualize sights and sounds such as a rosebud, their bedroom, a changing traffic light, or the patter of rain.

3. *Assure participants that it's okay if they experience difficulty visualizing what you describe*. Some participants initially block before they are relaxed enough to visualize. Tell them to be patient with themselves. All participants find that other thoughts drift into their mind at times. When this occurs, suggest that they simply bring themselves gently back to the subject being described.

4. *Give imagery instructions slowly and with enough pauses to allow images to develop*. If you use imagery scripts written by others, practice reading them in advance so that your delivery is smooth and well-paced. Keep your voice soft enough to be soothing but loud enough to be clearly heard.

5. *Invite participants to share their imagery*. Sharing should always be voluntary. Keep the reports brief (lengthy disclosures can be boring to the other participants). Participants can also recount their imagery experiences in a journal.

Examples of Mental Imagery Exercises

The following script can be used as a warm-up exercise to promote relaxation breathing with imagery:

> "With your eyes closed, draw and exhale several very deep breaths. Notice the rising and falling of your abdomen. Each time you breathe in, imagine that you are taking in energy from the universe. This is exactly what you are doing. As you exhale, notice that your body is becoming more and more relaxed, more and more peaceful.

"Now imagine that you are seated on a large rock, overlooking a quiet pool of water in some pleasant forest or wooded area. Imagine that nothing disturbs the tranquility of this scene except the occasional jumping of a small fish to the side of the pond. Imagine that, in slow motion, you have picked up a small round stone near where you are sitting, and in very s-l-o-w motion, you are lobbing this stone into the air and watching it descend s-l-o-w-l-y into the very center of the glassy pond. Watch the stone as it travels up and then down through the air. Watch it slowly enter the water, and watch the ripples begin to form. Watch the ripples spread slowly outward toward the edges of the pond. Watch the surface of the water until it is completely still once again.

"Stay with this scene until you are aware of feeling very relaxed and refreshed. When you are ready, notice the sounds around you in the room, gently open your eyes, and go about your day's activities."

Source: Richard McKnight, PhD, *Staying Relaxed in a Tense World* (Learning Project Press, 157 E. Lancaster Avenue, Wynnewood, Pennsylvania 19098, 1985). Used with permission.

Here is a sample script used to help lead a group of employees through the process of preparing to receive a performance appraisal.

I'd like you to close your eyes for a few moments as we explore how to prepare to receive your next performance appraisal. Close your eyes, slow your rate of breathing down, and listen as I walk you through the evaluation process. (pause) First, I would like you to imagine yourself working at your job. Consider aspects of your job that you truly enjoy. (pause) Think about the satisfaction that you receive as you complete that task. (pause) Now, imagine how you would describe the accomplishment of that task to your closest friend. Go ahead, brag about yourself. Explain just how well you like doing that task and why. Consider why you do that task better than anyone else.

"As you continue to keep your eyes closed, I would like you to turn your thoughts in another direction. This time, I would like you to consider an aspect of your current responsibilities that you really do not enjoy. Think carefully about a task related to a responsibility that you do not enjoy. (pause) What is it about this task that you do not like? (pause) Consider all of the different components of this task. Are there any that you believe that you could improve upon? Imagine yourself improving your performance of this task. Consider how you would feel if you handled this task to the best of your ability.

"Now you are ready to walk into your managers office. Instead of being nervous, you feel confident in your abilities. Think back on the images you have just seen. Consider that in an appraisal both positive and negative evaluations of work performance will be discussed. Think back to how you evaluated your own performance as you discuss your appraisal with your manager."

Source: Carol Auerbach. Reprinted with permission.

The following exercise is used in a training program for Dealing with Difficult People.

1. Acknowledge that coping with especially difficult people is a challenge.

2. Invite participants to identify difficult people in their lives and pick one. Then ask them to close their eyes (or use some other focusing technique) and imagine the worst thing that this person could say to them (for example, "You don't care").

3. Next, direct participants to bring to mind their first reaction to that statement, one that reveals how they might respond if the other person "pushed a button" or "struck a nerve." Give an example of your own to guide their thoughts.

4. Continue the imagery experience by directing participants to take a deep breath and then to imagine acknowledging what the person said, even if it was stated offensively. Suggest the response, "I can sense how angry you are." Next, direct participants to imagine asking the other person to be more specific about the complaint. Suggest the request, "Tell me more about what you want from me or what you are feeling about me." Have them imagine a positive response to their query.

5. End the imagery experience and ask participants to identify which suggestions were helpful and which they wished to question.

6. Remind participants that difficult people typically have trouble managing their own stress and tend to attack whoever is accessible. Taking their statements personally allows you to be a victim.

7. Obtain reactions to this observation.

Source: M. Silberman, "Negotiating to Win/Win," in *The Best of Active Training*, ed. M. Silberman (San Francisco: Pfeiffer, 2004), p. 363.

WRITING TASKS

Yet another experiential medium to consider is writing. Like mental imagery, writing is usually an individual activity. It allows each participant to reflect slowly on her or his own understanding of and response to training input.

Writing activities range from short responses to long essays. The most common short form is a *worksheet*, like the ones at the end of each chapter in this book. A worksheet provides specific instructions concerning what the participant is to write. It can be used at any time during a design. For example, a trainer in a course on customer relations might ask participants to fill out a worksheet that asks for brief descriptions of recent encounters with customers. A worksheet might also be assigned at the end of such a course, perhaps asking the participants to set goals for applying course techniques back on the job. *Longer writing* generally works best in the middle of a training design; assigned at the beginning or the end, it can make a program drag. One example of longer writing comes from a course on dealing with problem employees. Participants were asked to recall an especially disturbing incident that happened to them in the past. Then they were asked to write an action account of the incident in the present tense, as if it were happening in the "here and now." This writing assignment was used to help the participants distinguish behaviors from the feelings that accompanied them.

In addition to being used to describe events, writing tasks are useful when any written skill, such as business correspondence, is being taught. Furthermore, trainers can ask participants to record plans, develop verbal scripts, and review material in written form.

Guidelines

When you are about to introduce a writing task, keep these five tips in mind.

1. *Help participants to get in the mood to express themselves in writing*. Do something beforehand to inspire or challenge them. Make them feel that the writing has a good purpose and is not just busywork.

2. *Make sure your instructions are crystal-clear*. If appropriate, you may even want to provide a model for participants to emulate.

3. *Arrange a good work environment for writing*. Establish privacy and quiet. Invite learners to bring their laptops or tablets for a writing project to the session.

4. *Allow enough time for writing.* Participants should not feel rushed. They may need time to get started. On the other hand, don't be overly long. Involvement will slacken. In a virtual environment ask participants to complete writing projects between sessions.

5. *Allow enough time for feedback*. When participants have finished, they may want to share what they have written. One alternative is to invite a limited number of volunteers to read their finished work. A second alternative is to have seat partners share their writing with each other.

Examples of Writing Tasks

EXAMPLE: In a training program on interviewing skills, participants were taught five steps to planning an interview: (1) study the job description, (2) gather information on the organization and career advancement, (3) study the resume of the candidate, (4) list the skills to evaluate in the interview, and (5) write a list of open-ended questions to ask in the interview. At this point, participants were asked to outline questions for use in an interview they might actually conduct. Figure 6.3 reproduces the written instructions.

FIGURE 6.3 INTERVIEWING SKILLS: PLANNING THE INTERVIEW

INSTRUCTIONS:

Outline questions for the job description you developed earlier in class. Please list at least two technical questions and six categories of performance questions. Remember that you will be asking follow-up questions to discover situation, action, and result. Here is an example of a preplanned question outline.

You are interviewing a candidate for the position of fitness trainer for our class using the job description already prepared for you. The list of preplanned questions includes the following:

TECHNICAL

1. Are you certified to teach aerobics?

2. Do you have knowledge of first aid?

FIGURE 6.3 continued

PERFORMANCE

1. In the past, when you sensed that a previous class was losing interest in maintaining their workout schedule, what did you do? (team building)

2. When conflicts arose among class members concerning _____ _____, what did you do? (problem solving)

3. Describe a typical class. (planning)

4. Suppose that several class members had back problems. What would you do to accommodate them? (adaptability)

5. Tell me about the largest group you've had and describe how you maintained control over the group. (controlling)

6. How would you design or market a new aerobics class for a fitness center? (organizing)

YOUR PREPLANNED QUESTIONS

TECHNICAL
1.
2.

PERFORMANCE
1.
2.
3.
4.
5.
6.

EXAMPLE: Participants in a training session on assertiveness are asked to write down a situation in which they would like be more assertive about saying "no" or expecting someone else to do something they need. Following this, they are given a worksheet that invites them to respond to three questions:

1. What exactly do I want in this situation?

2. How insistent am I?

3. What reasons would I give for my refusal or request?

Taking the time to write out their responses to these questions helps participants clarify their goals in the situation, a crucial step in asserting their needs effectively.

EXAMPLE: In a program on organizational vision, the trainer asks participants to think about how their company would be functioning eighteen months from now if anything were possible. They are asked to imagine the following:

- The unique contribution their team or unit is making to the company

- How the team or unit is perceived by others in the company

- The effective ways people in the team or unit are relating to each other

- How much enjoyment people are having because they are part of the team or unit

Participants are then asked to write about this vision as if it were true now and email it to others in their team or unit.

ACTION LEARNING

Action learning involves assigning tasks in which participants, as individuals or as teams, take action on critical, real problems while explicitly seeking learning from having taken that action. These tasks should challenge them to obtain additional information not given by the trainer or to apply what they have learned back on the job. If you design action learning projects that participants find meaningful, you will find that this method has significant learning value.

We will describe and illustrate five kinds of action learning projects commonly used in training programs.

In-Basket Assignments

In-basket assignments are a form of the project method in which letters, emails, phone messages, and so forth are given to the participant playing an assigned role. The participant is then given time to write actual responses to the items in her or his in-basket. Figure 6.4 provides instructions for such an assignment. This assignment could be used in its present form as part of a time management program for managers. It can easily be adapted and the materials downloaded for a virtual classroom.

FIGURE 6.4 IN-BASKET

For the purpose of this exercise, you are to assume the role of Pat Ladder, manager of the operations department in the J. R. Jones Company. As manager of the operations department, you report to the division head, Kelly MacDonald. The following people report to you:

- Jamie White, secretary

- Mike Crossman, facilities maintenance supervisor

- Linda Stevens, property and supplies supervisor

- Stan Powell, security supervisor

- Jay Snyder, transportation supervisor

All of them are capable people and have been in their respective jobs one year or more. The situation this exercise deals with is as follows.

Today is Monday, December 14. You have been away for several days, so you have come into your office at 8:00 a.m. (early) to catch up and get ready for the day. The normal working day begins at 8:30 a.m. Promptly at 8:30 a.m., you must leave to attend a training meeting. Therefore, you only have about thirty minutes to organize your work, and you want to get as much done as possible. You do not expect to return to your office from the meeting until 10:00 a.m. As you reach your desk at 8:00 a.m., you find items in your in-basket.

As you go through the material, take whatever action is needed, assuming that you are Pat Ladder. Use your own experience as a basis for your decisions.

Make notes to yourself or to others by writing directly on the message, email, or voice mail message. Draft or write notes and emails where appropriate. List phone calls you plan to make, including information about when you plan to make the call and whom you plan to call. Note follow-up dates when further action is necessary. Write on the items that need further action, such as "Follow up 12/15" or "File."

After the exercise, you will have an opportunity to compare your actions with others in the group. Remember:

- Put yourself in the position of Pat Ladder.

- Today is December 14.

- You have come in before regular working hours. There is no one else available to help or call.

- You want to get as much out of the way as possible in the thirty minutes you have to spend organizing.

- Record (make mention of) every action you make or intend to make.

- Be prepared to discuss how you handled the exercise with the group.

Research Projects

If preparation time and the necessary data are available, asking participants to conduct some research and present their findings is a valuable
form of learning. This research can be done in small teams or individually. Teams or individuals can have the same or different assignments.
Data can be obtained either from people, from written materials, or
from the Internet.

EXAMPLE: An interesting example of a research project comes
from a course for insurance claims adjusters. The trainer in the
course wanted to avoid long periods of dry presentations intended to
give participants a crash course in tort law and medical terminology,
two things adjusters dealing with accident claims need to know.
Instead, she divided participants into small research study groups.
Every evening during this week-long course, participants were given
assignments (and reference material) that they did individually. For
one hour each afternoon, the groups met to study the information
they obtained and to draw up test questions for the other study
groups. Twice during the week, test questions were swapped among
the groups and the answers discussed. In post-tests, knowledge of
tort law and medical terminology was shown to have increased 60
percent over that gained in previous courses.

Field Observation

An excellent way to do action learning is to set up a "field trip" to
a real-life setting relevant to the training topic. You might begin by
dividing the participants into subgroups of four or five and ask them
to develop a list of questions and/or specific things they should look
for during their field trip. After the subgroups put their questions or
checklist items on flip-chart paper, post them, and share them with the
rest of the group; the total group can discuss the items and develop a
common list for every person to use. You can then give them a deadline
(for example, one week) and direct them to visit a site or sites, using
their list of questions or checklist items to interview or observe. Allow
participants to choose their own sites, or you may want to make specific assignments to avoid duplication or to get good distribution. For
example, with customer service, participants could identify different
types of organizations or businesses such as retail, fast-food, restaurant, health care, hotel, or car repair. They would visit these businesses
as customers and, using their checklist, record their experiences. This
is a perfect between-session activity for virtual classrooms.

Be sure the questions are specific and lend themselves to comparison with each other's findings. For example, with customer service, the following observation items would be appropriate:

- How long did the employee take before acknowledging the customer?

- Did the employee smile?

- Was the employee courteous and polite?

- Did the employee ask open-ended questions to identify the problem?

- Did the employee use active listening techniques? Give examples.

- Did the employee resolve the problem?

- Were you as the customer pleased with the experience? Why or why not?

You might ask the participants to share their findings with the rest of the group through some clever or creative method, such as a skit, mock interview, panel discussion, or game.

Here is an example of action learning using field observation.

EXAMPLE: In a training session entitled "Implementing the Americans with Disabilities Act," participants were given handouts and other information identifying architectural barriers and what business owners are required to do in order to make their buildings accessible. The participants were divided into five groups, with each group assigned a particular barrier such as (1) entrances; (2) parking facilities; (3) workspaces, lounges, and lunchroom; (4) bathroom facilities; and (5) hallways. Each group developed its own checklist for the barrier assigned and identified businesses to visit in order to determine how well the business or organization was meeting the Act's guidelines. They sought answers to the following questions:

Entrances

1. Is there a ramp to the entrance?

2. Are the doorknobs three feet from the ground?

3. Is the door light enough to be opened by someone in a wheelchair?

Parking Facilities

1. Are parking spaces reserved for people with disabilities?

2. Are the parking spaces near the entrance to the building and twelve feet wide?

3. Are there curb cuts so that people in wheelchairs can pass easily?

Workspaces, Lounges, and Lunchroom

1. Are the aisles in these rooms at least thirty-two inches wide?

2. Are work stations, desks, tables, and so on high enough so that a person in a wheelchair can roll up closely enough to sit comfortably?

3. Are the lunchroom and lounges accessible?

Bathroom Facilities

1. Are the doorways to the bathrooms at least thirty-three inches wide?

2. Are the sinks low enough to be used by someone in a wheelchair?

3. Are grab bars installed in the bathrooms?

Hallways

1. Are flashing lights installed for fire alarms so that people with hearing impairments will know there is a fire?

2. Are picture signs displayed to show the purpose of each room so that people who cannot read will know where to go?

3. Are Braille markers posted on the door and in the elevators?

Teaching Projects

It is said that someone really has learned something if she or he can teach it. Another project assignment is to ask participants to teach new information or skills to each other. The teaching can be performed by either individuals or teams in front of the full group or in small groups.

EXAMPLE: In a four-week course on family therapy, participants were formed into teaching teams. Each team was assigned one model of family therapy. In the last week of the course, the team was expected to teach others about the assumptions, key concepts, and intervention methods of its assigned model. Teams were urged to use active training methods. A natural competitiveness usually developed among the teams, which had the effect of producing teaching designs that were creative and of high quality.

EXAMPLE: A team-building trainer assigned teams to demonstrate one of the following attributes: flexibility, interdependence, trust, and openness. Some groups composed skills, some conducted meetings, and some used visual aids such as flip charts or banners in their teaching exercises. Once the demonstration was complete, the rest of the participants critiqued it, highlighting the positive aspects.

Task-Force Projects

The purpose of these kinds of projects is to give participants confidence in their ability to do the same task back on the job. Typically, groups are asked to generate a plan or other specific outcome that can be used by other participants in the actual work situation.

EXAMPLE: In a course on planning and organizing skills, participants were given a planning task based on a real case situation in their company. Task-force groups were formed, relevant materials were given out, and each group was asked to complete its work on a specific form, which was then duplicated and shared among the groups. A debriefing of the work of the task forces followed. The case study (minus the exhibits) and the planning chart that was to be completed are presented in Figure 6.5.

FIGURE 6.5 TASK-FORCE ASSIGNMENT

You are the director of distribution services and planning and you have been given approval by the president of XYZ Company to pilot a new teleselling program (or telemarketing as it is more commonly called). You have been waiting some time for this moment, and the decision represents a victory for your department.

Now the hard work of planning and organizing the project must begin.

BACKGROUND

The teleselling approach is a new one for XYZ. In teleselling a small, highly trained team uses advanced telephone technology to sell to a broad group of customers. To be successful, the teleselling team needs strong training in product knowledge as well as in telephone selling and communications techniques.

Typically, the XYZ sales force has operated on a face-to-face basis. The teleselling team would not supplant the regular sales force. Instead they would be an adjunct to the sales force and would help it reach smaller accounts more efficiently.

Upper management feels that teleselling would be especially useful in reaching accounts between $500 and $2,500 with a special emphasis on products other than hypertensives. In 1985 the company had fifteen thousand Class 19 accounts with total sales of just over $6 million for the year. Teleselling is viewed as a way to boost these sales.

Most of these accounts are too small for regular visits and detailing by the sales force. On the other hand, they would represent an excellent source of business if there were a way of reaching them efficiently. That is why upper management at XYZ finds teleselling so attractive.

But there are problems, too. For one thing, the wholesalers would feel that XYZ was impinging on their turf. The wholesalers are a key link between XYZ and its customers, both large and small, and relationships with the wholesalers would have to be handled carefully.

There are also turf issues within XYZ. The sales force feels that teleselling should be under its control. On the other hand, regional sales offices are located at most of the distribution centers that also handle inventory and transportation control. Ultimately, upper management decides to put the administration of the teleselling program in the hands of distribution, but the sales force will set the criteria for whom to call and what to sell and will provide the training. Thus, to be successful, the program will require excellent relations between sales and distribution personnel.

CURRENT STATUS

It is now August 1 and the president has passed on to you final approval to pilot the teleselling program in the Chicago region. Ultimately, he would like to see four teleselling locations set up, including the pilot. He wants the pilot up and running by the beginning of November. The company has set the following objectives for the program:

- Provide consistent coverage of mid- to low-volume Class 19s and allow more detailing time to field sales

- Increase market penetration

- Increase coverage of ethical and consumer products

- Improve XYZ's image with customers

- Increase sales at less contact cost

The president has given you a list of target products and has suggested that you work closely with the sales and marketing groups on strategies for promoting these products through special offers and other approaches.

You have on your desk the draft of an introductory letter to be sent to accounts in the Chicago region by the branch operations manager.

You have also been working up proposed staffing and budgets for the program.

Current plans call for two part-time telesell workers at the Chicago pilot site who will each work four hours per day. Each worker should be able to make thirty calls a day. You know that a key issue will be training and continued motivation for those involved in the program. From what you have been reading about telemarketing, burnout among workers in such a program can be very high. The total budget for the Chicago pilot program will be $152,000.

Under current plans, distribution will handle the operations of the teleselling program but will work closely with sales representatives. The division manager will send a list of all accounts below $2,500 to the sales representative. The sales rep will in turn determine which of these accounts should be called under the teleselling program, and this information will be given to the branch operation manager.

You have very little time to put the program together, and you are now mulling over how to plan and organize the work for the pilot. You are reviewing a memo prepared by a member of your staff on some of the key issues that will arise in the program. You know that the first and perhaps the most important step is to organize the work well and to plan for any contingencies that might arise.

PLANNING CHART

Prioritized Action Steps   *Time Reference*

_____   _____

_____   _____

_____   _____

_____   _____

_____   _____

WORKSHEET

USING EXPERIENTIAL LEARNING APPROACHES

Now that you have been introduced to these experiential learning approaches, consider which ones you would want to utilize to achieve the objectives in your next training program.

_____ Role playing

_____ Games and simulations

_____ Observation

_____ Mental imagery

_____ Writing tasks

_____ Action learning projects

STRATEGY OUTLINE:

_____

_____

_____

_____

_____

_____

_____

_____

_____

_____

_____

_____

_____

_____

_____

_____

_____

_____

_____

◆　◆　◆

Chapter Seven

Designing Active Training Activities

With objectives set and a variety of training methods at your disposal, you are in a position to develop all of the specific training activities you will need in an active training program.

THE THREE MAJOR INGREDIENTS OF ANY DESIGN

Earlier, we compared opening exercises to appetizers at the beginning of a full meal. Continuing with this delectable analogy, let's consider all the separate activities in an active training program as items on a menu or, if you prefer, dishes in a meal. Each item or dish has certain ingredients. Individual training activities have three: an **objective,** a **method,** and a **format**. How the objective, method, and format combine together is the basic recipe for the design. Your decisions about what is to be accomplished (objective), how it is to be accomplished (method), and in what setting it is to be accomplished (format) will determine the design you wish to create. Let's examine two activities to illustrate these points.

The first example is an activity called "The New Contract." In this activity, the following major decisions have been made:

1. The **objective** is to compare the "old contract" that described the historical employee-organization relationship to the "new contract."

2. The **method** employed is jigsaw learning, described in Chapter 5.

3. The **format** is pairs.

Figure 7.1 presents the details of this design.

FIGURE 7.1 THE NEW CONTRACT

---

1. Make the following points:
   - Change in the workplace is happening at an unprecedented rate.
   - Change is fueled by globalization and technology.
   - Change is likely to be ongoing, and things will not return to their original state.
   - Understanding change and developing strategies to thrive in it have been shown to be very helpful.
2. Ask the participants to form pairs.
3. State that many people today believe that a shift is occurring in the workplace. We are moving from the old implied social contract, which promised lifelong employment in exchange for hard work and loyalty, to a new contract where work is based on situational need and productivity rather than longevity.
4. Ask each pair to assign the number 1 or 2 to each of its members. Hand out the form below and ask the 1s to read about the "old contract" and the 2s to read about the "new contract."

OLD CONTRACT

Organizations value longevity and reward it through benefits programs.

Organizations expect you to work hard and be loyal.

Organizations are hierarchical in their reporting structure.

Organizations are paternalistic and take care of their employees.

Employees' career paths are directed and decided by managers.

Employees are expected to do work assigned to them by their managers.

Employees have job security for life if they work hard and are loyal.

Putting time in and doing the job is highly valued.

Employees expect regular promotions and pay raises if they do the job well.

NEW CONTRACT

Organizations value productivity.

Organizations expect you to work effectively, producing results.

Organizations value employees who keep their skills and knowledge up to date.

FIGURE 7.1 continued

Organizations are made up of clusters of teams that direct their own work.

Organizations empower employees by giving them decision-making authority.

Organizations provide learning opportunities for their employees but do not force employees to participate.

Employees manage their own careers.

Employees remain employed as long as they can make a contribution and their skills and knowledge are needed by the organization.

Organizations are flat and employees may have several lateral moves during a career.

Organizations value employees who are multiskilled.

Employees get pay raises and promotions when they do work that merits them.

Employees are loyal to their professions and engage in lifelong learning.

5. Ask pair members to explain to each other in their own words what they read.

6. Encourage pair members to discuss these different contracts with each other.

7. Reconvene the entire group and facilitate an open discussion on the new contract.

Source: Mundhenk, 1997, p. 33. Used with permission.

The second example is a follow-up activity to "The New Contract" called "Point-Counterpoint." In this activity, the following major decisions have been made:

1. The ***objective*** is to clarify the virtues and liabilities of each contract.

2. The ***method*** employed is a debate.

3. The ***format*** is a fishbowl (group-on-group), followed by a meeting of the full group.

Figure 7.2 presents the details of this design.

FIGURE 7.2 POINT-COUNTERPOINT

1. Divide the participants into two teams and assign a contract to each team, with one team getting the "old contract" and the other getting the "new contract."

2. Explain that the teams are going to debate the virtues and liabilities of each contract.

3. Describe the debate as follows:

    • The old contract team sits on chairs in the middle of a circle formed by the new contract team.

    • One old contract team member starts by reading the statements from the form describing the old contract.

    • All participants in the inner circle engage in a discussion defending the old contract, using their experience and imagination.

    • The teams then change places and repeat the process with the new contract team defending the new contract.

4. Reconvene the entire group and ask participants to add additional insights.

5. State that the new contract isn't necessarily better, that there are benefits to both contracts, but that most supporters see it as liberating and, since it is here to stay, it's important to understand how it is changing our work lives.

Source: Mundhenk, 1997, p. 34. Used with permission.

For many topics, it is possible to make a variety of choices concerning the objective, method, and format of the designs intended to cover them. Let's take, for example, the topic of leadership behavior and, in particular, the concepts of authoritarian, democratic, and laissez-faire leadership styles. Your objectives as a trainer may range from deepening participants' understanding of the consequences of each style (cognitive learning) to allowing participants to experience their differing levels of comfort with each style (affective learning) to providing them with practice in utilizing each style in appropriate situations (behavioral learning). Just as the same menu item can be prepared with different recipes, so, too, can each of these objectives be achieved by a variety of methods and group settings. For example, participants could experience their comfort levels with each style through role playing, mental imagery, or a writing task. Any of the basic formats (full-group, individual, pairs, small-group, or intergroup) could serve as well. In training, as in cooking, art, or music, a desired end can be accomplished by varied means.

When shaping a design, there are several considerations to take into account.

1. *Does the design achieve the activity's objective?* This is the most important consideration. To take an obvious example, a demonstration may show participants a skill or procedure in action without giving them actual practice. Even when the choice of method is appropriate, a particular design may not achieve its purpose. For example, a role play, if poorly designed, may provide little skill practice for participants.

2. *What knowledge or skill level does the design require of participants?* Your assessment of participants is often critical in creating a specific design. For example, a complicated task-force exercise on project planning might be premature for novice project managers. Or another design might not be sufficiently challenging for a particular situation.

3. *How much time will it take?* At any particular point in a program, you may feel that time is limited or, conversely, that a longer design is perfect for the occasion. In general, it is a good rule to keep afternoon activities shorter than morning ones. Further, it rarely pays to skimp on time when you are seeking to accomplish an especially important objective. You would not want, for instance, to give only ten minutes to a discussion of a company's controversial system for disciplining employees.

4. *Is the design slow-paced or fast-spaced?* Regardless of the overall time needed for a design, some activities are slow-moving and others have a quicker pace. Fast-paced activities work best to get the total group involved. Leisurely activities are more appropriate in a small-group format.

5. *Is it suited to the size of the group?* Some designs simply don't work well with large groups. For instance, dyadic role-playing practice is very hard to monitor when the training group consists of more than thirty people. On the other hand, some designs require a critical mass. For example, it can be uncomfortable to participate in a mental imagery exercise in a very small group

(fewer than seven people); the anonymity of a somewhat larger group helps participants to relax.

6. **What skills are required to conduct the design?** It's important to assess how much expertise or facilitation skill a design demands. For example, a study group approach to cognitive material requires less in the way of Socratic skills than does a guided teaching mode.

It is not always possible to answer these questions in advance. Experience is the best teacher when it comes to designing; often the most you hope for is to anticipate what might occur if a particular design is used. Taking small risks is absolutely essential to your development as a trainer: The only way to find out if a design will work for you is to give it a try. A good approach is to change the design of *one* part of your module or course every time you teach, in order to expand your repertoire.

THE REMAINING DETAILS

When the objective, method, and format for a single design have been chosen, several details remain:

1. **Time allocation**. How many minutes will the design take?

2. **Buy-in**. What will you say or do to get participants involved?

3. **Key points and/or instructions**. What are the major ideas in the presentation, and what exactly do you want participants to do?

4. **Materials**. What do you or the participants need in the way of materials to implement the design?

5. **Setting**. How should you set up the physical environment for the design to succeed?

6. **Ending**. What remarks do you want to make and/or what discussion do you want the participants to have before proceeding to the next activity?

Once these decisions have been made, a design is complete. Let us illustrate this process.

EXAMPLE: Assume that you are conducting a course on assertive behavior for a group of sixteen managers. You are using a large training room with four windows. Participants are seated around U-shaped tables, which occupy only half the room. It's right after lunch. During the morning, you discussed and demonstrated the differences between nonassertive, aggressive, and assertive styles of coping with conflict. Your goal for the early afternoon is to teach how body language is a large part of style. *You decide that the purpose of your first design is to introduce the topic of body language in a dramatic way and to help participants become aware how they now use body language during a power struggle.*

The next decisions concern method and format. Looking over several possibilities, *you decide to use a game that involves every participant.* This decision allows for a fast-paced, active activity, which is desirable after lunch. With sixteen people to accommodate and with the need for practice time later in the afternoon in mind, *you decide to use pairs as the most efficient format for the game.*

With these tentative decisions in mind, you now need to find a game or, if necessary, invent a game that will achieve your purposes. Luckily, a colleague has told you about a nonverbal "persuasion" game that might suit your purposes. The only problem is that this game usually takes forty-five minutes and appears to you to be too threatening for your clientele. You decide to redesign the game, paying attention to such details as time allotment, buy-in, activity instructions, materials, physical setting, and ending. Your final design might resemble the one in Figure 7.3.

FIGURE 7.3 NONVERBAL PERSUASION

After greeting the participants who have just returned from lunch, say the following:

"I thought it would be a good idea to conduct a lively activity this afternoon. It will help us to introduce the topic of body language and its effect on our style."

No materials are needed for the activity, but the instructions are very important and the physical setting plays a role. With those factors in mind, do the following:

1. Ask participants to pair off with a partner and to establish whose birthday falls earlier in the calendar year.

2. Give the person with the earlier birthday in each pair an index card with the following instructions: "Leave your seat and go somewhere else in the room (for example, look out a window, stand in the corner of the room, play with some object). Soon, your partner will come to fetch you and will want to bring you back to your seat. Resist him or her, saying or doing whatever you like. Don't go back to your seat until you feel persuaded to do so."

FIGURE 7.3 continued

---

3. After these participants leave their seats, ask their partner to go and fetch them. Explain to them that they can approach the task in any way they like except for one condition: they may not talk (or write) during the entire time they are trying to get their partner back to his or her seat. (Allow the "resisters" to overhear your instructions to the "persuaders.")

4. When all participants have eventually returned to their seats, ask the resisters to privately give feedback to their persuader. Urge them to identify which kinds of nonverbal communication were effective and which were ineffective. (Effective nonverbal communication tends to include some of the following: good eye contact, decisiveness, firm but gentle physical movements, persistence, and calmness.)

5. Ask the resisters to brag about their partner's effective nonverbal behaviors to the rest of the group.

6. Invite the partners to reverse roles and redo the exercise.

7. End the activity by stating that research indicates that the nonverbal aspects of communication (vocal, facial, and postural) influence the impact of our messages more (some even say 93 percent more) than does the verbal content. Display a PowerPoint slide that says, "It's not what you say but how you say it." Invite participants to react to the statement.

THREE TIPS FOR CREATIVE DESIGNS

Many trainers wish they were more creative. However, creative designers are not a special breed; they *work* at being creative and use several tricks to help them do their best. Here are some of their tips.

One Design Can Accomplish Two Things at Once

Economy is the trademark of a good design, and with a little care, most designs can serve double duty. For example, you could brief participant observers about nonverbal aspects of communication to watch for while their peers are giving sales presentations. By watching how you change your own facial, vocal, and postural communication during the briefing, the observers could gain observation practice before trying it out for real. Or suppose that you wanted to help a participant through a role play requiring the participant to coach a confused employee. As you did this, you could provide a demonstration of effective coaching behavior.

The Same Design Can Often Be Used for Different Purposes

Many creative trainers have a few exercises in their repertoires that they use over and over again with different topics because the exercises are easily adaptable. Here is an example.

EXAMPLE: For an energizer late in the afternoon, a trainer of a team-building course had participants make paper airplanes and attempt to hit a target. Noticing that some participants helped each other out with their airplane designs while others did not, he initiated a dramatic discussion about teamwork. At a problem-solving course, he used the same exercise to point out that many people changed their designs when their first attempts didn't work while others repeated the same essential solution (design) with each attempt.

Published Designs Can Often Be Modified to Suit Your Own Needs

Whenever you examine a published design, think how you might change its purpose, its direction, its length, and so on to achieve the design you are seeking. Here is an example.

EXAMPLE: A well-known activity based on a drawing that is either a young girl or an old woman, originally published in *Puck* in 1915, uses the ambiguous picture to examine stereotyping and group pressure on perception. Typically, participants are asked to relate their feelings and opinions about the woman they see in the drawing, not realizing that it can be viewed in two different ways. Instead of using this drawing for its traditional purpose, a trainer used it as the basis for an interesting coaching or teaching exercise, employing the following instructions:

1. Obtain two volunteers. One is to serve as a teacher. She should be a person who has previously seen the drawing. (You will always have some participants who have seen it.) The other volunteer is to portray a student who needs assistance in seeing both women.

2. The teacher should try to show the student how to see both women. (If the student is successful in a matter of seconds, replace him with someone else.)

3. After the student has seen both women, observers should tell the teacher in terms as descriptive as possible what she did to cope with the student.

4. Then discuss what behaviors were helpful or harmful in loosening up the student's perceptions of the drawing. Compare these behaviors to common teaching or coaching situations.

EXAMPLE: In a popular exercise, teams compete to build the best construction-paper tower. The towers are judged by height, aesthetic appeal, and sturdiness. A trainer was looking for a team-building activity to help in the development of new teams that would eventually work cooperatively with each other. He decided to change "towers" to "houses" and asked each team to construct a model of the dream house in which all members would like to live. Instead of using construction paper, teams were given index cards. With these noncompetitive instructions, three completely different and highly creative designs emerged and each team was able to proudly display a model of its dream home. Through a simple change in design, the activity had gone from a competitive to a noncompetitive experience.

WORKSHEET

DESIGNING A TRAINING ACTIVITY

Try your hand at designing a training activity. Choose an objective of your own and develop a creative design with the suggestions you have been given.

Objective:

Method:

Format:

_____ Individual

_____ Pairs

_____ Small-group

_____ Full-group

_____ Intergroup

Outline:
(*Include time allotted, buy-in, key points and instructions, materials, physical setting, and ending.*)

_____

_____

_____

_____

_____

_____

_____

_____

_____

_____

_____

_____

_____

◆　◆　◆

"I first met Mel Silberman in the early 1970s. I was a doctoral student at Temple University and Mel was one of a group of young professors who made the programs in education, curriculum and program development, group and organization dynamics come alive. Mel was a superb teacher and facilitator. He was highly creative and even in those early years, he was brilliant in the ways he bridged theory and practice. It was in the 1970s that Mel constructed the building blocks of what would later become his concepts of active teaching and active learning. Later in my career, Mel became a valued external resource we used to strengthen the program design skills of the Learning and Leadership Development functions that I had the privilege to lead. Mel never disappointed and was always very easy to work with and ever so generous of his time and attention."

"Respect for Mel in our home is a family affair. Mel served as my wife Nila's doctoral program and dissertation committee chairperson also during the 1970s. Nila's respect for Mel endures today. I asked Nila this morning about her memories of Mel. She described Mel as a great advisor...smart, caring, proactive, and organizationally savvy. These are all attributes that are of high value for any graduate student."

"We lost Mel way too soon. He made very important contributions to many people and to many organizations. Most importantly, Mel was a mensch (a good man). No better compliment can be made of a person."

Ed Betof, EdD
Sr. Fellow, The Conference Board and
President, Betof Associates LLC

Chapter Eight

Sequencing Active Training Activities

What you do as a trainer is not all that counts. Equally important is *when* you do it.

No matter how well you design a particular activity or presentation, its impact and value for the participants may diminish greatly if it is misplaced in the overall sequence of events. For example, participants may be tired just when you need them to be alert. Or the group may not be able to grasp abstract ideas before experiencing concrete examples.

Further, an active training module is not a string of exercises. Nothing could be a greater waste than having participants go through one activity after another without a thoughtful plan. How well you weave activities together is of paramount importance to your overall effectiveness.

Every concept in this chapter is something you will consider whether you are sequencing activities for a physical or a virtual classroom.

Sequencing is partly an art; some trainers just know where to place different pieces in their overall design and how to obtain a good mix and flow. Most trainers, however, learn to master sequencing through experience and trial and error. Nonetheless, some basic guidelines remove the mystery from effective sequencing.

BASIC SEQUENCING GUIDELINES

The following guidelines apply to most sequencing of training activities and should be considered fundamental to effective designing.

1. ***Build interest and introduce new content before you delve more deeply.*** Set the stage for learning by using an activity that hooks participants' interest or gives the big picture.

2. ***Place easy activities before demanding activities.*** Get participants settled in and warmed up before you put them through hard work.

3. ***Maintain a good mix of activities.*** Vary training methods, the length of activities, the intensity of activities, the physical setting, and the format. Variety is the spice of good training.

4. ***Group together concepts and skills that build on each other.*** Generally, we learn more easily when one idea is an outgrowth of another.

5. ***Provide sub-skills before practicing complex skills.*** It's better to learn the parts before the whole.

6. ***Close training sequences with discussion of "so what" and "now what."*** Have the participants consider the implications of the course content for themselves and plan their next steps back on the job.

How would you apply these guidelines to specific situations? Figure 8.1 presents an opportunity for you to try your hand at sequencing. There are no correct answers. Use your own judgment.

FIGURE 8.1 SEQUENCING ACTIVITY

You have been asked to design a training module for supervisors on giving feedback to their employees. The design is to be based on the handout containing the following text.

WHAT MAKES FEEDBACK USEFUL?

Constructive feedback is a way of helping other people to look at their own behavior without putting them on the defensive. It is communication to a person (or group) that gives that person information about how she or he affects others. If we wish to avoid creating defensiveness with our feedback, we must not appear to be attacking the person but rather commenting on the behavior.

FIGURE 8.1 continued

Here are some criteria for useful feedback:

1. ***It is descriptive rather than evaluative.*** Describing one's own reactions leaves the individual free to use or not use the feedback or to use it as he sees fit. Avoiding evaluative language reduces the need for the individual to react defensively.

2. ***It is specific rather than general.*** Telling someone that she is "dominating," for example, would probably not be as useful as saying, "Just now when we were deciding the issue, you did not listen to what others said. I felt forced to accept your arguments or face attack from you."

3. ***It takes into account the needs of both the receiver and giver of feedback.*** Feedback can be destructive when it serves only our own needs and fails to consider the needs of the person on the receiving end.

4. ***It is directed toward behavior that the receiver can do something about.*** Reminding a person of some shortcoming over which he has no control only causes frustration.

5. ***It is solicited, rather than imposed.*** Feedback is most useful when the receiver herself has formulated the questions that those observing her answer.

6. ***It is well timed.*** In general, feedback is best offered as soon as possible after the given behavior (depending, of course, on the person's readiness to hear it, the support available from others, and so on).

7. ***It is clear.*** Feedback is worthless if the receiver misinterprets it. One way of checking is to have the receiver try to rephrase what he has heard to see if it corresponds to what the sender had in mind.

The training activities you have chosen to support the handout include:

A. Asking participants to assess themselves as *givers* of feedback

B. Setting up role plays so that each participant can practice giving feedback to a difficult employee

C. Dividing participants into small groups and asking them to discuss and clarify the handout

D. Setting up skill-building exercises to practice each skill suggested by the handout

---

FIGURE 8.1 continued

    E. Asking participants to discuss what they value when *receiving* feedback

    F. Having participants identify employees to whom they would be willing to give feedback according to the guidelines in the handout

In what order would you sequence these activities? Why?

1. _____

2. _____

3. _____

4. _____

5. _____

6. _____

Remember that there are many viable sequences. Here is one way to sequence the module in Figure 8.1:

1. E. Ask participants to discuss what they value when *receiving* feedback. (A good lead-in to the handout)

2. C. Divide participants into small groups and ask them to discuss and clarify the handout. (A study group method for teaching about feedback)

3. A. Ask participants to assess themselves as *givers* of feedback. (A useful way of reviewing the handout and motivating participants to improve their skills)

4. D. Set up skill-building exercises to practice each skill suggested by the handout. (An activity that allows the group to learn the sub-skills of giving feedback)

5. B. Set up role plays so that each participant practices giving feedback to a difficult employee. (An opportunity for participants to pull together the skills learned in the previous step)

6. F. Have participants identify employees to whom they would be willing to give feedback according to the guidelines in the handout. (A consideration of on-the-job application of the skills taught in the module)

APPLYING SEQUENCING GUIDELINES

Active training programs contain sequences of activities or modules that adhere to the six guidelines presented at the beginning of this chapter. Figure 8.2 presents an example of a one-hour training sequence on the topic of encouraging feedback from others. As you read the design, note (1) the use of several methods described in previous chapters and (2) the way in which sequencing guidelines are respected (interest building, easy activities first, a good mix, and so on).

FIGURE 8.2 ENCOURAGING FEEDBACK FROM OTHERS

---

1. Objectives
   Participants are told that during the next 60 minutes, they will:

   - Discuss the reasons why people withhold feedback

   - Learn ways to encourage honest, constructive feedback from others

   - Identify the kinds of feedback they really want to receive

   - Develop an action plan to obtain feedback from someone in their workplace

2. Opening Exercise
   Participants are shown a 4x4 matrix and asked how many squares they see. At first glance, the typical participant sees 16 squares. In fact, there are 30! The facilitator points out that just as the exercise shows that there is more that meets the eye than what appears at first, when it comes to how we see ourselves, there are always things we don't see (our "blind-spots") and it helps to hear the perspectives of other people.

3. Self-Assessment
   Participants are asked to rate themselves on five statements that assess their openness to obtaining feedback from others.

4. Experiential Exercise
   Participants obtain a partner. They are given a list of animals and asked to choose one that best describes their partner. They are told not to reveal their choice to their partner. After two minutes of reflection, they are told: Before you tell your partner the animal you have chosen, I have two questions for you. The first question is: How many of you are eager to tell your partner the animal you've chosen? [Participants are asked to note the number and speed with which people raise their hands.] Then, they are asked: How many of you are eager to find out what animal your partner has chosen? [The participants will notice after this question that more people raise their hands and do so with greater enthusiasm.]

FIGURE 8.2 continued

These key points are given:

- People usually prefer to *receive* feedback than to *give* it.

- Because of this fact, very little feedback is given. If nearly everyone wants to *receive* feedback more than *give* it, nearly everyone will *not* receive any feedback . . . except for mandated performance appraisals.

Then, the following directions are given: *Now, it's time to find out from your partner the animal he or she has chosen and the reasoning behind the choice . . . but instead of just telling each other this information, I want each of you to INVITE your partner to reveal it. Your job is to ask for the animal feedback in such a way that your partner feels ENCOURAGED to tell you. Say something so that your partner feels that you really want the feedback and that it's safe for him or her to be honest.*

Five minutes is given for partners to invite and receive the animal feedback from each other. The activity is then debriefed by asking a few participants to share how their partner "encouraged" them to reveal the feedback.

1. Presentation: Why People Withhold Feedback

    The facilitator presents five reasons why people withhold feedback. Participants are invited to share brief examples about when these barriers apply in their work situations.

2. Writing Task: Encouraging Feedback from Others

    Participants are given a worksheet that contains six suggestions on how to encourage feedback from others. They are asked to study the suggestions with their "animal" feedback partner. Next, they are asked to list the names of people (co-workers, supervisor, customers, and direct reports) with whom they work closely. Then, they are requested to select one person from whom they would like to receive feedback and to specify the feedback they are seeking from that person.

    Following the previous actions, participants are asked to review the suggestions on how to encourage feedback from others and select one or more they would like to use to encourage feedback from the person they have identified. Then, they share their plan with their partner.

Source: Adapted from Silberman, 2005.

Another sample sequence is given in Figure 8.3. Taken from a parenting course, the topic is that of obtaining support from other adults. Again, take notice of the techniques and guidelines as they are employed. Notice, in particular, how each part of the design flows into the next part.

FIGURE 8.3 OBTAINING SUPPORT FROM OTHER ADULTS

This session is devoted to how a parent obtains support from (and gives support to) other adults who care for their child, such as spouse, relative, teacher, and child caregiver. The key assumption is that parenting does not occur in a vacuum. There are always other significant adults who can support or undermine an individual parent's efforts.

I. The Lone Ranger (Game)

A. Ask participants to stand up and form a line. If they see themselves as a person who usually faces personal problems alone, they should go to the head of the line. By contrast, if they typically seek the help of others in solving their personal problems, they should find a place to the rear of the line. Participants who do not identify with either choice should find a place somewhere in the middle. Don't allow participants to "bunch up" in the middle. Urge them to create a "single-file" line. Use humor to help participants feel relaxed during the activity.

B. When the lineup is completed, ask participants to form a semicircle so that they can see each other while keeping their place.

C. Interview the two participants at each end of the semicircle as to the factors influencing their self-placement. Ask them if they feel good about their position in the line.

D. Indicate that a parent needs to combine both ends of the spectrum: He must stand on his own two feet and also be willing to involve others in the problems posed by his children. Compare this notion to the Lone Ranger, a rugged individual crime fighter who nonetheless had someone to depend upon: Tonto.

II. The Need for Support, Feedback, and Planning (Presentation)

A. Ask the group to sit down.

B. Write *support, feedback,* and *planning* on a chalkboard or flip-chart paper.

FIGURE 8.3 continued

C. Point out that adults in charge of the same children need to give and receive these three things in order to maximize their effectiveness as a team. *Support* is available if you can count on someone else to help out, listen to your frustrations, and appreciate your efforts. *Feedback* is a constructive evaluation of your strengths and weaknesses as a parent. *Planning* is a joint commitment to discuss rules, expectations, and discipline strategies for specific problem behavior.

III. Your Own Resistance to Team Collaboration (Discussion)

A. Indicate that every parent has some resistance to including others in the parenting of his or her children. Share your own resistance in order to give participants an example of what you mean. Perhaps you consider yourself more interested, better informed, and more capable of helping children than someone else. This attitude, although understandable and maybe even true, nonetheless blocks a team approach to parenting.

B. Request participants to form pairs and share with each other some of their resistance to including others in the parenting of their children.

IV. How Adults Disqualify Themselves (Guided Teaching)

A. Illustrate the five major ways adults "disqualify" each other:

- Allowing others to parent their children
- Keeping a rigid role division
- Acting impulsively
- Not standing on their own two feet
- Directly interfering with the other adult

B. Ask participants to provide examples from their own lives.

V. Guidelines for Team Parenting (Study Group)

A. Divide participants into small groups and ask them to read and discuss a handout—"Guidelines for Team Parenting." Be sure to indicate that these are general guidelines, not hard-and-fast rules.

B. Ask participants to share their questions and comments about the five guidelines. Remind participants that the major activities done in this course are useful to do with their partners.

FIGURE 8.3 continued

VI. Making Requests (Mental Imagery and Role Playing)

A. Share with participants that they are more likely to practice team parenting if they feel comfortable and skillful making specific requests of other adults.

B. Ask participants to select someone (spouse, relative, teacher, child caretaker, and so on) to whom they wish to make a request. The request should be something they want from that person that will improve their relationship with that person or the person's relationship with his or her child. Invite the participants to relax (perhaps closing their eyes) and then ask them to imagine making the request of the person they selected. Ask further, "When would you do it?" (wait fifteen seconds), "Where would you be?" . . . , "What exactly would you say?" . . . , "How do you think the person you selected would respond?" . . . , "How would you respond back?" . . . , "Can you make your request more specific?"

C. Ask a volunteer to describe the dialogue he or she just imagined. Role-play the scene with you as the other person. If the person experiences difficulty, provide coaching.

D. Ask participants to pair off and role-play making their request to their partner.

VII. What's Next for Me (Ending Activity)

A. As a closing event, ask participants to share their completions to any of the following sentence stems:

1. Something I'm going to do as a result of tonight's session is

   _____.

2. I'm still not sure that _____.

3. Tonight, I learned _____.

B. Explain that participants can share any of these thoughts as the spirit moves them. There is no need to raise hands or agree or disagree with what others have said.

Source: The Confident Parenting Program, 303 Sayre Drive, Princeton, NJ 08540.

Figure 8.4 contains one more example of a training sequence. It is a module from a day-long training program on conflict management. Its purpose is to help participants assess "what they bring to conflict situations." Note the variety of training activities.

FIGURE 8.4 WHAT YOU BRING TO CONFLICT SITUATIONS

Over their lifetime, most people have developed an approach they take in conflict situations. Although a person's *conflict style* often influences how she or he will behave in a given situation, many people are unaware of their own style. This module helps participants to reflect on their own conflict style.

I. Feelings About Conflict (Physical Continuum)

    A. Ask participants to stand up and form a line. If they see themselves as people who usually "hate" being in conflict situations, they should go to the head of the line. By contrast, if they typically "relish" conflict situations, they should find a place to the rear of the line. Participants who do not identify with either choice should find a place somewhere in the middle. Don't allow participants to bunch up in the middle. Urge them to create a single-file line. Use humor to help participants feel relaxed during the activity.

    B. When the lineup is complete, ask participants to form a semicircle so that they can see each other while keeping their place.

    C. Interview the two participants at each end of the semicircle as to the feelings influencing their self-placement. Ask other participants to share their feelings about conflict. Note that discomfort with conflict is rather normal.

II. Looking at Your Conflict Style (Game)

    A. Use one or more game-like exercises that place participants in a conflict situation.

    B. Examples are:

        • Thumb wrestling.

        • Debating someone. Find an issue that two partners truly disagree about such as abortion, capital punishment, or American foreign policy.

        • Breaking balloons. Have each participant blow up a balloon and tie it to his or her ankle with a string. Then give a signal to begin a game in which participants try to break one another's balloons by stepping on them. The last person to have an unbroken balloon is the winner.

FIGURE 8.4 continued

C. Process participants' feelings of aggression, defensiveness, defeat, and victory. Note strategies or styles for coping with conflict.

III. Assessing Your Conflict Style (Questionnaire)

A. Distribute the Conflict Management Style Survey and ask participants to complete and then score their survey.

B. Allow participants time to share their results with people seated near them. Obtain reactions and questions.

IV. Experiencing Different Conflict Styles (Role Play)

A. Divide participants into groups of four (if possible). Explain that each group will be asked to pretend that they are a group whose job is to distribute $10,000 to one cause.

B. Before starting their meeting, give participants a copy of the attached form.

Discussion Styles

	Person 1	Person 2	Person 3	Person 4
Round 1	C	P	I	R
Round 2	P	I	R	C
Round 3	I	R	C	P
Round 4	R	C	P	I

Key: C = Confrontational (aggressive, judgmental)
P = Persuasive (assertive, standing up for oneself)
I = Introspective (analytical, somewhat conciliatory)
R = Reactive (withdrawn, accepting)

C. Ask each group to designate who will be person 1, 2, 3, and 4. Explain that the meeting will be interrupted every five minutes, thereby creating four "rounds." During each round, each participant will behave with the style she or he is assigned on the chart. Thus, over the twenty-minute discussion, each member will adopt each one of the four styles (though in a different order).

D. Suggest that participants act out their style in subtle ways. It is generally not helpful to exaggerate any style.

FIGURE 8.4 continued

E. When the four rounds are completed, invite each group to process the experience. You might use these questions:

- Which style or styles were easy or hard for you to perform?

- What feelings did you have from this experience about each style?

V. Your Conflict Style Is Situational (Checklist)

A. Explain that we tend to vary our style depending on the situation and, in particular, the relationship in question. Some people are confrontational with one person and reactive with another.

B. Ask participants to assess this matter for themselves by completing the following checklist. (After writing the names of three significant others, ask them to check how they see their predominant style when interacting with each person.)

Name	Confrontational	Persuasive	Introspective	Reactive
1.				
2.				
3.				

C. Have participants show this checklist to a partner and discuss it with each other.

Source: Adapted from Silberman, 2005, pp. 355–378.

THE FINER SIDE OF SEQUENCING

Now that we have looked at some basic rules of thumb about sequencing, we can explore more subtle sequencing issues. You have a number of sequencing choices at your disposal. In this respect, you can be compared to musical composers. Although composers follow certain "rules" in writing music, they still have a seemingly endless variety of directions to take. Sometimes, like Beethoven, they may even pull off breaking the basic rules and obtain a stunning result. Likewise, the content you are teaching may seem to dictate a certain logical sequence, but content is not the only determining factor.

Imagine, for example, that you were teaching somebody how to use a digital camera. If the learner knows little about such a camera, what would you do first? We've posed this question to several groups of trainers, and the most common response we get is to "start from the beginning"—show and explain the camera's parts (shutter, lens, and so on) and their function; discuss the difference between auto focus and manual focus and when to use each.

It seems logical to start at the beginning, doesn't it? Yet starting at the end could be just as effective. You could show a series of photographs, some unfocused, some too light, some too dark, and so on, then invite your learner to speculate about why these results occurred and lead, in a Socratic fashion, to the unfortunate actions taken by the photographer. Along the way, you could explain the parts of the camera and how they interact to get different results.

In this example, the learner, rather than the content, influences the sequence. By beginning with the end result, you immediately involve the student, stirring up curiosity and grabbing his or her attention from the start. Nor is this method the only alternative to the more traditional approach. There are many other possibilities. The critical thing to avoid is to continually use the same sequence. *The hallmark of active training programs is the variety of sequences employed to keep participants not only awake but also learning.*

Let's consider four ways to alter a training sequence:

1. *Your design can go from the general to the specific or from the specific to the general.* You are teaching participants how to establish customer credit. You could define what makes a good payment record and then give a case example illustrating the positive payment history of one customer. Or you could reverse the sequence by providing the case example followed by the definition.

2. *When teaching a procedure, you could start with the first step or the last step of the procedure.* You are teaching participants how to compile a profit-and-loss statement. You could start by explaining the basic elements and proceed with a step-by-step demonstration of compiling the statement. Or you could present a completed financial statement and work backward, showing how the bottom line represents a profit or loss.

3. *You could place an experiential activity before a content presentation or follow a content presentation with an experiential exercise.* You have decided to discuss four manipulative communication roles people play (blaming, distracting, placating,

and intellectualizing). To reinforce the presentation, you have designed a role play in which the different members of groups of four each exhibit one of these roles. Placing the role play before the presentation would allow you to hook immediate participant interest and provide examples to refer to in the presentation. However, placing the role play after the presentation would also work well, helping to clarify (experientially) what has already been presented (didactically).

4. ***You could teach from theory to practice or from practice to theory.*** You begin a counseling module by explaining how direct confrontation increases resistance in defensive employees. You follow your theoretical input with a chance to practice indirect ways to correct performance and lower resistance. Alternatively, you might begin by practicing indirect approaches and then discussing why employee resistance is lower when this strategy is used.

In addition to reversing sequences, you can also place design components in a variety of *positions*. Take, for example, practicing a complex skill. The practice session usually is placed **at the end** of a long sequence of explanation and demonstration. It often makes sense, however, to have participants practice a skill **at the beginning** without benefit of prior instruction just to see how well they do. You can then go back and examine the skill, piece by piece. Frequent practice sessions can also occur **during** the explanation and demonstration phase. The trainer can show the skill as a whole, and the participants practice it; the trainer then focuses on a specific aspect of the skill, and the participants practice the entire skill again. Each time, the skill is broken down further and further by the trainer, but the participants always attempt to practice it as a whole.

The success of an effective training sequence often lies in the *flow* from one piece of the design to the other. The worst kind of training sequence is a steady progression of topics with little regard for building participant interest, highlighting the links between pieces, recycling earlier material, or concluding satisfactorily. Here are some tips to improve the flow of a design:

1. Use what Ruth Clark (2014) calls the "Zoom Principle." When introducing participants to new information, give them a broad picture before going into the details. The learner needs what

Clark calls an "advanced organizer" before being able to sort new information out. After presenting the big picture, the trainer "zooms in" on some detail, returning to it periodically to show the participant how each detail relates to the whole. Clark provides the following example.

> When teaching the customer service representative job to new hires, you could describe the process flow of work among functional units in the customer service department. Then you might proceed with an explanation of the representative job, returning at critical moments to the flowchart to show the interfaces between the job and other departmental functions. The new customer service representative could also be presented with an overview of the major types of customer calls he will be taking and how they relate to each other. Then, as detailed information is given about each call type, the big picture can be presented again, giving more detailed information on how the call types relate to each other.

2. A training sequence should look like a spiral rather than a straight line. Reintroduce later on skills and ideas taught earlier in a sequence. If the skill or idea in question is complex, introduce it first on a simple level and then teach it at greater levels of complexity as the course unfolds. Training in conflict management provides a good example.

> A core skill in conflict management is the ability to listen attentively to one's opponent. Typically, active listening skills are stressed early in the program. As she introduces mediation and negotiation techniques, the trainer can easily point out how active listening is the basis of these more sophisticated tools. Moreover, being in the difficult spot of mediating or negotiating these intense conflicts of interest dramatically tests the ability to listen attentively.

3. Avoid the urge to plunge right into an important part of your design. Add a brief activity or short presentation to set up the main event and build motivation. Before an important task, warm up a group with a lighter exercise similar to but not as serious as the one to follow. Sometimes, a shift in the design that widens or redirects the focus is necessary for the next experience to be more effective.

In team-building or leadership development programs, a crucial moment occurs when each participant is about to receive serious peer feedback about her or his behavior in the program thus far. The anxiety level of the group rises precipitously. Before giving the final instructions, a trainer can use the following analogy: "Feedback is like a gift. Take it as such. Like any gift, you may not like it. But, if it's from a reputable source, you can always return it 'to the store' without the giver knowing." Inserting this piece in the design helped to reduce the tension, and participants were more receptive to their first experience receiving peer feedback.

4. From time to time, build a training sequence around a critical incident, a problem to be solved, or a task to be accomplished rather than a set of concepts or skills to be learned. Often, trainers employ didactic teaching methods when the participants can learn instead from their own inquiry. Inquiry modes of learning are always more active than trainer-dependent ones.

Novice bank tellers are required to learn how to identify counterfeit bills. The usual training sequence is an orderly presentation, with handouts, of the flaws to watch for, such as the whiteness of the portrait, broken sawtooth points around the rim of the seal, uneven spacing of the serial numbers, and blurry lines in the scrollwork surrounding the numerals. A more active approach would be to ask the learners to attempt to distinguish between counterfeit and non-counterfeit bills without benefit of prior instruction, sharing their evidence as they do so. The trainer could then point out other telltale signs of forgery. Yet another approach would be to ask the learners to examine some genuine bills and develop hypotheses about how they are printed to discourage counterfeiting.

5. Closing a training sequence can be climactic or reflective. Sometimes a sequence should end with a bang to emphasize the accomplishment. For example, a dramatic finish could consist of a scintillating final presentation, an intergroup competition, a role play that serves as a dress rehearsal for later application, or a challenging case study. At other times, however, it may be more appropriate to wind down by processing reactions to the material, making connections to skills previously learned, generating final questions about topics that are still unclear, or providing prompts to remember back in the real world.

In designing the closing of a virtual training module on Leadership Skills for a VUCA world, the trainer informed the group of the designated Twitter hashtag (#1Thing___ for example, #1ThingLeadership). She asked the participants to log into their Twitter accounts and, in 140 characters or less, share one key point they learned from the session by posting a tweet. Search and display their key points as they are posted. Tell them to do this exercise 3 days, 1 week, and 2 weeks after the session to refresh their memories when they're back at work. Results were "Learned the importance of self-awareness of my own strengths/weaknesses. Not enough to know theirs. #1ThingLeadership." "Wow, I never thought about assigning tasks based on their strengths instead of their typical responsibilities. #1ThingLeadership."

Source: Wendy Gates Corbett, MS, CPLP

EXPERIENTIAL LEARNING SEQUENCES

The sequencing of strongly experiential training requires special consideration. In such training, learning flows not from didactic presentations but from what participants discover for themselves as a result of powerful experiences the trainer has designed for them.

The value of any experiential learning activity is enhanced by asking participants to reflect on the experience they just had and explore its implications. This reflection period is often referred to as a *processing* or *debriefing* period. Figure 8.5 describes a three-stage sequence for processing a rich learning experience called "What? So what? Now what?"

FIGURE 8.5 WHAT? SO WHAT? NOW WHAT?

What?
Take participants through an experience that is appropriate to your topic. These experiences might include any of the following:

• A game or simulation exercise

• A field trip

• A video

• A debate

• A role play

• A mental imagery exercise

FIGURE 8.5 continued

Ask participants to share *what* happened to them during the experience:

- What did they do?
- What did they observe? Think about?
- What feelings did they have during the experience?

So What?
Next ask participants to ask themselves *so what?*

- What benefits did they get from the experience?
- What did they learn? Relearn?
- What are the implications of the activity?
- How does the experience (if it is a simulation or role play) relate to the real world?

Now What?
Finally, ask participants to consider *now what?*

- How do you want to do things differently in the future?
- How can you extend the learning you had?
- What steps can you take to apply what you learned?

The best way to explain each step is to do so with an example. As mentioned in Chapter 6, many games resemble the classic competition-cooperation exercise, the Prisoner's Dilemma Game. One example is a game appropriately called The Game of Life. Figure 8.6 presents the instructions.

FIGURE 8.6 THE GAME OF LIFE

This is a game to be played by six groups of any size, although adjustments can be made to accommodate fewer groups. Each group should have approximately the same number of players. The objective is for each group "to win as much as you can."

FIGURE 8.6 continued

PROCEDURE

There are six rounds to the game. For each round, each group chooses either Y or X (without knowing what the other groups have chosen) and writes its choice on a slip of paper. All slips are handed to the trainer, who tallies them and announces the results. Each group's payoff depends on the combination of choices made by the groups. For six groups, there are seven possible combinations:

Combinations	*Payoffs*
All choose X	All lose $2
Five choose X; one chooses Y	Xs win $2; Y loses $10
Four choose X; two choose Y	Xs win $4; Ys lose $8
Three choose X; three choose Y	Xs win $6; Ys lose $6
Two choose X; four choose Y	Xs win $8; Ys lose $4
One chooses X; five choose Y	X wins $10; Ys lose $2
All choose Y	All win $2

Other payoff schedules can easily be generated for fewer than six groups.

After the third and fifth rounds, allowance is made for a ten-minute negotiation session between single representatives from any group that wishes to participate. The negotiations, if held, are to be loud enough for everyone in the room to hear. Before these opportunities for negotiation, the trainer announces that the payoff (wins and losses) will be tripled for the fourth round and multiplied tenfold for the sixth (last) round.

After experiencing The Game of Life, participants will have many reactions, especially anger at teams that did not cooperate (the six groups rarely choose to cooperate by all choosing Y) and disdain for any groups that used deceit. Some participants will protest, "It's only a game," while others will take it very seriously. In the ***what?*** portion of the process, it is crucial to obtain these reactions and observations in order to realize the potential of this experiential activity. The biggest mistake is to analyze the game too quickly before allowing feelings to be expressed.

After noting what happened during the game and what participants were feeling, the skilled facilitator guides the group into the ***so what?*** stage. Here, participants begin to develop many insights.

They note that the world is not simply divided into good guys and bad guys. They understand that behaviors could have occurred during the negotiations that would have inspired trust and cooperation. They also observe how groups that were losing heavily often behaved like victims and failed to see that they had the power to turn their fortune around.

After achieving these insights, participants can now be helped to do some generalizing. Among the principles and learnings that might emerge are these:

- All parties in an organization are responsible for creating its ultimate climate.

- The actions of one unit invariably affect the actions of the others.

- Groups with power are reluctant to negotiate.

- Negotiation is most effective when each side acknowledges its needs in a straightforward fashion and acknowledges its differences with others in a non-blaming manner.

At this point, participants are usually motivated to start applying the experience to their own organization in the final *now what?* step. When all participants belong to the same organization, discussion can address the intergroup competition within their own ranks and ways to alleviate it. When participants come from different organizations, individual participants can share case situations for the advice and counsel of peers.

As you can see, following this cycle allows you to base an entire training sequence on one experience. Two ingredients are key to an effective experiential training sequence: a structured *experience* that is rich in potential and a set of *questions* to follow it up, including these:

1. What happened?

2. How did you feel about it?

3. What did you observe about your behavior and the behavior of others during this experience?

4. What can we learn from this experience?

5. How can you apply these learnings to your life or work?

WORKSHEET

SEQUENCING ACTIVE TRAINING ACTIVITIES

Consider all the sequencing ideas in this chapter and select one or more to use in designing or redesigning your own training module. Outline your thoughts below.

Objectives:

Areas for change:

_____ Obtaining a different mix of activities

_____ Improving the flow

_____ Reversing commonly used sequences

_____ Altering placement of activities

_____ Improving beginnings and endings

_____ Providing experiential learning cycles

Outline:

_____

_____

_____

_____

_____

_____

_____

_____

◆　◆　◆

"I first met Mel when I began speaking at a national conference. The room I presented in was always next to Mel. In the first few minutes of his presentation a train whistle would go off and the entire session would have to stop and adjust. I would always say, 'Hey—Mel is next door—be sure to not miss his next presentation!'"

"When I told Mel what I was doing he laughed. But then a minute later he said, 'You aren't using this opportunity to the fullest!' He then told me that I should say 'Hey—hear that train whistle! That is the train for evaluating training. This is your last chance to get on the train or be left at the platform!'"

"It sounds funny but it really worked! The participants would stop and look at me and then start taking notes and asking better questions as a result."

"Mel became a mentor to me and helped me increase my business and my potential as a consultant to our profession. The training and development world lost a mentor but Mel's impact will live on, and when I hear a train whistle I want to get on that train!"

Teri B. Lund
Strategic Assessment & Evaluation LLC

Chapter Nine

Planning Active Training Programs

At this point in the design of your active training program, you've established your objectives and sequenced activities to support them. You have now reached the point where you can organize all of your design ideas on a given topic into a complete program. This final step in designing involves the creation of the outer shell of the program, sometimes referred to as the *"macrodesign."*

THE MACRO-DESIGN OF AN ACTIVE TRAINING PROGRAM

The introduction to Part Two proposed that an active training program was characterized by

- A moderate level of content
- A balance between affective, behavioral, and cognitive learning
- A variety of learning approaches
- Opportunities for group participation
- Utilization of participants' expertise
- A recycling of earlier learned concepts and skills
- Real-life problem solving
- Allowance for future planning

With these characteristics in mind, let's review a macrodesign for a total program of a minimum of six hours length. If your time is limited, it may be difficult to employ all aspects of this plan. In this case, adjust the macrodesign that follows to your time constraints.

Opening Activities

Design activities that build interest in the entire course and introduce some of the major ideas of the first part of the program. Also use this time for group building and learning about the participants. An initial case study that invites participants to start thinking about the subject matter may be a good starting point. This is also the time to solicit participants' initial questions about the topic being studied. If the course is skill-oriented, ask participants to try out the skills without the benefit of prior instruction just to see how well they do.

Building Blocks

Design activities that both teach the basic knowledge and/or skills and explore participants' attitudes and feelings about the topic. Actively involve the participants by interspersing presentations with opportunities for group participation. Utilize alternative methods to lecturing and experiential learning approaches for variety.

Middle Activities

Design activities that help participants review the building blocks and introduce ideas to be covered at the next stage of the program. Role playing, simulation, and observation exercises; case studies; assigned projects; and other comparable methods can be featured.

Advanced Knowledge and Skills

Design activities that teach the course material at a more advanced level. Emphasize real-world problem solving. Be careful to recycle the information and skills presented earlier. Be especially mindful of utilizing the participants' expertise. Draw out their feelings about what they are learning.

Closing Activities

Design activities that help participants test their knowledge and skill and encourage them to apply these activities to new problems and on-the-job (or back-home) situations. Allow time for goal setting, action planning, and consideration of on-the-job or back-home application issues.

To illustrate this five-part macrodesign, examine Figure 9.1, a training program on coaching and counseling skills that was designed as part of an ongoing development program for a group of new managers in a large pharmaceutical company. The details of each activity have been eliminated so that you can easily follow the general outline of the macrodesign. As you read this outline, keep in mind that the program design was developed as an intensive two-day seminar. If the program had been longer in duration or allowed for time back on the job during it, the specific designs of each section could have been quite different. A program you are designing will differ due to the nature of your training topic, your assessment of the participants, and your overall training objectives. Still, you should find this macrodesign adaptable to your situation.

FIGURE 9.1 COACHING AND COUNSELING PROGRAM

This two-day program is designed to increase a manager's skills as a coach and as a counselor. As a coach, the manager identifies a need among employees for instruction and direction, usually related directly to their current work assignments—for example, an employee may be having difficulty learning a new computer system. In a coaching relationship, employees are open to advice and show little defensiveness. As a counselor, the manager identifies a problem that is interfering with employees' work performance—for example, an employee may be suffering from burnout and lack interest in the work. A manager needs to switch from a coaching to a counseling mode when employees are not as open to his or her input. In a counseling relationship, the manager builds trust by approaching the employee in an especially supportive, nonthreatening manner.

The program gives equal weight to affective, behavioral, and cognitive aspects of the topic. It builds on training that participants have already received about the Myers-Briggs Type Indicator (MBTI), a tool in which the effects of personality type on performance as a manager can be examined.

I. Opening Exercises

    A. Introduction and Objectives

        1. Key terms

           a. Coaching

           b. Counseling

        2. Objectives

           a. To value the role that coaching and counseling play in a manager's work

           b. To learn and practice coaching skills

           c. To learn and practice counseling skills

FIGURE 9.1 continued

(The trainer begins with remarks about the terms coaching and counseling and shares her or his objectives with the training group.)

    B. The Role of Coaching and Counseling

        1. Discussion: Ask, "What experiences have you had being coached and counseled by others?" "What coaching and counseling behaviors have been effective and ineffective?"

        2. Activity: Have participants identify specific examples in which coaching and counseling have taken place (or might take place) in your work as a manager.

        3. Discussion: Ask, "What are the benefits of coaching and counseling effectively?"

        4. Videotape: Watch "Coaching and Counseling" (an overview of the two skills).

(This section is a sequence of activities designed to achieve team building, on-the-spot assessment, and immediate learning involvement. Although participants already know each other, they become reacquainted by discussing their prior experiences and current views. At the same time, the trainer can assess participants' attitudes about the training topic. The video is used not only to clarify further the distinction between coaching and counseling but also to stimulate interest in further skill development.)

II. Building Blocks

    A. Coaching Employees

        1. Activity: Do a paper-tearing exercise that proves that coaching is not merely telling someone what to do.

        2. Activity: Have participants observe a role play in which someone is learning something new.

        3. Activity: Have participants practice teaching a new skill or procedure to an employee.

        4. Discussion: Ask, "How does your MBTI profile affect how you coach employees?"

(The first major training sequence begins with an exercise demonstrating common foibles in coaching another person. Participants are then asked to observe effective coaching procedures and apply what they have observed in their real-life work situation about teaching a skill or procedure to another participant. The sequence concludes with an interesting exchange between participants with contrasting MBTI profiles concerning the needs each has in a coaching situation.)

FIGURE 9.1 continued

B. Counseling Employees

   1. Discussion: Ask, "How do you feel when you have to counsel a resistant employee?"

   2. Presentation: Provide guidelines for giving performance feedback.

   3. Activity: Have participants practice feedback skills.

   4. Activity: Have participants learn ways to actively listen, reflect back what people are saying, and ask probing questions.

   5. Demonstration: Have participants participate in a counseling interview.

   6. Activity: Have participants practice counseling interviews.

   7. Discussion: Ask, "How does your MBTI profile affect how you counsel employees?"

(The second training sequence begins with an affective consideration of the problems inherent in counseling employees. It then presents basic counseling skills [feedback, listening, questioning, and reflecting] and provides opportunities for practice. At the end of the sequence is a second discussion of the MBTI, this time examining how contrasting styles affect the success of the counseling experience.)

III. Middle Activities

A. Case Review Problem

   1. Activity: Have participants determine whether a case situation requires coaching or counseling and outline the actions needed.

   2. Discussion: Ask, "What questions remain for you concerning when and how coaching and counseling skills are applied?"

(Before launching into advanced topics, the trainer asks participants to reflect on what they have learned by clarifying their understanding of the respective roles of coaching and counseling.)

IV. Advanced Skills

A. More Issues in Coaching and Counseling

   1. Demonstration: Demonstrate dealing with anger and resistance.

   2. Activity: Have participants practice dealing with anger and resistance.

FIGURE 9.1 continued
---

3. Demonstration: Demonstrate motivating higher performance.

4. Activity: Have participants practice motivating higher performance.

5. Discussion: Ask, "How confident do you feel about handling your role as a coach and a counselor?"

6. Activity: Have participants perform, critique, and redo role plays of a variety of coaching and counseling situations.

(The purpose of this section of the program is not only to consider new issues [anger or resistance and motivating higher performance] but also to process emerging feelings and polish difficult skills. The last two activities recognize that coaching and counseling are a confluent mixture of affective and behavioral elements. Participants are asked to rehearse their newfound skills in a variety of situations to maximize the transfer of training back on the job.)

V. Ending Activities

A. Peer Consultation

1. Activity: Have participants use fellow participants as consultants on back-on-the-job problems with difficult employees.

B. Action Planning

1. Discussion: Discuss the steps needed to ensure retention of skills.

2. Activity: Have participants develop a self-contract for improving their coaching and counseling skills.

(When the trainer asks participants to act as consultants for each other, the peer consultation activity becomes a review of the knowledge participants have gained. Action planning is incorporated into the design to motivate back-on-the-job application.)

WORKSHEET

PLANNING AN ACTIVE TRAINING PROGRAM

Use the space provided in this worksheet to outline a total active training program of your own. Check the results against the characteristics of an active training program.

Opening Exercises

_____

_____

_____

_____

_____

_____

_____

Building Blocks

_____

_____

_____

_____

_____

_____

_____

_____

Middle Activities

_____

_____

_____

_____

_____

_____

_____

_____

WORKSHEET continued

Advanced Skills

_____

_____

_____

_____

_____

_____

_____

_____

_____

Ending Activities

_____

_____

_____

_____

_____

_____

_____

_____

Qualities of my program:

_____ Moderate level of content

_____ Balance between affective, behavioral, and cognitive learning

_____ Variety of learning approaches

_____ Opportunities for group participation

_____ Utilization of participants' expertise

_____ Recycling of earlier learned concepts and skills

_____ Real-life problem solving

_____ Allowance for future planning

◆   ◆   ◆

Chapter Ten

Incorporating Active Learning in All Training

*T*he number of tools available to trainers has expanded rapidly within the past decade; no longer are trainers constrained to the time and expense of in-person training sessions. With the assistance of technology, trainers can now design programs without worrying about geographic proximity. Online courses, webinars, and web conferences are all practical and cost-efficient options when designing your active training programs.

While technology has provided many great advances for learners, it is important for trainers to know when and how to use that technology most effectively. Not every problem requires a training solution; similarly, not every training solution requires technology. The trick is figuring out how technology can best enhance and extend the learning experience for the participants while still adhering to the key principles of active training.

A few points of clarification are necessary before we explore the options at your disposal. The use of technology in training is commonly referred to as *e-learning*. E-learning has different forms and a multitude of definitions. Until the entire industry settles on exactly the same definitions, the following will serve our needs for this book. We have separated technical learning opportunities into four categories.

1. **Asynchronous E-Learning:** web and computer-based training that can be taken by anyone at anytime

2. **Group-Based E-Learning:** synchronous webcasts or webinars, usually with limited interaction, but held at one time

3. **Virtual Classroom Training**: highly interactive synchronous online instructor-led training using a web-based classroom platform (Huggett)

4. **Blended Learning**: e-learning (synchronous and asynchronous) combined with instructor-led classroom training, independent learning, virtual reality, a flipped classroom event, and social media, taking advantage of the delivery mode that is necessary each time

The term *asynchronous* is used to describe learning that does not have to take place at the same time. So, participants can take a course when and where they choose. A *synchronous* learning event is one in which participants learn at the same time. Virtual training classrooms are highly interactive and blended learning takes advantage of both asynchronous and synchronous modes to create additional types of learning experiences. Let's look at each one in greater detail.

ASYNCHRONOUS E-LEARNING

An asynchronous e-learning course is self-paced instruction taken on the computer, usually downloaded from the Internet. These courses are best for situations when you want to deliver consistent training to a group of participants who may not be located in the same place. E-learning is an excellent choice for training situations where learners need access to the material 24 hours a day, 7 days a week. It also works well when the content needs to be exactly the same for every participant.

Before you make the decision to replace your classroom training programs with e-learning, you must take into account the relative disadvantages of these types of courses. Engaging, interactive e-learning requires extensive development time by trained instructional designers, and that cost is transferred to the buyer. The course may be a technical marvel yet fail to match learners' prior knowledge, aiming the course content either too high or too low for its audience. Online courses also may not meet participants' expectations because many learners want to talk and share their experience with others. E-learning is convenient because it is an independent activity, yet that same independence means learning takes place in isolation, without the benefit of peer support.

E-learning may be developed in your organization or is available through various training vendors, each of whom provides varying levels of sophistication in their products. Here are questions to consider when you are evaluating a vendor's e-learning program:

- How easy is it for new users to navigate their way through the course?
- Does the course offer a pre-test and a post-test to assess participant learning?
- Does the course offer a way for knowledgeable learners to bypass basic instruction?
- Does the course offer more than simply text on a screen?
- Are the situations used in video clips realistic?
- Is there a progress bar that shows how much a learner has completed throughout the course?
- Does the course offer remediation for wrong answers within the course modules?
- Does the course provide printable documents as takeaways for the learner?
- Would you want to take this course yourself?

An important key to success with e-learning is to diagnose exactly what the training problem is and determine if online learning will provide the best solution. Here are three examples of independent e-learning in the workplace, two of which were successful and one which was not.

EXAMPLE: A large food company had manufacturing facilities throughout the United States. The government required each of these plants to follow Good Manufacturing Principles (GMPs), as well as provide regular training on mandated safety programs. The training needed to be available to employees on every shift, and it had to be consistent with each delivery. Although many of these facilities set aside Safety Days, during which employees received a day's worth of safety training, these were only scheduled once a year. If an employee joined the company a month, a week or a day after Safety Day, they were left out of the regular instruction of safety topics and were potentially at risk within the plant. Supervisors and safety managers spent a great deal of their time during the year personally educating new employees on programs they missed on Safety Day.

Online learning provided a fairly straightforward solution to this training dilemma. Through the use of computer workstations placed near the manufacturing floor but far enough away to prevent distraction, employees could access safety training when and where it was most convenient to them. Employee training was not dependent upon a supervisor's schedule or the safety manager's availability. The consistent format guaranteed that each employee would receive every part of the training course every time. Additionally, a post-test with a set passing rate insured that each employee had at least a basic knowledge of the course material before returning to the plant floor. In this case, e-learning was the right solution to this particular problem.

EXAMPLE: Internal management boards offered high-potential employees an opportunity to work on projects and activities to improve the overall success of a large company. The leaders of these boards were looking for a way to provide training to their members on the topic of change management. An instructor-led course on this topic had been offered throughout the company in prior years, but the boards were interested in trying something new. They investigated online options and decided to choose one offered by a very well-established training vendor.

The board members received information on how to access the course via the Internet. They were given several weeks to complete the course, and then were asked to provide an assessment of their experience. Here were some of their comments about the online training:

> "I liked taking the course at my desk, although I'm out in the open—it was sometimes hard to concentrate with people around me. Next time I would try to borrow an office."

> "I prefer the personal interaction of a live course and the ability to share examples and learnings with others during the course. I learn better through seeing and doing rather than reading."

> "I would have liked to be able to get feedback on my action plan. I think we can share this with our supervisors for feedback, but we've missed the opportunity for immediate feedback with an online course."

In this situation, the training did not require technology. The board members were all centrally located, the learning experience did not need to be exactly the same for every participant, and the course content was such that participants would have benefited from the direct sharing of ideas and experiences in a live environment. Peer interaction and discussion is what these board members were looking for, as it related to managing change efforts. What they received was a technically sound program that turned participants into passive learners and low-level thinkers. Many participants started the program and did not finish it, or they rapidly clicked through the screens to achieve a completion mark without fully processing the content.

EXAMPLE: Employees in a large law firm attended semi-annual training courses on a variety of legal topics. These training sessions were mandatory, and no one liked their one-size-fits-all quality. Training consultants moved all the legal topics to an e-learning format with pre-tests and three different versions of the course content. The paralegals and lawyers could test out of what they already knew, and then spend their time on courses matched to their existing knowledge base. The convenience of taking these courses at their own pace and on their own time schedules increased compliance, and had the side benefit of generating some competition among the employees to see who could complete their training first.

Creating Active Independent E-Learning

How can you make a participant's individual e-learning experience more active? Here are some ideas for increasing involvement in e-learning experience. Notice that many of the tactics are exactly the same that you would use if you were developing a classroom training.

- Make sure that the course content is well suited to an independent learning format.
- Build interest and curiosity by beginning an e-learning course with an opening question, a lead-off story or visual, or a case problem.
- Maximize understanding and retention by presenting major points upfront, providing user-friendly examples, employing analogies, and inserting visuals with impact.
- Intersperse text with activities such as quizzes, spot challenges, and brief exercises to keep the learner mentally alert.
- Recommend that participants set aside approximately 30–45 minutes for each learning session. After approximately 45 minutes, many learners get bored with what they are viewing and end up rapidly clicking through screens in an effort to get to the end.
- Reinforce learning with requests to recap major points, consider ways to apply the material, or solve a final case problem.

GROUP-BASED E-LEARNING

A second type of e-learning involves group training facilitated through technical delivery tools. Although not all participants have to physically be in the same place for the learning event, the training takes place at the same time and is therefore synchronous. Many types of technology may be incorporated into these group experiences, ranging from telephones to computers to video studios. Here are three of the most frequently used delivery tools for group assisted e-learning.

Webcasts

A webcast is an audiovisual event which is accessed either just through the computer or through the computer and a conference call line. It is typically based upon one-way communication, with a presenter speaking from prepared notes and slides to a widely dispersed audience. Frequently the prepared remarks end with a question and answer session in which participants ask questions directly of the speaker through the conference call. All webcast participants listen to the answers and may respond in turn. Some webcasts are taped and can be accessed on the Internet at a later time, thus turning a synchronous learning event into an asynchronous experience.

EXAMPLE: The training department at an international company offers a management orientation program to newly promoted managers. As part of this program, company executives provide their perspectives on the company as a whole as well as their own area of expertise. New managers dial into a webcast to listen to prepared remarks, and then have the opportunity to ask questions of the executives about specific points of interest. If the participants want to revisit the experience sometime after the initial program, they can log onto the company intranet and replay the webcast from beginning to end.

A webcast works in this situation due to the time constraints of the guest speakers. International executives do not have the time to travel to the corporate headquarters to meet new employees, yet have a vested interest in getting their message out in a consistent manner. As a trainer, you can take this e-learning delivery tool to another level by adding interactivity. Here are some ways you can use a webcast to create a more active learning experience:

- Send an email in advance with instructions or a form indicating how participants should take notes during the webcast. This guided note-taking strategy will help to channel listeners' thoughts and provide clues to key learning points.

- Interrupt the flow of prepared remarks with on-the-spot questions from the presenter to the participants. To increase the challenge and make sure everyone is paying attention, address specific listeners by name.

- Offer a panel of speakers on a webcast to provide differing perspectives on a controversial topic. Model your webcast after a radio call-in show, in which participants can ask questions of speakers with very different viewpoints.

Webinars

A webinar is a more interactive version of a webcast. Although computers and conference call lines are used for both types of group-based e-learning, webinars differ from webcasts in application sharing between the trainer and the participants. Application sharing is a great way to demonstrate features and capabilities of new software; as an active trainer, it is also a good starting point for more collaborative exercises as well.

Most webinar vendors offer interactive features such as polling and quizzes. These tools allow for efficient communications between the dispersed participants and the remote instructor, and are best used to quickly test comprehension in a situation where the trainer cannot physically walk around a room to check for understanding. Be careful of overuse of these tools, however; polls and quizzes may not be the best choice when another interaction might be more appropriate to the course design.

EXAMPLE: A national retailer decided to upgrade their computer systems across the company to a brand new application. The sheer number of employees affected by this change made on-site training prohibitively expensive. In addition, management wanted to limit the amount of time employees were away from their stores. Trainers found a solution to this dilemma by offering webinars at various times and locations across the company. Employees went to computer training rooms at regional office buildings when time and coverage allowed, logging into a predetermined site on the Internet and dialing into a conference call through a speakerphone. Employees worked at individual computer terminals, listening to a trainer speak about the application while watching the new process on their own computer screens. Trainers used data gathered from quizzes and polls to match the pace and level of detail with each group of participants.

A downside to the typical webinar is the lack of individual instruction and hands-on help from an instructor. Learners tend to passively watch what is happening on the screen without fully experiencing the application for themselves. Here are some hints for making webinars more active:

- Create instructional slides using limited text and plenty of white space. Slides should focus on concepts and graphics that encourage conversation, not overwhelm with information.
- Alternate between having the instructor talk through an exercise and having the participants work through exercises independently from a prepared guide.
- Pair participants who have a high degree of comfort with the new application with those who are less comfortable, building in time within the webinar for the "on-site coaches" to assist others.
- Schedule several short webinars over a period of time rather than one extended session.

Webinar technology can actively support skill building, as shown in this innovative case.

EXAMPLE: Trainers at a credit card collection agency struggled with how to best improve employee skills in situations that required both telephone interactions and data entry. Ten participants signed onto the webinar through the Internet on which the trainer launched the data entry software. Participants also dialed into a conference call so they could hear one another speak. One participant at a time played the role of the collector, initiating a conversation with the trainer. Throughout the conversation the rest of the participants could not only hear the role play, but also could watch how the collector handled the data entry transactions. At the conclusion of the conversation, the trainer debriefed what the participant had done well and what could have been improved. The role play then rotated to the next participant until everyone had had a chance to work with the trainer, using different scenarios each time to teach new skills for a variety of situations and to retain the group's interest.

Video Training

Though not nearly as popular as webcasts or webinars, training through a video studio offers a way to create personal contact with a training group without the time and expense of travel. Although this group-based e-learning approach requires the investment in video equipment in at least two locations, it can be a cost-savings alternative to standard classroom instruction. A video studio complete with production equipment and alternative camera views allows participants to look at more than just a talking head; it creates an interactive experience in which the person on the TV communicates in real time with the learners.

It takes time and practice for both participants and trainers to adjust to live video sessions. Participants are typically very quiet the first time they are in a video classroom setting, as they are not sure when to speak. Trainers have to get used to looking at the camera as they deliver their instruction, and may not have the same degree of mobility they have in a standard classroom setting. Room set-ups may have to be adjusted to accommodate camera views, microphones and flipchart easels. Despite the initial awkwardness, video training sessions can deliver high-quality learning experiences to groups who might otherwise miss out on worthwhile training.

EXAMPLE: A U.S.-based corporation recently purchased a manufacturing operation in mainland China. The new employees had little to no experience with American human resource practices around yearly goal setting discussions and performance appraisals. The forms, concepts, and approach were totally different than what employees had experienced within a Chinese company. American trainers used live video sessions to introduce employees to these procedures, taking them step-by-step through the goal setting process and engaging the participants in exercises to illustrate complex points. Additionally, video training sessions created personal connections between the Americans and Chinese that could never have been achieved with a standard training manual, yet saved thousands in travel expenses.

To prevent participants from "zoning out" as they participate in a video training session, employ these active learning techniques:

- Conduct video training sessions as if you were in the classroom by asking lots of questions, pairing up participants for discussions, and encouraging small group work.

- Increase participant involvement by having them call on the next speaker in group discussions.

- Maximize retention through the use of interesting visuals on a document camera.

- Find alternatives to lecturing through case studies, demonstrations, and study groups.

- Sequence training activities to the learners' best advantage, with more frequent breaks and a shorter training day.

VIRTUAL CLASSROOMS

Trainers usually create virtual classrooms through a software platform that supports online course instruction. The time savings afforded by not having to create a course website from scratch allows trainers to create interesting, effective opportunities for extending learning outside a face-to-face classroom environment. A typical virtual classroom includes tools for synchronous delivery like chat rooms and online whiteboards. They may also include asynchronous tools like discussion boards and email that students can use at a time that is convenient for them. With the use of email, chat rooms, and whiteboards, your choice of options on how to incorporate technology in a virtual classroom environment expands exponentially.

Before you decide to design a virtual classroom experience for others, make sure to enroll in an online session yourself. The simple process of participating in an online course will sensitize you to some of its inherent challenges, such as email overload or dominating personalities in a chat room. As a participant you can also take note of what tools your online instructor used well and what you might use differently as you plan for your own virtual course.

EXAMPLE: Participants in an online supervisory training program were asked to email the trainer a real-life example of dealing with a difficult employee. The trainer changed names and other identifying information from several of the cases to use in a live and online session. The trainer created a slide with a case study and asked the supervisors to comment through a whiteboard on how they would suggest handling the situation. The trainer then presented a new slide outlining a formal process for dealing with difficult employees. Participants used the whiteboard to describe how they would apply this process to two additional real-life cases.

EXAMPLE: Nursing students in an online case management course received their homework assignments through email. One such assignment involved accessing a prepared PowerPoint presentation from the course website, and then responding independently to a series of application questions on a discussion forum. Although these activities were both asynchronous, the online instructor extended the assignment using synchronous tools available through their virtual classroom. The instructor posted a series of questions in a chat room, one every minute or so. The students had to answer all of the questions in the chat room, and then review their fellow students' responses. The combination of independent study and peer review provided students with an opportunity to explore how the presentation content would affect their future patients.

EXAMPLE: A construction management company was looking for a way to encourage the cross-fertilization of ideas from employees in their New York and Los Angeles offices. They hired an outside training consultant to assist them with a group brainstorming session on effective time management techniques. The employees signed into a virtual classroom and found a whiteboard slide with three related questions on time management. Participants from both locations answered each question with as many responses as possible. The groups wrote their answers as separate text lines in the chat area of the classroom. The instructor gave the participants a short break while he reviewed the results and prepared to debrief the exercise. He quickly created a slide with the most intriguing responses using the annotation tool on the whiteboard. The two employee groups then reconvened for a whole group discussion on key time management techniques.

Creating Active Virtual Classrooms

Resist the urge to simply dump classroom content into a tedious slide or text presentation when your course goes online, using these ideas to energize your virtual classroom:

- Keep your course focused by thinking of learning objectives first and delivery tools second. Design an online course based upon what makes the most sense for your content, not upon technical tools.
- Use asynchronous discussion boards to exchange ideas on provocative questions, case studies, and brainstorming sessions.
- Use polls to get quick interaction by asking participants about their opinions or knowledge.
- Use breakouts to create virtual teams that work together in synchronous mode to search for information, clarify challenging data, answer discussion questions, and solve problems.

- Maximize understanding by including directions for all synchronous activities and exercises in a participant guide. Read the directions from the guide aloud and encourage clarifying questions before beginning any exercise.

- Reduce presentation time by sending articles for participants to read in advance, using "live and online" time to answer questions about the article in a chat room.

BLENDED LEARNING

A fourth option for trainers is to blend e-learning with traditional classroom instruction to create courses that mix delivery methods. Blended learning has gained popularity because it combines the best of both worlds: offering reduced training costs and time spent away from jobs with the value of peer-to-peer interaction. With a blended solution, trainers can use e-learning to deliver informational content, assess performance, and provide individual feedback. A flipped classroom, where content is provided prior to the classroom portion, is a hybrid of blended learning. Time spent in the classroom is reserved for whole group discussions, practice and rehearsals, and face-to-face interaction.

EXAMPLE: A social service agency was looking for a way to increase the effectiveness of one of its employee training programs on case documentation. Evaluation forms revealed the social workers found much of the classroom training to be lengthy and boring. Agency trainers decided to take a novel approach to the situation, blending independent e-learning with classroom instruction utilizing the jigsaw training technique. Here's how it worked: Each participant received one of four different online videos two weeks in advance of their scheduled training session. The videos contained information on one type of case documentation, complete with real examples and a post-test. Participants worked through their videos prior to the course, then came to the classroom prepared to teach others what they had learned. The small group instruction dramatically increased knowledge retention, and time previously spent on instructor presentations became time spent discussing particularly difficult cases.

EXAMPLE: A trainer was looking for a way to capture and share work created by participants over the course of a seven-week project management series. She created a group website as a repository for project documentation drafts, and asked students to submit samples of their work to the site. The trainer used the website's discussion board feature to create a forum for peer review. Each participant was required to comment on at least one other person's work each week through the discussion forum. The online group site offered participants immediate feedback on their work at each stage of the project management process, while the weekly onsite session provided an opportunity for follow-up questions and answers. The entire group benefited from real-life documentation they could use to review course material, share with colleagues, or reuse in the event they encountered a similar project in the future.

EXAMPLE: A global manufacturing company, which previously had offered leadership training only to employees at its corporate headquarters, decided to expand its monthly leadership series to include employees at a remote location. Video training became a key factor in making this expansion work. Home office–based trainers traveled to the remote sites to kick off the series and establish an initial personal connection with the employees. The following month, the next course in the series was delivered via a video studio at corporate headquarters. An onsite facilitator handled administrative chores and helped with the video equipment at the remote location. This alternating schedule continued throughout the seven-month series, concluding with onsite training on graduation day. The program was so successful it later expanded to three additional remote sites.

Creating Active Blended Learning

Here are some ideas for actively blending e-learning with classroom instruction:

Before the course:

- Pre-test participants to assess their current knowledge and skill levels, using the information from the pre-test to modify the course content specifically for that group.
- Provide a case problem for the participants to read and reflect upon before the session.
- Ask participants to send surveys to co-workers, family members, or friends for feedback prior to taking a course.

During the course:

- Engage participants in exercises requiring them to use a database to complete a software testing task during the session.
- Extend a classroom presentation on business principles with simulations on product development, project management, sales, and finance.

After the course:

- Create discussion guides for small group use after the online learning takes place.
- Use game templates to reinforce learning through online crossword puzzles and quiz shows.
- Create a role-play environment on a website where participants can practice additional scenarios not used in the session.

Sometimes trainers feel challenged to choose between high-tech and high-touch learning experiences as they design active training programs. Actually, it doesn't make sense to do 100 percent or 0 percent of either in a training environment; sessions based on technology need interactive pieces for the learners to connect to the course content, and sessions based on interaction can be improved with the addition of technology. It is through the blending of high-tech and high-touch that an active trainer can create memorable learning experiences that extend far beyond the hours spent either in a physical classroom or in front of a computer screen.

SOCIAL MEDIA EXPANDS ACTIVE TRAINING AND DEVELOPMENT

Web 2.0 technology has initiated growth in the use of social media tools and social networking activities. Growing communities through social networking benefits organizations. Employees use social media tools to obtain information straight from the source. Trainers use social networking tools to continue the development of employees. Social media can extend and expand training and development beyond the virtual and physical classroom.

Social media and networking are not new. The software has been around since the times of the Plato bulletin board system in the late 60s. Some of the older networks and discussion boards such as Compuserve and Usenet have not been used by the general public due to their unwieldy interfaces. This isn't the case today. Social media technology is easier to use, making the strongest case for trainers and employee developers to embrace the technologies to support their organizations' needs. Today's tools empower both the trainers and the learners.

The easy to use environment ensures a more interactive and informal relationship between learners and trainers. But what? How? Social media tools extend the discussion beyond the classroom whether it was in an online classroom or a physical classroom. Social media provides new active learning tools and a wider breadth of content. Social networking provides trainers with more ways to meet learners and to more easily find out about their needs. Social learning opens an opportunity for the organization, training department, and learners to more quickly and accurately identify employees needs and provide content when and where it is needed.

What can the tools do? It can be a trainer's dream. The biggest advantage is that the tools bridge geographical gaps around the world. Imagine that Ken Blanchard is visiting your organization to discuss "Ethical Leadership." Skype or Google Hangouts can be set up in conference rooms in Bogota, Beijing, Berlin, and Baltimore so others can join in.

You probably already use GoToWebinar to develop online seminars. If you record presentations or seminars, employees can go back and review them at any time. Blogs and Facebook wall posts are useful for delivering in-the-moment content, and short messages can be sent through Twitter accounts. LinkedIn groups encourage corporate-wide conversations and continued live with Skype, while Q&A threads can be created on Yammer. Pinterest and Flickr can be used for static visuals, and sites such as YouTube can be used to make and share instructive videos. Facebook and Twitter provide tools to create quizzes, games, and polls. The possibilities are endless. Many social media tools, such as LinkedIn Group and Facebook Group are used to create online virtual spaces that can be limited to corporate use only.

EXAMPLE: A food manufacturer recently created a Leadership Development Program for its High Potential employees. The three-year program puts young promising employees on a fast track to develop skills and obtain experience. There are twenty-seven employees in this HiPo group located in five different countries. Since teamwork and collaboration are two of the critical elements for the company, the training and development department has set up a LinkedIn Group for them. A schedule has been developed so that a new concept paper will be posted every other week. Each member has been assigned a particular date and is responsible for uploading one of these concept papers once during the year on a topic that the individual feels is critical for the rest of the members of the group to know. Discussions will take place via Skype the week after the paper is posted. They will also be sharing questions and ideas daily.

EXAMPLE: Digital Round Robin (Bozarth). Following a module in human trafficking, participants were asked to continue their discussion by sharing ideas using Twitter. Learners were assigned numbers and provided with a hashtag. They were told to respond in order. Number one asked a question; number two answered it and asked a new question. Number three answered that one, and so on. The last participant wrote one last question to be answered by number one. When topics like this one (actual comments) occur on a public site like Twitter, a secondary advantage provides the information—in this case, awareness of issues around human trafficking—to a larger sphere than just those enrolled in the course.

- Learner 1 [@Name]. What are some less well-known reasons that victims of human trafficking don't identify themselves to law enforcement or hospital staff? #HT101

- Learner 2 [@Name]. Fear of law enforcement, embarrassment, fear of retaliation on family members. #HT101

  Learner 2 [@Name]. What are some strategies being used in Indonesian communities to reduce human trafficking? #HT101

- Learner 3 [@Name]. Engaging girls early in moneymaking activities, helping young women start small businesses, implementing detailed checks of potential employers #HT101

- Learner 3 [@Name]. What are some red flags that might indicate you have encountered a victim of human trafficking? #HT101

  Learner 1 [@Name]. Living with employer, employer holds travel documents, unable to speak with individual alone, answers appear scripted or rehearsed. #HT101

It is key to remember that using social media and technology are not that different from creating effective classroom training. One of the experts in the field is Jane Bozarth, author of *Social Media for Trainers* and *Better than Bullet Points*. She shares her thoughts in Figure 10.1.

FIGURE 10.1 TECHNOLOGY IS NOT THAT DIFFERENT

Sometimes the idea of separating "classroom" and "digital/virtual" activities suggests that they are really entirely different undertakings. Many activities used all the time in traditional face-to-face training translate very easily to other environments: For instance, the "Digital Round Robin" activity above started life as an index card exercise. Experienced trainers have the skills needed to facilitate these: starting and redirecting conversations, facilitating for an answer or outcome, drawing out quieter participants, harnessing more dominant ones. If you are mostly engaged in live-classroom work, start paying attention to the times you already conduct activities that are social and collaborative—group work at small tables, games, debates, role plays, case studies, group discussions—and think about how you might make them work in another environment.

One thing that gets little attention in conversations about face-to-face versus digital work: Sometimes activities are better when done online. For instance, the virtual classroom environment (WebEx, Adobe Connect, and others) allows participants to write on a whiteboard anonymously, which can be a huge advantage in a focus group on a sensitive topic. A collaborative list of resources can take on new life if created with a tool that can be easily accessed and allows for updates even after the training event. Consider products like Diigo, Google Docs, and Pinterest for that. Running an activity on a public platform, like Twitter, can make your content more visible to the public (important with content like "human awareness trafficking"), to supervisors (whom we need to support the learning on the job), and to potential participants. Of course, your judgment here is crucial: not everything needs to be public. But not everything needs to stay locked inside the walls of the traditional classroom, either.

M-LEARNING OFFERS INSTANT OPTIONS

Learning in the palm of your hand. What could be better? M-learning, short for mobile learning, has more than one definition. We will use what appears to be the most commonly accepted definition: learning that occurs via a mobile device such as a smartphone or tablet. Mobile learning has been a major topic of conversation for a number of years. Even though many are talking about m-learning, it has been slower to move forward than anticipated.

Smartphones are used for many things, but everything cannot be called specifically "learning." Facebook, for example offers a free mobile application for smartphones that provides functionality similar to that offered on the regular site. You can do almost everything on your smartphones as on the site: comment on someone's status, update your status, post photos, and post videos. You can play YouTube videos on your smartphone. You can download a free application that gives functionality equal to that of the full version online site.

Many conversations center around "bring your own device" or BYOD for short. And there is probably more concern at this point than necessary. What you as a trainer need to focus on instead is what does an effective learning "module" look like on a mobile device?

- It is concise—probably less than five minutes long.

- It is something that encourages a response from the reader.

- It is something that is straightforward and easy to understand since the user will not likely be in a distraction-free environment.

- Ideally it should offer support or knowledge required just-in-time, like an updated policy, a job aid, or a short communication skill.

EXAMPLE: A trainer taught a speaking skills class for 12 participants who were preparing for various speaking roles in the company. Many were nervous because the speaking events were important to their career advancement. Throughout the next weeks she would text the group short questions such as, "Have you practiced your breathing exercises today?" or "Which practice techniques did you use today?" or "What organizational pattern will you use?" All participants were reminded of what they learned as they read responses from their cohort. In addition, since she had a schedule of the participant speaking dates, she could customize information at just the right time for each participant.

M-learning allows you to pair a tiny but critical (either time or importance) data point with a skill check, giving you a quick connection with your learners. This accomplishes several things. It provides the learner with content, allows the learner to provide you with an update, and it keeps the relationship between the two of you alive.

According to Clark Quinn, "Ultimately the 'm' will disappear; learning will be ubiquitous and seamless, taking advantage of where we are and what digital technology is at hand to leverage our actions, add unique value to what we are doing, make us more effective in the moment, and develop us overtime. There is, or will be, an app for that, and you should be preparing to capitalize on the opportunity. Are you ready?"

WORKSHEET

BLENDING IN TECHNOLOGY

Use this worksheet to determine whether e-learning is right for your active training program.

Consider *asynchronous e-learning* if:

☐ The participants are widely dispersed.

☐ The participants do not need to take the training at the same time.

☐ The course content is stable.

☐ The course uses highly structured problems to build comprehension.

☐ The course content is based upon a transfer of consistent information.

Consider *group-based e-learning* if:

☐ The participants have significant time and/or travel constraints.

☐ The participants have access to required technical resources.

☐ The course content is based upon the evaluation of information and shared experiences.

☐ The group is large and widely dispersed.

☐ The instructor is skilled in the use of group-assisted e-learning technologies.

Consider a *virtual classroom* if:

☐ The participants are geographically dispersed.

☐ The course content is based on less-structured problems that require application, analysis, synthesis, and evaluation.

☐ The content can be delivered to relatively small groups.

☐ Participants will benefit from highly interactive instructor-led content.

☐ The instructor is adept at using tools such as chat, breakouts, polls, and other interactive tools.

Consider *blended learning* if:

☐ The participants prefer a mix of independent and interpersonal learning experiences.

☐ Content requires at least some time to practice or discuss face-to-face.

WORKSHEET continued

☐ Participants can use time saved from a physical classroom setting to engage in critical thinking, analysis, and application.

☐ The course content is based upon peer interaction and group discussion.

☐ The instructor is experienced with both synchronous and asynchronous delivery modes.

◆ ◆ ◆

"Mel and I worked together on the first three editions of Active Training in addition to collaborating on four other training-related publications. The practical philosophies that he espoused have staying power because they work. Any time an individual takes on the task of designing, developing, delivering or evaluating a learning event, *Active Training* is there to help. It is a trusted resource when many of us are at our most vulnerable, knowing others will be looking to us for guidance, instruction, and understanding. As my professor, then my mentor, and finally, my friend, Mel and his insights have helped me and many other professional trainers make connections that last far longer than a specific training event. Thanks, Mel."

Carol Auerbach
Co-author, *Active Training*

Part Three

Conducting an Active Training Program

An Internet search on best practices for trainers might include the following responses:

- Involve participants in an activity in the first five minutes.
- Frequently check for understanding.
- Be prepared to modify plans based on participant feedback and technical difficulties.
- Use self-disclosure and humor to develop an open climate.
- Listen carefully and match what's happening to the needs of the participants.
- Use a wide variety of learning methods.
- Give participants the "what-why-how" for every training activity.
- Review where the group has been, give an overview of where it's going, and summarize periodically along the way.

Yes, you can build active learning into the design of your program, but it is in the delivery of that program that your efforts are truly tested. As we have already stressed, designing is not complete at the time of delivery. Instead, the delivery phase of a training program is a period of continually adjusting, refining, and redesigning.

Ensuring the successful delivery of a training program is a process that actually begins before the participants arrive. Preparation is one of the most important ingredients for success. Since much will happen during the actual program, you need to make sure that materials and equipment are ready and that the physical layout of the training room is suitable. As the trainer of this event, you need to be mentally prepared as well. Greeting participants, establishing early rapport, presenting your training agenda, and inviting feedback are also important beginning steps.

Once you have *connected* with your participants, you have the opportunity to *lead* them through the program. Your credibility as a leader depends on your ability to set group norms, eliminate training time wasters, get the group's attention, win over wary participants, and manage difficult behaviors. This can be a daunting task for many trainers. Fortunately, there are a wide range of techniques to help you gain control and establish yourself as an effective leader of the training group.

The challenge of delivering an active training program is most apparent during the middle section of the program, where the majority of your content is covered. Here, you have two different roles as a trainer: as a *stimulator* when you give presentations and lead discussions and as a *facilitator* as you guide participants through structured (and often team-based) activities. At this point, your success will depend upon how well you present information, lead discussions, direct participants through exercises, and make effective transitions from one event in the program to another.

Concluding a training program can be as difficult as beginning one. Among the key skills are how you review the program, handle remaining questions, guide back-on-the-job application, and end on a celebratory note.

The five chapters that constitute Part Three focus directly on your actions as you conduct active training programs in traditional settings, blended learning environments, and online classrooms. Chapter 11 tells you how to prepare yourself mentally and arrange the physical layout of a training room and illustrates four ways to establish immediate rapport with participants and introduce the training program. Chapter 12 suggests ways to foster constructive group norms, control timing, assert positive authority, and use humor to handle difficult situations that occur in training programs. Chapter 13 describes ways to overcome anxiety, make eye contact, maintain a natural and positive body language and voice quality, handle props, and make smooth transitions. It also outlines a ten-point menu of training behaviors that facilitate discussion. Chapter 14 explains how to motivate participants to buy into a training activity, give clear instructions, manage group behavior, and assist participants in processing what they have learned and examining its implications. Special suggestions are made for fostering collaboration in long-term learning teams. Finally, Chapter 15 identifies techniques for reviewing program content, eliciting final questions and concerns, promoting self-assessment, focusing on back-on-the-job application, and expressing final sentiments.

Each of the chapters in Part Three is filled with examples of how the ideas it contains have been translated into many different types of training programs covering a wide variety of content areas. As it did in Part Two, every chapter ends with a worksheet where you can practice applying the suggestions to your training situation.

At times, it will be helpful to refer back to the design ideas in Part Two as you apply the suggestions for conducting active training. Be alert to instances where material from Part Two should be considered side by side with material from Part Three.

"I first met Mel at an ASTD International Conference. I always loved his sunrise sessions—they were jam packed full of practical, active learning techniques. I had purchased his book, *101 Ways to Make Meetings Active* and stalked him in the bookstore for his autograph. He graciously signed my book and proceeded to ask if I would like to join him for coffee. It was the beginning of a wonderful friendship that lasted many years. I later became certified to teach his PeopleSmart course. I have had several mentors in my twenty-four years of training and Mel tops the list. He was generous, kind, inspiring, thoughtful, and so creative. He lived the words of Winston Churchill, 'We make a living by what we get. We make a life by what we give.' Thanks for giving me so much, Mel. I miss you."

Gale J. Mote
Gale Mote Associates

Chapter Eleven

Beginning an Active Training Program

*Y*ou have assessed your group participants, have written course objectives and an instructor's outline, and are now ready to conduct your active training program. If you have designed some effective opening exercises, you're likely off to a strong start. For added insurance, however, it is wise to think about these questions in advance: How are you going to arrange the physical setup of your room? What technology will you require? How are you going to establish rapport with participants as they walk in the door? And what are you going to say to introduce your program once it officially starts?

No training program can be totally successful based solely upon a written design. Programs that make sense on paper will not work if the trainer does not possess basic delivery skills. Even the most experienced instructors have seen programs fall apart due to a lack of upfront planning. Alternatively, a well-planned opening sets the stage for a successful experience. In this chapter, we will give you tips for conducting the beginning portion of a previously designed training program.

PREPARING YOURSELF MENTALLY

It's only natural for trainers to be a bit nervous when kicking off a program. That nervousness shows you care about the learning experience and are anxious to make it as positive as possible for the participants. The anticipation of the training is usually worse than the actual experience; most trainers feel an adrenaline rush once the program begins that carries them through the day. If you have thought through your exercises and follow a well-structured outline, there is a good chance the nervousness will pass. If, on the other hand, you forget to take care of preparation details until the last minute and do not carefully think out your design, you will have a far greater chance of losing the confidence necessary to help sell the group on your ideas.

The preparation of materials and activities for a training program begins weeks or days before participants walk into the session. Typical preparations include determining the date and time for the course, deciding on a delivery platform, preparing course materials, reserving room space or conference lines, and confirming course attendance. People who are not directly involved with training themselves usually don't consider all of the little things that go into making a program successful—that is, until something "inconsequential," like a miscommunicated date and time or a training room without enough chairs interferes with the overall conduct of the session. Attention to all of the details required to put together a successful active training program sets an atmosphere of order, organization, and professionalism.

In addition to preparation, you will find making the effort to connect with participants before you begin will reduce your tension and build your confidence. This way you avoid the self-absorption that breeds anxiety. Remember it is the participants who are responsible for producing skills or information as a result of the training experience. The purpose of their coming to training is not so you can impress them; it is so they may take something back with them when they leave the training session. Here is a case of someone who needed this advice.

EXAMPLE: A trainer in a large service organization was well known for his sense of humor. Employees were always eager to sign up for his courses because he was known as the "fun" trainer. This style worked well until the trainer delivered a two-day influence skills course for global senior executives. The trainer's jokes fell flat with the international audience, creating an uncomfortable situation for everyone in the room. The senior executives began questioning the credibility of the instructor and then the course itself. By the afternoon of the second day, the trainer had lost half of his group, and the participants who remained weren't able to demonstrate any significant changes in their influence skills.

Another consideration is your own comfort level with the course content. Creating a training program from scratch and delivering it for the first time can be tremendously exciting as you participate in the learning process step-by-step with the participants. The drawback to presenting new material is the hesitancy and uncertainty with which you may deliver the course content.

If you are uncomfortable with the subject matter, you might be especially concerned about questions from the participants. Remind yourself that one way to handle questions when you don't know the complete answer is to draw upon group expertise by asking the question to the whole group to determine if collectively they can discover the answer. You can do this through the chat feature in an online classroom, on a flipchart in a more traditional setting, or simply verbally on a conference call. Make sure to get back to the learners once you, or the participants, have the correct answers.

A different kind of mental preparation is needed if the course content is something that's second nature to you. Boredom with subject matter is a problem faced by anyone who teaches a subject repeatedly. If you are in the position of teaching course material you could recite in your sleep, try to remember that although the information is not new to you, it is new for your participants.

EXAMPLE: A sales trainer was asked how she could possibly look forward to conducting a session on customer relations the next day in light of the fact she had conducted the same session three other times that week. Her answer was simple: "I just tell myself to focus on the participants and not myself. I find it interesting to watch the way they respond to what I'm saying and try to find as many opportunities as possible for them to contribute to the discussion. In that way I can learn from their experiences and add their contributions to the subject matter the next time I teach the course."

Other ways to prevent trainer burnout are as follows:

1. *Be flexible with your lesson plans and designs.* Use repeat sessions of the same program to try out new ways to deliver the same material or to try out different sequencing.

2. *Vary the location, the environment, and your choice of delivery platforms.* If you always teach in the same room, see if a different one is available instead. Try offering the training session at an alternative time or location to mix things up. Experiment with a variety of delivery platforms and see how well the material translates to each format. If you always use PowerPoint, try delivering the same content using flipcharts or live video conferencing.

3. *Watch others train the same program.* If an outside vendor offers a similar program elsewhere, attend the session to get new ideas on how to handle the same subject matter. If you can observe other trainers within your organization, drop in to pick up new delivery techniques and styles.

As a professional trainer, you may be asked to conduct a program many times more than you would prefer. However, the preceding tips may help you to extend your endurance and postpone burnout a bit longer than you would ordinarily expect.

One final recommendation as you mentally prepare for your training program ahead: Remember what works well for one audience may not work at all with another group of people. The course content may not vary from one session to the next, but the mix of people most likely will. Success in an active training program will depend upon your ability to modify the content and design of a course according to the overall goals of a particular group of participants. Focus your training on the particular knowledge, skills, or attitudes you want participants to learn. Think through your program with the participants you will be training in mind. Try to be as flexible as possible, always considering a backup exercise if a planned activity does not fit the characteristics of your current training group.

EXAMPLE: An instructor received frequent requests for training sessions on a well-known psychological test. These sessions could have easily become routine, as neither the test nor the training materials varied from one administration to the next. What did vary, however, were the participants and their results on the test. The instructor used these differences to construct exercises specific to each training group, creating a new learning experience each time she delivered the program. Instead of dreading the sessions, she looked forward to them as an opportunity to test her creativity and deepen her understanding of the assessment instrument.

ARRANGING THE PHYSICAL ENVIRONMENT

If you could design a training room from scratch with an unlimited budget, what would be at the top of your preference list? Most trainers would include the following:

- Flexible, lightweight tables
- Comfortable swivel chairs
- Natural light with easily manipulated window treatments
- Dimmers for overhead lights
- An easy-to-understand lighting, sound, and projection system
- Flat-screen display panels for the front of the room
- Power sources for every participant's laptop computer
- Reliable temperature controls

The physical setup of a training facility is the first impression that participants will have as they begin their session. Large conference centers are available with hotel-type accommodations and extensive recreation areas, but your program may very well be scheduled for a church basement or a community college classroom. Regardless of the level of luxury in your surroundings, take into consideration the number of ways you can directly affect the physical layout of the training classroom.

By considering the physical arrangement of a room to be a continually flexible backdrop to your active training program, you enable your room to provide continued action and support for your activities. Don't be afraid to move the furniture within your room, even with the participants' help. By asking the participants to work with you to rearrange the room differently than they found it, you offer them the chance to change things around, make use of the existing surroundings, and in a very subtle way make it their own. Training conducted in a less-than-optimal environment is sometimes more successful than training undertaken within the best possible facilities, because everybody has to pitch in to make things work. Here is a case in point.

EXAMPLE: A trainer walked into a room with twelve rectangular tables arranged in three rows (see Figure 11.1).

FIGURE 11.1 TABLE ARRANGEMENT 1

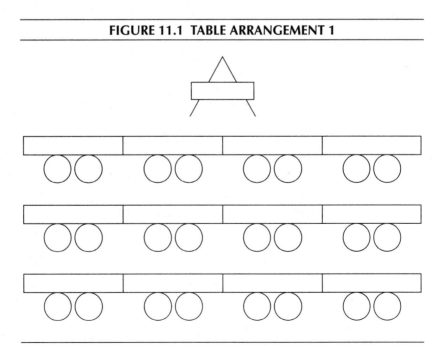

Since there was little time to rearrange the tables, he decided to leave things as they were for his opening remarks. When he needed participants to be seated as subgroups, he asked them to help him do some interior decorating, rearranging the tables as in Figure 11.2.

FIGURE 11.2 TABLE ARRANGEMENT 2

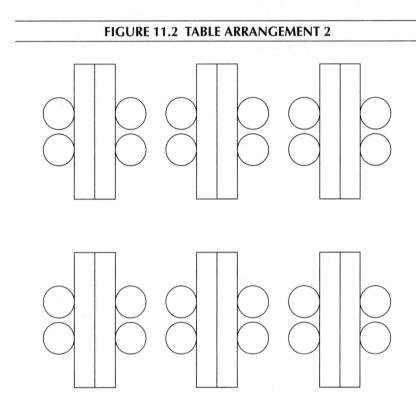

Later on, when he wanted a fishbowl design (one group surrounding another group), he used the arrangement shown in Figure 11.3.

There are times, of course, when nothing can be physically changed to create new arrangements. Even then, however, all is not lost, as evidenced by this case example.

FIGURE 11.3 TABLE ARRANGEMENT 3

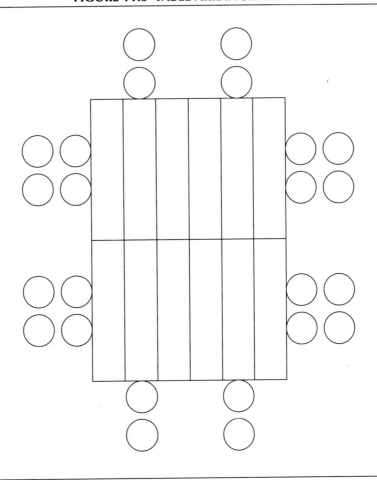

EXAMPLE: A trainer had designed a fishbowl activity as part of a course on conflict management. She walked into a small room furnished with one large rectangular conference table and space enough only for chairs around it. Her solution was to treat each side of the table as a fishbowl group. Participants along one side of the table at a time became the center of the discussion, with all those seated elsewhere acting as observers (see Figure 11.4).

FIGURE 11.4 MUSICAL FISHBOWLS

First fishbowl group

Fourth fishbowl group   Third fishbowl group

Second fishbowl group

Even fixed seating in an auditorium does not have to inhibit interaction. Participants can still have dyadic conversations with seat partners and can also be divided into groups of four, with two of the participants sitting directly in front of or behind the other two.

Probably the most common seating arrangement in the training world is a horseshoe (see Figure 11.5).

FIGURE 11.5 SEATING ARRANGEMENT 1

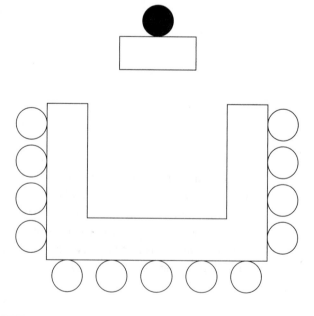

The virtue of a U-shaped layout is that participants can see each other while a traditional teacher-in-the-front presentation is going on. Whenever the trainer wants to break into full group discussion, participants can interact face to face without having to move. The arrangement is also convenient for handing out materials as the need arises: The trainer simply moves into the U and gives a stack of handouts to participants at each side of the horseshoe. If the room is large enough, participants can pull away from the tables and form small groups. For a more intimate full-group discussion, some participants can move their chairs into the mouth of the U to create a circle.

Another common seating arrangement is to have all chairs gathered around a conference table. In many cases this situation is difficult to change, as the only table available is the one occupying the entire center of the room. Use the conference room set-up for whole group discussions, and then ask participants to pull their chairs away to the corners of the room for small group work (see Figure 11.6).

FIGURE 11.6 SEATING ARRANGEMENT 2

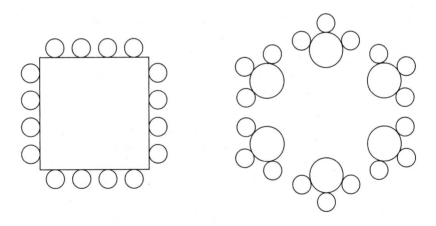

If you plan to have the participants work in subgroups, try to locate groups as far from each other as possible so they do not disturb one another. In these circumstances, if you must address the full group at any time, keep your remarks brief because you will be too far away to connect with your entire audience for a long period of time. Use breakout spaces, if available, for maximum privacy for the subgroups, but do so only when the task is sufficiently lengthy to warrant physical isolation between groups. For short tasks, sending groups to breakout areas may be too time-consuming.

In the event your design involves little need to write, take notes, or read from training manuals, you can do away with tables entirely. With only chairs to maneuver, any layout can be set up easily and quickly. Circles for small or large groups are easiest to achieve without any tables as obstacles. Removing the tables decreases the formality of a training environment and encourages more open group discussions.

GREETING PARTICI- PANTS AND ESTAB- LISHING RAPPORT

The first moments of getting acquainted with group members can be an awkward time for both the trainer and the participants. Consider the following example.

EXAMPLE: A new trainer put together a one-day program on team building for two recently merged small manufacturing companies. He scheduled the program to run from 9:00 a.m. to 4:00 p.m. at the in-house training facility of one of the two companies. A confirmation email informed the participants that coffee and donuts would be available beginning at 8:30 a.m.

By 8:35, the first few participants had walked into the training room and began helping themselves to the refreshments. This was the first opportunity for employees from the two companies to meet each other, and, even within the same company, some of the faces were unknown to fellow workers. As more people entered the training room, small groups of participants began to form, with little interaction between the groups. A few participants made no effort to socialize; after getting coffee, they began to check their phones and open up laptops at their seats. Several other participants wandered around the room, looking unsure of where to sit. The trainer did not help himself to coffee and donuts. He was in his office around the corner from the training room checking his emails. When he looked at his watch and discovered it was 8:50, he realized he still had a chance to make a couple of phone calls before the official session start time. When he did enter the room at 9:00, he quickly said hello and launched directly into the content of the program.

By 9:45, the trainer experienced his first feelings that perhaps all was not going as planned. Although he could not identify exactly what was wrong, he noticed that no one volunteered answers when he posed general questions to the group. When he opted to direct his questions to participants individually, the responses were quite short and defensive in tone. A small group exercise on sharing team experiences ended quickly due to a lack of conversation.

The trainer decided to give the group a morning break a little earlier than he had planned to give himself a chance to figure out why the group wasn't relating to his material. He kept asking himself, "What went wrong?"

Consider this trainer's experience to be a warning of what can happen if you do not take the time to greet participants and connect with your group. A simple way to ease the tense early moments of a training program is to make sure you are available and ready to greet participants at least fifteen minutes prior to the program's start. Walk around the room casually as people enter, make eye contact, and try to shake hands with participants as they make themselves comfortable in the training environment. *Learn as many names as you can. Introduce participants who don't know each other.* This getting-to-know-you process may relax your nerves as well, for you will begin to see the group members as individuals with whom you can share your interests. If you have not had a chance to do a thorough assessment of your group previous to the session, informal conversations with the participants can help you to gain valuable information before you begin the program.

Informal conversations are also valuable for establishing rapport with your participants. This can be very difficult with a new group, yet is essential if you are to gain your participants' acceptance and respect. Consider the following approaches as you attempt to connect with your audience, whether in informal conversations or in the first moments of your training program. Not all may work for you, but utilizing even one of these approaches will create a bond between you and the participants.

1. *"I've got something for you."* Let participants know about your expertise and your ability to transmit it to them. Don't be boastful, but do let them know you are confident about your knowledge and skills.

   EXAMPLE: Management training is a difficult subject to deliver unless you can convince participants of your expertise and experience. In a management training session designed for newly promoted supervisors, one trainer began the session with, "I'm pleased to be your trainer for this session. For those of you who aren't familiar with my background already, *I'd like you to know*

I've worked at this company for the last twelve years, eight of them in the plant. I've been a line worker, supervisor, manager, and trainer. I hope these prior experiences will help me to relate to your questions today."

2. *"I've been through this, too."* If you have been through the same training and work assignments as the participants, let them know you can identify with them.

   EXAMPLE: A trainer used this approach to connect with her group when she delivered a program for employees in a manufacturing environment. The employees were responsible for high production volumes and often had to rotate through off-shift assignments. Before beginning a session on quality awareness, the trainer let the participants know she had also worked an off-shift at one time in her career. She began the session by encouraging participants to compare stories about the difficulties of coping with irregular work schedules. The group was pleased to discover the trainer understood some of the pressures of their work. Without this mutual exchange of stories, it is doubtful the employees would have paid as much attention to the new information presented in the program.

3. *"I admire you."* Express your admiration for qualities you respect in your participants. Praising their efforts, their intelligence, and their goodwill can help you to build a positive rapport.

   EXAMPLE: A trainer asked customer service representatives in a program on selling skills to describe what it was like to be on the firing line with angry customers. The initial response was hesitant. When a participant told a real-life story about her job, more and more participants joined what quickly became a very animated discussion. The trainer wrapped up the conversation by saying, "It's very interesting for me to hear about some of the frustrations you face daily. I really respect you for having the patience and control to be able to deal with so many customers. I'm not sure I could do as well."

4. *"You interest me."* Get to know the participants and express interest in their backgrounds, life experiences, and concerns. The more you let participants know that you care about who they are, the more they will care about what you have to offer to them.

EXAMPLE: A group of Indonesian managers came to the United States for a two-month training program. One of the trainers in the program began the first day of his section of the program by asking the participants if they already missed home. Most nodded affirmatively. A participant added that that day was a special national holiday back home. The trainer asked the group if they would sing their national anthem for him to hear. Immediately, all twenty-eight participants rose and sang in unison. The trainer tried to learn the melody by humming along. To the delight of the participants, he successfully got through the opening notes. A tradition was then started, and, during breaks in the program, the participants taught the trainer several Indonesian songs. Showing this degree of interest in the participants' native music enabled the trainer to form a strong bond with the group.

GETTING THE BEST FROM THE FIRST THIRTY MINUTES OF TRAINING

Any progress you might have made toward establishing rapport with your group can go to waste immediately if you are not careful during the most important time period of your training program: the first thirty minutes. The first half-hour is a kind of "grace period" during which any overt hostility or antagonism will be submerged under a veneer of politeness, watchfulness, and, reserve. It is during this initial segment of time, however, that participants decide how they perceive you, what role they expect to play during the training program, and what they intend to accomplish during the course. As a trainer, it is your responsibility to make sure that each of these concerns is resolved positively during the first thirty minutes of your program. Be aware that participants may be asking themselves any of the following questions about their involvement with you and the training:

1. When are we actually going to start learning? How long will this thing last? (impatience)

2. What am I doing here? I already know this stuff. Does the trainer really know what she's doing? (competence)

3. I don't think that I'm going to like this trainer. I wonder what the trainer thinks of me? (compatibility)

4. Is he really interested in solving *my* problems? I wonder if what I say will get back to my manager? (trust)

5. Who will handle my regular work while I'm here? Should I keep my cell phone on? When can I check for messages? (out-of-session concerns)

Knowing the first thirty minutes of your training sets the tone for the entire program, try following these tips for making a positive first impression on your group:

1. ***Impatience:*** Begin the session promptly at the time previously announced for the start of the course. Work to focus the group on the course objectives, trying to hook the participants' interest onto the course content as opposed to what time they will be released for breaks and lunch.

2. ***Competence:*** Don't assume everyone in a course needs exactly the same content delivered to the same degree. Assess the range of participants' knowledge, skills, and attitudes, either as part of a formal needs assessment or during informal conversations before the session. Opening exercises also can be used to explore participants' skills more fully. Let the participants know you are confident in your abilities without pretending you have all the answers or the final word, and never pretend you know more than you really do.

3. ***Compatibility:*** Neutralize the traditional teacher-pupil relationship as quickly as possible during the opening moments of a training program. Let participants know your purpose is not to preach *at* them, but instead to interact *with* them. Establish a community-like atmosphere in which contributions from the group are welcomed and supported by you and by the other members of the group.

4. ***Trust:*** Emphasize that you respect confidentiality. Show the participants you want to hear what they have to say and you will be responsive to their needs.

5. ***Out-of-session concerns:*** Allow the participants the opportunity to speculate about how the training program will affect their work. Begin to establish the transition from the session back into the real world during the first, not the last, hour of the program. Set some rules around electronic communications by determining as a group whether cell phones should be on or off.

REVIEWING THE AGENDA No discussion of the beginning moments of a training program would be complete without a reference to reviewing the agenda or program objectives. After your introductory remarks, clue the audience into what they can expect out of the training program and detail what is expected of them. There are several ways to do this:

1. Include your training objectives in the participants' manuals or online materials. Briefly clarify what you mean by each objective. Giving participants a copy of the objectives up front allows them to be clear about what learning is expected of them. Figure 11.7 presents an example.

FIGURE 11.7 OBJECTIVES

After completing this time management course, you will be able to

- Complete a time-study analysis
- Specify time savers and time wasters that have an impact on your personal productivity
- Establish priorities to maximize your work in the future
- Develop a time plan to use both at work and at home

Identify what you hope to accomplish in the program. You can include your goals in your materials or can express them verbally as you make your opening remarks.

EXAMPLE: A trainer began a management training program for new supervisors by saying, "The transition from coworker to supervisor can be difficult. Many first-time supervisors ask questions such as these:

- How do I manage relationships with former coworkers?
- Do I need to keep my distance?
- How do I define my role as supervisor to them?

"Today's workshop is designed to help you adjust to your new position."

In addition to informing participants about your goals, be sure to tell them how the program is structured and what you need from them in order for the program to be successful. Include the following information:

1. A content outline

2. A description of the kinds of training activities you have designed

3. The schedule

4. Requests you will make of participants during the program

5. Housekeeping information (eating arrangements, location of restrooms, coffee breaks, access to phones and laptops)

INVITING FEEDBACK TO THE AGENDA

One of the basic decisions you face at this point is the degree to which you will solicit participants' feelings about the scheduled session. Some trainers are reluctant to risk the possibility of comments, so they enthusiastically present their agenda and then proceed directly with opening exercises. There is little problem with this if time is limited and you have every reason to believe that everyone is looking forward to the program. In most instances, however, you have much to gain by inviting feedback. How else can you check whether your agenda fulfills the participants' expectations?

The simplest approach is to ask directly, "Does this match what you hope to gain from this program? Is there anything you would like to add to the agenda?" By asking these questions, you are not implying the agenda is up for grabs. You are merely expressing your willingness to consider any wishes the participants may have. Most participants will understand when their wishes cannot be accommodated.

Another common approach is to ask participants, once they have learned about your plans, what hopes and concerns they might have. This formula allows them to express a wide variety of wishes, from wanting the program to have more real-life application to allowing for more time for breaks. Some trainers prefer to separate the discussion into two parts. First they elicit from the group *what* they want to learn. Then they encourage the participants to discuss *how* the program will proceed and *how* they will work together as a group.

If you have gathered assessment data about the participants prior to the program, it makes sense to share a summary of that information at this point. Let the participants know you have done your homework and are aware of their needs. This recognition is particularly important if you learn the participants have some resistance to the program. Instead of ignoring their resistance, you are better off bringing it out into the open. Showing interest in their misgivings is a sign you are supportive and not afraid to listen to negative comments. Even if you do not agree with the participants' views, you can still empathize with their feelings and acknowledge their valid points without compromising your own beliefs concerning the value of the program you have planned.

By the time you have completed your agenda review, your training program should be well under way. You can now continue with the opening exercises outlined in Chapter 3. Remember that a well-planned beginning can save you hours of frustration and prepares the stage for the rest of your active training program.

WORKSHEET

BEGINNING AN ACTIVE TRAINING PROGRAM

Use this worksheet to think about the beginning of your next program.

In-Person Training Physical Layout

Table and Chairs Configuration:

_____

_____

_____

Virtual Training Delivery Platform

Access, Connection, and Tools to Use:

_____

_____

_____

Establishing Rapport

"I've got something for you" (describe):

_____

_____

_____

"I've been through this, too" (describe):

_____

_____

_____

"I admire you" (describe):

_____

_____

_____

WORKSHEET continued

"You interest me" (describe):

_____

_____

_____

Reviewing the Agenda

_____Presentation notes

_____Informal remarks

_____Inviting participant feedback

Notes:

_____

_____

_____

_____

_____

_____

◆   ◆   ◆

"Before I ever met Mel, I used his *Active Training* book in the college-level courses I taught on instructional design. His ideas helped make the models I was sharing with my learners come to life in important ways; his audience-centered approach was critical to my students who were new to the field. I'm honored to have had submissions in three of Mel's past books. I admired these books, too, for their simple, practical, and applicable ideas. The fact that he was so willing to share ideas openly with the training community showed his true generosity of spirit."

Sophie Oberstein
New York University

Chapter Twelve

Gaining Leadership of the Group

*I*n the early stages of a training program, the group needs to see you as a strong leader. Even though all learning does not depend upon you, your active training program requires your professional direction and guidance. Setting appropriate group norms, controlling the timing and pacing of the program, getting the group's attention, communicating your message effectively, and dealing with problem participants are all important aspects of gaining leadership within a training group.

SETTING GROUP NORMS

One of the first steps in gaining leadership of the group is to set appropriate group norms. Consider what behaviors you want to foster within the training and then focus on guiding the group in this direction. Establishing firm ground rules lets everyone understand how the training program will operate and where it will go. Watch out for setting ground rules without enforcing them; model and reinforce the rules continuously throughout the session. Group norms that are firmly established from the outset of the training program help to guide the remainder of the course.

The following group norms have been found to be helpful within an active training environment:

1. ***Encourage participants to express themselves honestly.*** Let them know the open expression of ideas, concerns, and attitudes is appreciated and will enhance the overall learning process.

Sample script: "Please feel free to add your own opinions to our discussions; your ideas and experiences will contribute to the value of this session for all of us."

253

2. *Ask that confidentiality be respected.* Let participants know you want conversations during a session to remain confidential. Conversations about people outside the training group should not be disclosed to others once the session is over.

Sample script: "I realize many of you know the same people within your organization. Let's have a rule of trust between us that whatever we say and do as individuals during the training session will remain in this room."

3. *Urge risk taking.* A training session is a unique opportunity for participants to step away from their usual roles and responsibilities and consider information from another point of view. Encourage participants to use the training environment to their advantage by taking risks they normally would not consider.

Sample script: "Sometimes people shy away from role plays because they feel uncomfortable acting in front of a group. It is my hope you will find role plays to be quite useful for examining your own behavior in a variety of situations and you will feel comfortable participating in the activities planned for today."

4. *Expect participation from everyone.* Remind participants if they hold back initially from participating, it becomes increasingly more difficult to join in as time goes on. Tell them you have planned opening exercises designed to encourage participation.

Sample script: "Do you remember when you were a student in high school or college how the same people seem to answer every question? I don't want that to happen here, so I have put together some introductory activities designed for all of you to contribute right from the beginning."

5. *Promote the value of performance feedback.* Let participants know they are expected to give feedback to each other and all comments, both given and received, should be considered as helpful information.

Sample script: "As part of this interviewing skills training course, I will ask each of you to participate in an exercise that will be recorded and then critiqued by the group. I hope you will view this as an opportunity to sharpen and enhance your existing skills and not see it as a personal attack on your own interviewing style."

6. ***Require participants to sit in different spots.*** This way more people meet each other, the social climate of the group evens out, and cliques cannot form.

Sample script: "We will be together for two days. During this time, we'll be switching seats frequently for small group work. This will give you the chance to work with everyone in the room."

7. ***Reassure participants their questions are welcomed.*** Let them know you expect them to ask questions whenever they are confused and to speak up when they don't understand.

Sample script: "The best questions are those that, at first, you might think are dumb. These questions truly seek an answer and are asked at a risk. These same questions might also be on the minds of many others."

8. ***Insist on punctuality.*** Let participants know you will be able to start and end on time as long as they return promptly from breaks and lunch. (Note that this norm applies to the trainer as well!)

Sample script: "We have a jam-packed program, and I need your cooperation to make it run smoothly. One thing that will help me a lot is if you are punctual when it's time to resume after a break. Even one person missing can be a problem because often we will be involved in team activities and therefore can't start until all members are present."

As an alternative to stating norms yourself, you can invite group members to express their own norms. You may wish to have them add norms to your list. You may also want to ask them for norms and then add yours following the discussion. Be sure to allow time on your agenda for either of these.

Norm setting does not, of course, have to rely on direct verbal statements. The opening exercises you have designed can set in motion positive group behavior without any direct suggestions from you. Setting positive group norms through opening exercises can go a long way toward preventing negative situations from arising within your training program.

CONTROLLING TIMING AND PACING

Losing control of time during a training session often feels like you are losing your grip over leadership of a session. Few feelings are worse than the discovery that you have only one hour left to cover half a day's worth of material. Running out of material also can be embarrassing and can give participants the feeling they have been cheated out of time that they have already allocated and purchased. And, although you may decide during the design phase of development how you would like to pace your program, it is not until you actually begin delivering that program that you will be able to ascertain the appropriate timing and realize its benefits. Both the participants and you will feel a sense of completion and organization when a program remains on target and moves at a steady pace through the planned agenda. On the other hand, a program that moves too slowly or too rapidly will leave participants either bored or breathless.

Consider a leisurely pace for small-group activities to allow sufficient time for each person to be heard and directly involved in the activity. A much faster pace is necessary to keep the attention of all the participants when you are working with the group as a whole. Regardless of the format, stay alert to signs of restlessness and conclude any activity before the participants' interest is lost. Keeping things moving will help to give the entire program a sense of organization and accomplishment.

Also make sure no time is wasted during your training programs. This may mean giving shorter breaks, letting participants know work will begin as soon as the break is over, and taking care not to waste time when you move from one part of your program to the next. Potential training time wasters and their more efficient alternatives are shown in the following list:

Time Waster	*Alternative*
Starting late after breaks or lunch	Start exactly at the time you indicated. If all of the participants are not yet in the room, begin the session with a discussion or filler activity for which complete attendance is not necessary.
Starting an activity when the participants are confused about what they are supposed to do	Give clear and precise instructions. If the directions are complicated, put them in writing beforehand to avoid the need for lengthy oral instructions.
Recording presentation points while participants watch	Prepare key points ahead of time. Or, ask a participant to record information as you moderate a discussion of responses using only key terms.
Distributing participant materials	Prepare handouts ahead of time, or distribute packets to others and ask for assistance.

Time Waster	*Alternative*
Demonstrating every part of a new skill	Show only the parts of a skill that are new to the participants or are key for their understanding of the whole skill.
Having every subgroup report back one by one	Have each team report only one item at a time so everyone can listen for possible duplication. The groups should not repeat what has already been said.
Letting discussions drag on and on	Express the need to move on but be sure to call on those who were cut off during a subsequent discussion. Or begin a discussion by stating your time limit and suggesting how many contributions time will permit.
Waiting for volunteers to emerge from the group	Recruit volunteers during breaks in the program, or call on individual participants when there are no immediate volunteers.
Pulling ideas or questions from a tired or lethargic group	Provide a list of ideas or questions and ask participants to select those with which they agree. Often your list will trigger thoughts and queries from participants.

You can affirm the value of your training program by monitoring how you allocate time within the session. A program that provides both adequate time for participants to learn and a quick pace to ensure participant attention helps to establish your control. You maintain that control by eliminating busywork and time wasters.

INCREASING RECEPTIVITY TO YOUR LEADERSHIP

The way a trainer talks to adult participants makes a big difference in how receptive they will be to her or his leadership. As you converse with your group, particularly in the early stages of the program, try to use some of the following approaches to win participants over.

1. Make "liking" statements:

"I'd like to get the chance to know all of you."

"I hope that, through the comments I give you, you will feel as though you're getting some personal attention."

2. Convey respect and appreciation:

"Don't worry about waiting for a break if you need to use the restroom."

"Thanks for having me here."

3. Share what you have in common with participants:

"I guess we all struggle with this at one time or another."

"A lot of us don't plan."

4. Phrase your advice and directives indirectly:

"I'd like to start by asking you…"

"Let me tell you how I propose we do this."

5. State what's positive about participants' contrary viewpoints:

"It's exciting for me to try out these ideas with you."

"Thanks for providing us with a different point of view."

6. Encourage disagreement:

"I want you to know that nothing is carved in stone here."

"Although most people are resistant to this part, stick with it and I think you'll find it worthwhile."

7. Convey a desire for collaboration:

"You're going to have a lot of input in this program."

"I'd like to hear how you would handle this situation."

HANDLING PROBLEM SITUATIONS

Any experienced trainer can tell you anecdotes about difficult moments with training groups or with individual participants. The unfortunate truth is a trainer is an easy target for hostile participants' frustrations. Dealing with those feelings of hostility and a lack of interest can be the most difficult aspects of delivering a training program.

EXAMPLE: Project managers responsible for implementing a multimillion-dollar enterprise management system at a pharmaceutical company decided all employees needed to go through a four-hour change management session. There were no exceptions; every employee had to go through the training whether or not they would be using the new system. The general reaction to these sessions was so negative the trainers dreaded these sessions almost as much as the participants did.

Why might an **entire group** become hostile toward you? Quite simply, because participants are likely to turn any dissatisfaction or frustration that they are feeling at the time of the program on you. The hostility may have nothing to do with you personally but instead may stem from irritation at having to attend your program or anxiety about learning new skills. Additionally, the participants may make an "us-versus-you" distinction in which they perceive you as the natural opposition.

As we mentioned in the prior chapter, acknowledging group resistance is the first step to overcoming it and breaking through the us-versus-you barrier. A well-known strategy is to acknowledge that often participants do not come to a training program as voluntary, eager *learners*. Instead, they may have been sent by their managers and feel like *prisoners*. Or they might have just wanted a break from the daily grind of their job and may be attending essentially as *vacationers*. You might try asking participants to identify their role and place themselves in a group with fellow learners, prisoners, or vacationers. Ask them to discuss these questions:

1. Why are you in this group?
2. Why do you feel the way you do?
3. What can you get from others in the room?
4. What can you give?

The more you encourage group members to explain their position, the better chance you have of reducing their hostility. This may mean leaving the course content for a while, but more productive learning in the long run will make up for the time spent dealing with the situation. An efficient approach is to use the conflict as a learning tool by incorporating it into the discussions and exercises planned for the course.

If you sense resistance when introducing a new skill or some new information midway through a program, take time to focus on the resistance and identify it before the situation gets out of control. Don't be afraid to stop the program, ask what's happening, and propose a discussion of the problems at hand.

Negative behaviors of **specific individuals** create another difficult situation. Fortunately, you can prevent a lot of negativity by using active training methods. Further, the frequent use of pairs and sub-groups minimizes the damage individuals can do to you and the rest of the group. Following is a list of some common behaviors you might face within the training environment:

1. **Monopolizing:** constantly trying to provide all of the answers

2. **One-upping:** trying to appear more skilled and knowledgeable than the others in the group, including the trainer

3. **Complaining:** continually finding fault with the procedures

4. **Intellectualizing:** excessively rationalizing and justifying one's ideas and beliefs

5. **Withdrawing:** not participating (and sometimes distracting the group by doing so)

6. **Arguing:** taking vocal exception to any comments with which one disagrees

7. **Questioning:** stopping the flow of presentations by frequently asking questions

8. **Clowning:** joking at inappropriate times

9. **Distracting:** using cell phones and electronic devices during the session

EXAMPLE: You've worked with the same group of participants once a month for the last four months. You've got six more sessions to go, and you've noticed a huge change in the training environment. Personality traits that were well concealed early on are now fully evident in the group. One person loves to openly challenge you, another makes it clear he's got more experience than you or anyone else in the room, and several of the participants seemed to have mentally "checked out" of the program. Two individuals actually dared to pull out their laptops during a small group exercise and were exchanging humorous emails. You cannot believe you are stuck with this group through the remainder of the training program.

The key to handling such behaviors is to not take them personally. There are several reasons for problem behavior by a participant that have nothing to do with you:

• She may have been ordered to attend the training to shape up.

• He may be hiding fears about failing to do well in the program.

- She may be a long-time employee who doesn't believe anything will change.
- He may feel too old to deal with new approaches.
- After years of hostility toward her boss, she may be displacing her anger toward you.
- He may like the attention he attracts with his behavior.

Coping effectively with participants' problems is an extremely important training skill. When a participant exhibits problem behaviors, the whole group likely will become involved and therefore will be distracted from the actual training program. Negative behaviors also tend to rattle the trainer and distract from the delivery of the course content.

Your responsibility is to the entire group and not just to one participant. You should not allow the disrupter to monopolize your attention to the point where the program begins to suffer. If you do need to say something to a participant exhibiting a problem behavior, however, it is far better to do so privately. Introduce your request with a statement such as "I think that it would be helpful if…" or "I'd like to ask you to…"

One way to control potential troublemakers is to periodically remind the whole group to adhere to the norms or ground rules established at the beginning of the program. In addition, make some new requests from time to time to prevent problems from occurring. Following are some common requests used by experienced trainers:

- "Please hold your questions for a few moments."
- "I think it would be helpful for people to speak only for themselves."
- "Let's just have one comment per person for now so everyone has a chance to speak."
- "Try to build on each other's ideas."
- "When you go into your groups, I'd like to ask you to listen to the opinions of each member before getting into further discussions."
- "Let's have a rule that a different spokesperson be nominated every time a subgroup is asked to report its findings."
- "Watch how you treat each other."

As conflicts between you and one or more participants arise in a session, you may begin to feel annoyed with the other participants. Be wary of becoming unsettled by the conflict: *Managing your feelings and remaining in control are important to your overall leadership of the group.* Do everything you can to defuse and depersonalize the situation. Try to acknowledge the challenge openly and to respond in a warm but businesslike tone of voice. This will tell the rest of the group you are confident and in charge. Following are some tips on maintaining control in the face of participant conflict.

Don't get caught in one-to-one power struggles.

Acknowledge the value of a participant's views even when they are contrary to your own (for example, "You've got a good point"). Empathize with his feelings. Show interest by asking the participant to go into more detail about his concerns. Summarize the participant's position. Agree to disagree. Offer to discuss the matter further during a break.

Use good-natured humor.

Deflect conflict by humoring the combatant. Be careful not to be sarcastic or patronizing. Gently protest the harassment (for example, "You must be related to my in-laws"). Humorously put yourself down instead of the participant (for example, "Don't mind me; I'm not human until I have my second cup of coffee").

Connect on a personal level.

Whether the problem participant is hostile or withdrawn, make a point of getting to know her during breaks or lunch. It's unlikely she will continue to give you a hard time or remain distant if you've taken an interest in her.

Broaden the participation of others.

The more you use small groups and other devices to involve everyone, the harder it will be for just a few individuals to dominate the group. Also ask for the opinions and comments of others (for example, "I'd like to hear from those of you who haven't spoken so far").

Protect participants as needed.

If a participant or a subgroup is being attacked by a barrage of criticism, find something positive or provide a plausible explanation for what occurred (for example, "I agree John came on a bit strong in that role play, but I did really like his honesty").

Here is a list of several problem situations that can occur in training programs. How would you handle them?

1. A participant monopolizes discussions.
2. A participant goes off on a lengthy tangent unrelated to the current discussion.
3. A participant continually holds private conversations with another participant.
4. A participant disrupts the session with jokes.
5. A participant strongly expresses disagreement with what the trainer says.
6. A participant has a distracting habit (for example, tapping a pencil, clicking a pen, shuffling papers, or checking his phone).
7. A participant does other work during the training session.
8. A participant does not adhere to time schedules, arriving late or coming and going at will during the session.
9. A participant does not participate at all during discussions.
10. A participant falls asleep.

Here are potential solutions to these situations:

1. Monopolizing
   - Break eye contact.
   - Summarize the participant's viewpoint (active listening), then move on.
   - Ask other participants direct questions.
   - Change the discussion into a small groups or pairs exercise.
2. Tangents
   - Ask the participant to hold off till later in the seminar.
   - Summarize the participant's viewpoint and move on.
   - Address directly the fact that a tangent has been raised—"That seems to be a different issue"—and restate the purpose of the discussion, asking others for input.

3. Private conversations

- Use nonverbal methods to regain the participant's attention (make eye contact, move closer).
- Lower your voice or pause.
- Ask one of the participants a question (making sure to say the participant's name *first*).
- Ask the participants to refrain from talking (privately, if possible).

4. Jokes

- Come up with a quick retort and then resume your regular content immediately.
- Reinforce the person by complimenting his or her sense of humor.
- Privately ask the participant to minimize jokes.

5. Disagreeing

- Try not to personalize anything the arguer says.
- Summarize the participant's viewpoint; ask others for their opinions.
- Turn the opposing statement into a question for the group.
- Agree *in part*, then state how you differ and why.

6. Distractions

- Use nonverbal signals, such as eye contact, to get the participant's attention.
- Ignore the behavior if it is not distracting from the session.
- Privately ask the participant to stop.
- Request that participants only use their phones during breaks.

7. Doing one's own work

- Switch into pairs.
- Use nonverbal methods to get the participant's attention.
- If a group activity is under way, ask all to participate.
- Ignore the behavior if it is not affecting others.
- Privately ask the person to participate actively in the program.

8. Time schedules

- Minimize the distraction of the latecomer by ignoring the behavior.

- Adhere to time schedules; don't let everyone suffer for one person's lateness.
- Remind participants of time frames.
- Privately request promptness (as a courtesy to the rest of the group, not just to you).

9. Nonparticipation

- Ask direct but nonthreatening questions.
- Connect with the participant during breaks.
- Ask the participant to be the leader in a small-group activity.
- Leave such participants alone (just because they're not participating doesn't mean they aren't learning).

10. Sleeping

- Walk near the person without being obvious.
- Vary your voice.
- Shift into pairs or subgroup discussion.
- Create a physical activity.

One final thought as you consider handling problem situations: Remember it may not be necessary for you to intervene every time a participant exhibits a problem behavior during your training program. Very often, other participants will make it known they find such behavior inappropriate and unnecessary. A good guideline is to intervene only if the problem behavior is repetitive or affects the entire training program. Also, realize participants who have been difficult often want to find a way out themselves. Give them some space to discover a graceful, face-saving way to change their behavior.

To effectively gain leadership of your training group, it is important to keep in mind that prevention and intervention are the keys to establishing and maintaining control. Setting positive group norms and modeling those behaviors throughout the session help participants know what guidelines to follow. Controlling the timing and pacing of your program prevents boredom and keeps participants focused on the course content itself. The way you handle problem situations will give further credibility to your leadership, allowing you to concentrate on giving presentations and leading discussions.

WORKSHEET

GAINING LEADERSHIP OF THE TRAINING GROUP

Use this worksheet to think through how you will establish your leadership in your next training program.

Group norms to be encouraged:

_____

_____

_____

_____

_____

Time wasters to be avoided:

_____

_____

_____

_____

_____

Comments to win participants over:

_____

_____

_____

_____

_____

Ideas for preventing problem behaviors:

_____

_____

_____

_____

_____

_____

◆   ◆   ◆

Chapter Thirteen

Giving Presentations and Leading Discussions

*C*hapter 4 suggested several ways to design presentations to build interest, maximize understanding and retention, involve participants, and reinforce the content. The tips and illustrations of successful delivery techniques provided here are intended to complement those ideas. In addition, this chapter will cover ways to make smooth transitions between phases of your program and facilitate lively discussions.

KNOWING YOUR GROUP

To many people both in and out of the training profession, the ability to deliver an effective presentation is the mark of a good trainer. Sometimes, sessions that are called training programs are really just forums for presentations by speakers with expertise in a particular area. If a presentation is the only component of your session, don't expect much retention or application. You can expect better results if you include brief presentations at intervals during an otherwise active training program.

To be effective, first consider the nature of the participants. What are their concerns, their backgrounds, and their reasons for attending? Customizing your remarks specifically to your audience is the first step toward a successful presentation. If you originally designed a presentation on writing techniques for college undergraduates, for example, edit your examples to make sure that they are appropriate in an adult working environment before presenting the same information to a corporate audience. The more aware you are of the composition of your audience, the better your chances of suiting your remarks to its needs. Following these other tips also will help you to connect immediately with your audience.

1. *Make it personal.* Participants will be attentive if they think you are going to address the questions that matter most to them. Until these questions are answered to the participants' satisfaction, they will have difficulty relating to the information you are trying to get across. Here are some typical concerns:

   • "Why are you telling me this?"

   • "How does this affect me?"

   • "Why should I be here instead of elsewhere?"

If you do not address these concerns at the outset, you risk losing your listeners before you even begin and may have to spend valuable time fighting to regain attention and interest.

2. *Understand why you are there.* Have you been invited to speak as an expert consultant, a helpful intermediary, or a decision maker who is telling the group what is about to happen? If you have been asked to present information about a new benefits program that will require employees to make major concessions, are you prepared to handle hostility and angry responses from your audience? If you are lecturing as an expert consultant, do you have the credentials to back up your statements? Anticipate your group's perceptions of your role and plan your reactions accordingly.

3. *Speak their language.* Avoid jargon or unfamiliar terms that might confuse people or prevent your overall message from getting through. Provide examples that relate to your audience.

Following is an example of what a trainer might say when teaching employees how to handle upgrades to an existing purchasing system. Pay attention to how the trainer attempts to make it personal, explains her role, and uses language familiar to the participants as she opens her presentation:

"Welcome to training on the new version of our purchasing system. Today's session is intended to help you make an easy transition between what you are using currently and the upgrades we will be incorporating in the future.

"Although a full conversion will not take place until all employees have gone through training, you will find that as of tomorrow morning the new version will be available to you as a new application. It is important to try out the new version on your own as soon as possible so you can gain full advantage from your hours spent in training today. I have been tracking previous participants closely and have found those who have the best results use the new version immediately. I'd like to give you a follow-up call approximately three days from now to find out if you have accessed the new version and if you experienced any problems when using it. Before I go any further, what initial questions do you have for me?"

"Will we still be able to access our current system?"

"Yes, for a limited time period you will have access to both versions of the purchasing system. I will be explaining more about conversion time frames at the end of our session today.

"Let's start by finding out what's new. We have been searching for a way to integrate purchasing processes across our company for quite some time. The upgrade will offer you enhancements the old version simply didn't have. I think after you have a chance to test out the new version, you'll agree the enhancements are really terrific and make the purchasing process easier than ever."

"What if I decide I don't like the upgrades?"

"Any time you move away from something you're comfortable with you are bound to feel a bit awkward at first. However, I think once you experiment with the new version, you will be frustrated returning to the old one.

"Instead of just talking about what's new, let's go ahead and try out some of its features. Please sign on by entering your user ID and password."

In this example, the speaker addressed the participants' potential concerns by identifying the reason why she was giving the presentation as well as the short- and long-term impact of system upgrades. A concern the trainer had overlooked (giving up what was familiar) was brought up by a participant very early in the presentation. The trainer clearly identified the purpose of the session (to help employees learn how to use the upgraded version) and used jargon the audience would understand ("application," "upgrades"). The trainer made it personal to her audience and presented the information in a way they could understand.

Here is another example, this time from a presentation presented as part of a program entitled "Strategic Selling Skills." The immediate topic is sales presentations. As with the previous example, notice how the trainer focuses his initial remarks on the concerns of his listeners, understands his role in communicating this information, and uses a common language to bridge his experiences with those of the participants.

"Right now we're going to be focusing on the sales presentation framework. Taking a look at our list of course objectives from this morning, you may remember that several people mentioned improving their sales presentation delivery skills as one of their personal goals for our training program.

"I know from previous experience that making a presentation can be a nerve-racking experience, especially if this is new to you. However, you may find you already possess much of the knowledge you should have in order to be successful. What you will see by comparing the information covered this morning to this afternoon is that there are a lot of similarities between a sales call, a sales telephone call, and a sales presentation. Let's review the framework of a sales call now."

(The following list appeared on a slide labeled "framework of a sale.")

- Opening
- Client's Primary Needs
- Probing Questions
- Listening
- Positioning Product Knowledge
- Resolving Objections
- Close
- Action Step

"The framework for a sales presentation will follow that of a sales call very closely because all of the elements are very much the same. The skills required for handling a successful sales call will also be required for successfully handling a sales presentation, with some extra attention given to specialized delivery techniques such as voice inflection and positive body language. We will have a chance to practice these delivery techniques later in today's program.

"Let's begin, however, by discussing the opening or the introduction within the framework of a sales presentation. When you start giving a sales presentation, one of the most important things to do is to immediately thank everybody in the room for the opportunity to speak to them. You are taking time away from their work, so you want to thank them for coming and giving you the opportunity to speak about your organization.

"Another thing you want to do up front is to clarify just how much time you have to speak. Many of us will prepare for an hour's presentation only to have someone come in and say, 'I'm sorry, I have to leave in forty-five minutes,' or somebody might say, 'You're going to have to cut your presentation to twenty minutes because we have a big problem and we have to run out on you.' Some advice I'm going to give you is to always have a short program and a long program, because you never know what the situation is going to call for. Above all, you want to make sure you save enough time to get through your major points, close effectively, and allow time for questions and answers.

"So, initially, prepare yourself for your presentation by planning for both a long and a short program, and don't forget to thank your listeners up front for the opportunity to speak to them."

ORGANIZING YOUR PRESEN-TATION

Although the actual design of your presentation may vary widely from one course to the next, several organizational principles apply to all presentations regardless of content or structure. Some ideas to keep in mind as you organize your presentation follow.

1. ***Make sure your opening is effective.*** A good opening will help the rest of your presentation to go much more smoothly. An especially effective opening involves telling a story directly related to how you have used the content of your presentation in real life. Another option is to poll the group or ask the participants a few initial questions designed to elicit their opinions on your subject before you launch into your presentation. Asking the group to participate immediately will be as effective as the most humorous or captivating opening story.

2. ***Provide a preview of information prior to an explanation.*** An overview can familiarize participants with what you will present. It should be short and precise, providing a statement of the overall idea to be presented, the importance of the information, and a statement that outlines the structure of the content to be presented.

3. ***Cover a few points of information thoroughly rather than many points quickly.*** Set limits on how much you plan to

cover and stick to those limits during your presentation. All listeners have finite attention spans, no matter how interesting or scintillating the speaker. Trying to cram in as much information as possible can overwhelm your key points as well as confuse the listener.

4. ***Organize your information within a step-by-step sequence.*** Participants tend to get lost in verbal mazes. Carefully structure the presentation, arranging information logically and breaking down material into clear, coherent, and explicit steps.

5. ***Avoid tangents and getting off track.*** Prevent yourself from going off the deep end when delivering your presentations, especially in response to participant questions. Stay on target and in focus, and pace your presentations to keep everyone's interest in your subject matter alive.

6. ***Signal transitions between information.*** Use statements that move from the introduction to the body of the presentation, between major points and subpoints, and from the body to the conclusion. Make transitions explicit and then relate the previous information to the new information.

7. ***Keep your presentation as specific as possible.*** The clearer your message, the greater the likelihood your audience will understand what it is you are trying to convey. Give examples or make analogies that truly illuminate your points. Select dramatic examples to which participants can relate.

8. ***Provide for brief pauses at appropriate times during the presentation.*** Give participants adequate time to process the information and take good notes. (Most people are capable of taking notes at only twenty words per minute.) Also, consider using guided note taking (see "Guided Note Taking" in Chapter 4).

9. ***Review or allow participants to recap information frequently.*** This helps to "save" the information for later retrieval. Reviewing is especially important after a stretch of difficult material and at the end of the presentation.

10. ***Estimate the time each part of your presentation will take.*** By doing so, you can alter your remarks as needed. Sometimes you will need to shorten certain parts of a prepared presentation to fit into the time constraints of a particular training group. Before delivering the presentation, decide which segments can be shortened or lengthened if needed.

WATCHING YOUR BODY LANGUAGE

Underlying all presentations are your body language and the expressiveness of your voice. The maxim "It's not *what* you say but how you say it" holds true. In fact, research shows *what* you say accounts for only 7 percent of the impact of your presentation. The other 93 percent of how people will respond to you stems from *how* you are communicating nonverbally. The keys to effective nonverbal behavior are how you present yourself *vocally, facially,* and *posturally.* Remember the participants will primarily be focused on you as the presenter. The effective communication of your message can be sabotaged by delivery techniques that are annoying or irritating to your listeners. Following these suggestions will enhance your personal presentation skills:

1. ***Establish your comfort level with the group through natural, positive body language.*** Maintain good posture and a firm stance as you address the group. Avoid putting your hands near your mouth or your face, as those gestures signal insecurity. Watch out for bad habits such as fidgeting, playing with your hair, or jingling change, as they distract the participants from your message.

2. ***Individualize your audience by making eye contact with the participants.*** Resist the temptation to read from a written page or a screen. You are speaking to an audience, not to a piece of paper or a slide. Pick out a friendly pair of eyes in the audience and pretend you are having a one-on-one conversation with them. After approximately five seconds, switch to another pair of eyes and deliver your next thought. As you continue your presentation, keep telling yourself you are really just stringing together a series of individual conversations. This will calm your nerves and provide you with instant feedback from the participants.

3. ***Stay aware of the pace and volume of your voice.*** Speak slightly more slowly than you would in normal conversation so all participants can catch what you are saying. Speak at a volume loud enough for all to hear yet not so loud that you find yourself shouting. If you imagine a volume scale from 0 (inaudible) to 10 (painfully loud), try to keep your voice within the 6 to 8 range. Varying both the rate and the tone of your voice can help to keep the audience's attention, much as a master storyteller modulates her or his voice to complement the plot and characters of the story.

4. ***Alter annoying speech habits.*** Fillers like "ah," "um," and "er" are irritating when used repetitively by a speaker. Especially guard

against the continued use of "like," which is a popular conversational phrase but sounds out of place in a presentation. Excessive coughing or throat clearing also takes a listener's attention away from the presentation.

As you try to make any desired changes in your nonverbal behavior, be careful not to overdo it. Eye contact that becomes a stare, a forced smile, or an overly enthusiastic voice will diminish your credibility.

Listening to a recording of yourself giving a sample presentation may help you to pick up annoying speech mannerisms of which you are unaware. Viewing yourself (ask a friend or colleague to help) is even better, since you can both hear and see your delivery style.

Changing your presentation style may be difficult at first. Your habits have probably developed over a long period of time and may be hard to break. However, constant awareness of your body language and voice patterns while you speak in front of a group will help to ensure that your message not only is delivered, but also is heard and understood by your participants. If you wish, utilize the feedback form reproduced in Figure 13.1 to assess how you are doing.

FIGURE 13.1 FEEDBACK ON NONVERBAL BEHAVIORS

VOICE

Volume	(loud)	5	4	3	2	1	(soft)
Tone	(animated)	5	4	3	2	1	(monotonous)
Fluency	(smooth)	5	4	3	2	1	(halting)
Speed	(fast)	5	4	3	2	1	(slow)

FACIAL EXPRESSIONS

Eyes	(engaged)	5	4	3	2	1	(removed)
Mouth	(friendly)	5	4	3	2	1	(stern)
Forehead	(relaxed)	5	4	3	2	1	(furrowed)

POSTURE

Posture	(erect)	5	4	3	2	1	(slouched)
Movement	(controlled)	5	4	3	2	1	(fidgety)
Hand gestures	(natural)	5	4	3	2	1	(robotic)

**ADDING
VISUALS**

Visuals are expected as part of any professional presentation, so much so that they can often overwhelm the presentation itself. This is especially true if the lights are dimmed and the visuals incorporate animation, sound, and special effects. What active trainers need to remember, however, is that the participants are there to listen to what *you* have to say, not to stare at colorful graphics. The main purpose of visuals is to provide you with your notes or speaking points, as well as to create a lasting image to support your message.

You have numerous options to choose from when you create presentation visuals. The most basic of these is the classic flip chart, which is inexpensive, versatile, and fail safe. The drawback to the flip chart is it looks amateurish as compared to higher tech options, especially if you have bad handwriting. Flip charts are most effective if you tear off sheets as you use them and post them up on the walls of your training room. Participants then have constant visual reminders of the information you've covered during the session.

If you decide to use flip charts either as your main visual medium or to support other visuals, keep these hints in mind:

1. Improve readability by using print lettering, not cursive writing.
2. Limit the number of words you use on each flip chart page.
3. Use one color for the title and bullet points and another for the text.
4. Increase visibility by using black, green, blue, and red markers.
5. Leave a blank page in between flip chart sheets to prevent colors from seeping through.
6. Number, paper clip, or otherwise flag important pages so you can locate and flip to them quickly.
7. Build curiosity by posting all the flip charts you plan to use along a wall or blackboard. Fold up the bottom of the flip chart page and tape it to the top until you are ready to reveal the content.

The most popular medium for creating visuals is the slideshow. This type of visual is so prevalent that the phrase "death by Power-Point" is well known to many participants who have endured seemingly endless slides overloaded with text, charts, and graphs. Despite its detractors, ***slides are effective in adding impact to your presentations, especially when you are presenting to a large audience.***

The key to success is to keep your slides simple: clear, concise, and easy to read.

Here are a few important tips to follow when you create a slide presentation:

1. Use headers or titles on each slide to keep your presentation organized.

2. Limit yourself to one idea per slide.

3. Value white space. Don't feel as though you need to "fill up" a slide.

4. Follow the "6 by 6" rule: There should be no more than six lines on each slide, and each line should contain no more than six words per line.

5. Use phrases, not complete sentences, in your text.

6. Replace words with images whenever possible.

7. Limit your use of animation to approximately one third of your slides.

8. Don't stand in front of the light emitted by a projector.

9. Keep the lights on in the room! A darkened room will put participants to sleep and take the focus away from you. If you must dim the lights, do so only at the very front of the room.

10. Stay connected with your audience by stepping away from the screen to expound upon a point or engage in a group discussion.

11. Use your slides to increase interactivity within a presentation. Show a slide, and then ask participants to study it, talk in pairs, or do something with the information before you launch into an explanation of your content.

A ***handout*** spares participants the burden of note taking and provides a helpful reminder of the points that you covered in your presentation. Make sure, however, that your handout is concise and designed for easy reading. And think carefully about when you should distribute your handouts. Many trainers do so before their presentations and then wonder why they have trouble getting the group's attention when they begin speaking. If you want the group's full attention, let them know handouts covering the major points of your discussion will be available after you speak. They will then be free to concentrate fully on what you have to say rather than on what you have written on the handouts. If you feel participants will follow your presentation more easily if they have a handout in front of them, be explicit about asking them for eye contact when you need it.

Following the suggestions outlined in this section should assist you with any presentation that you are asked to make, regardless of the size of the group or the subject matter. Well-designed visuals can help you to communicate your message quickly and effectively to the participants in your training program, as well as provide a lasting image of your key points.

MAKING SMOOTH TRANSITIONS

Earlier in this chapter, we gave an example from a presentation on strategic selling skills. In this section on linkages and transitions, we will be taking a look at another passage from that same presentation. This time pay attention to how the trainer leads the group from one topic to the next.

"I hope you didn't forget the framework of a sales presentation over lunch because it's important that you keep that in the back of your mind as we move on to our next topic. By taking a look at our agenda, you'll notice we're going to be discussing differentiation. Mark, I believe it was you who asked me this morning about how to differentiate proposals, wasn't it? Now is the time when I finally get to explore your question in detail.

"As you'll see on this slide, I have listed three specific ways to differentiate your proposal from the competition. The first method listed, team strategy, focuses on introducing the team of individuals that is with you when you make your sales presentation and the expertise of those individuals. It's important you make sure to introduce whoever is accompanying you from your company and give the group a brief idea as to how and when they are going to be contributing to your presentation that day."

Making smooth linkages and transitions between one topic and the next in your presentation involves briefly reminding the participants of what you have already covered, then indicating what is to follow. The best transitions appear to be seamless and flowing, easily connecting what you have already covered to what you will be discussing next. There are several techniques for either tying together sections of your presentation or linking together various parts of your training program. Following are descriptions of these techniques and examples of how they can be used:

1. **References to periods of time.** Mentioning specific periods of time—"yesterday," "this morning," "today," "this afternoon"—helps participants to organize the sections of your training program in their mind and gives them a clear indication of where you are headed.

   "This morning, we took a look at what not to do in an interview; this afternoon we will be focusing on what positive approaches you can take to make the most out of an interview."

2. **Mini-subject review.** Taking a few moments to review what was previously covered allows participants the chance to reflect on what they've already learned and to prepare themselves for the next part of your presentation.

   "Let's quickly review what we've covered so far before we move on to our next topic of discussion."

3. **Agenda check.** Hanging your planned agenda on the wall not only helps to keep the group on track but also serves as an easy reference when you are making subject matter transitions.

   "Taking a look at our agenda for today, you'll see we have already covered writing and speaking communication skills and are now ready to address the topic of listening."

4. **Change of visual aid.** Introducing a new visual aid or changing to a different type of presentation tool indicates a transition to a new topic.

   "Turning to our flip chart, you'll see I have listed the five assertive communication techniques that we will be discussing today."

5. **Change of group format.** Reorganizing the group into a new configuration is probably the clearest way of marking a definite transition from one segment of your program to another.

   "I think it makes more sense for us to be together in one group for our next discussion topic. If you would just move your chairs from the small groups we were in for our last activity and form a large circle, we can begin."

Logical linkages between sections of your presentation ensure both you and your group are ready to address a new topic. With just a bit of practice, elegant linkages will become a natural part of your delivery style.

FACILITATING A LIVELY DISCUSSION

For many trainers, encouraging a discussion after a presentation consists of introducing a question-and-answer period with the classic line, "Are there any questions?" All too often what follows is an uncomfortable silence as the participants wonder who will dare to speak up first. After a few awkward moments, the trainer sighs and says, "Well, if there are no questions, I thank all of you for listening."

How do you coax discussion out of a group intimidated by the quiet aftermath of a presentation? Starting a discussion is no different from beginning a presentation. You first have to build interest. Note how the following opening remarks are designed to generate a discussion about the benefits and problems with work teams.

> "Now that we have looked at the nature of work teams, I'd like to take the next ten minutes to get your thoughts about their advantages and disadvantages. Everyone seems to think work teams are the way to go in business today. However, I think there hasn't been a critical enough look at when it makes sense to do things in teams and when it's better to get work done on an individual basis. I also know people who feel that work teams place an unfair burden on the 'responsible' people who have to take up the slack of the team members who don't pull their weight. It's as if there can be no individual accountability in work teams. You have a lot of experience working here at ABC Corporation. What do you think about the pros and cons of getting work done around here using teams?"

Start off the discussion with an open-ended question (for example: "How do you feel about...?" "What do you know about...?"). Most experts agree that open-ended questions trigger better discussions than closed questions. Avoid closed questions because they are too restrictive and don't require participants to think. They can also make your audience defensive and stifle participation. Therefore, avoid questions that can be answered simply yes or no, such as "Did you like this training video?" The question, "What are some things that you liked and didn't like about this video?" invites a longer response. In addition, avoid questions that can be answered with a fact, such as "When did that occur?" or "Which action would you take?"

Remember that once a discussion topic is introduced, you can use many interesting formats to obtain further participation. In Chapter 3, we discussed the following methods:

- Open discussion
- Response cards

- Polling
- Subgroup discussions
- Partners
- Go-arounds
- Games
- Calling on the next speaker
- Panels
- Fishbowls

Many of these options allow you to sit back and let the participants take charge. You might, for example, ask participants to form small groups to discuss the question, "What do you think about the pros and cons of getting work done around here using teams?" and then summarize their conclusions on flip chart paper or in an online chat room. Other options require your leadership. In such cases, your role is to facilitate the flow of comments from participants. Although it is not necessary to make an interjection after each person speaks, periodically assisting participants with their contributions can be helpful. Here is a ten-point facilitation menu to select from as you lead group discussions:

1. **Paraphrase** what someone has said so the participant knows she or he has been understood and the other participants can hear a concise summary of what has just been said at greater length.
   "So what you're saying is you have to be very careful during an interview about asking an applicant where he or she lives because it might suggest that you are looking for some type of racial or ethnic affiliation. You also told us it's okay to ask for an interviewee's address on a company application form."

2. **Check** your understanding against the words of a participant or ask a participant to clarify what she or he is saying.
   "Are you saying this plan is not realistic? I'm not sure I understand exactly what you meant. Could you please run it by us again?"

3. **Compliment** an interesting or insightful comment.
   "That's a good point. I'm glad you brought it to our attention."

4. **Elaborate** on a participant's contribution to the discussion with examples or suggest a new way to view the problem.

"Your comments provide an interesting point from the employee's perspective. We could also consider how a manager would view the same situation."

5. ***Energize*** a discussion by quickening the pace, using humor, or, if necessary, prodding the group for more contributions.

"Oh my, we have lots of quiet people in this group! Here's a challenge for you. For the next two minutes, let's see how many ways you can think of to increase cooperation within your department."

6. ***Disagree*** (gently) with a participant's comments to stimulate further discussion.

"I can see where you're coming from, but I'm not sure what you're describing is always the case. Has anyone else had an experience that's different from Jim's?"

7. ***Mediate*** differences of opinion between participants and relieve any tensions that may be brewing.

"I think Susan and Mary are not really disagreeing with each other but are just bringing out two different sides of this issue."

8. ***Pull*** together ideas, showing their relationship to each other.

"As you can see from Dan and Jean's comments, personal goal setting is very much a part of time management. You need to be able to establish goals for yourself on a daily basis in order to manage your time more effectively."

9. ***Change*** the group process by altering the method of participation or prompting the group to evaluate ideas that have been raised during the previous discussion.

"Let's break into smaller groups and see if you can come up with some typical customer objections to the products that were covered in the presentation this morning."

10. ***Summarize*** (and record, if desired) the major views of the group.

"I have noted four major reasons you have suggested that may account for managers' unwillingness to delegate work: (1) lack of confidence, (2) fear of failure, (3) comfort in doing the task themselves, and (4) fear of being replaced."

Any of these actions can be used alone or in conjunction with the others to help stimulate discussions within your training group. You may find that, as participants become more and more relaxed about contributing their ideas and opinions, you shift from being a leader to being an occasional facilitator and perhaps just another participant with an opinion. As your role in the conversation diminishes, the participants make the learning process their own.

Finally, there are many special formats for stimulating lively discussions. One excellent choice is to set up an "active debate" that involves every participant in the group, not just the debaters:

1. Develop a statement that takes a position with regard to a controversial issue relating to your subject matter (for example, "The FDA is taking too long to approve important new drugs").

2. Divide the group into two debating teams. Arbitrarily assign the "pro" position to one group and the "con" position to the other.

3. Next, create two to four subgroupings within each debating team. In a group of twenty-four participants, for example, you might create three "pro" subgroups and three "con" subgroups, each containing four members. Ask each subgroup to develop arguments for its assigned position. At the end of their discussion, have each subgroup select a spokesperson.

4. Set up two to four chairs (depending on the number of subgroups created for each side) for the spokespersons on the "pro" side and, facing them, the same number of chairs for the spokespersons on the "con" side. Place the remaining participants behind their debate team. Begin the "debate" by having the spokespersons present their views. Refer to this process as "opening arguments."

5. After everyone has heard the opening arguments, stop the debate and reconvene the original subgroups. Ask the subgroups to strategize how to counter the opening arguments of the opposing side. Again, have each subgroup select a spokesperson, preferably a new person.

6. Resume the "debate." Have the spokespersons, seated across from each other, give "counterarguments." As the debate continues (be sure to alternate between both sides), encourage other participants to pass notes to their debaters with suggested arguments or rebuttals. Also urge them to cheer or applaud the arguments of their debate team representatives.

7. When you think it appropriate, end the debate. Instead of declaring a winner, reconvene the entire group in a single circle. Be sure to "integrate" everyone by having participants sit next to people

who were on opposite sides. Hold a group discussion on what the participants learned about the issue from the debate experience. Also, ask participants to identify what they thought were the best arguments raised on both sides.

You can also use a debate format that is less formal and moves more quickly:

1. Select an issue that has two or more sides.

2. Divide the group according to the number of positions you have stated and ask each group to come up with arguments to support their issue. Encourage them to work with seat partners or small cluster groups.

3. Seat groups opposite each other.

4. Explain that any participant can begin the debate. After that participant has had an opportunity to present one argument in favor of his or her assigned position, allow a different argument or counterargument from another group. Continue the discussion, moving quickly back and forth between the groups.

5. Conclude the activity by comparing the issues as you, the instructor, see them. Allow for follow-up reaction and discussion.

Every training program, even the ones that are the most active, needs to incorporate some type of information sharing into a session. Providing essential content through a presentation or webinar is an efficient use of both the trainer's and participant's time but runs the real risk of leaving participants disinterested or bored. Using the methods and techniques described in this chapter will help you to involve participants in their own learning experience, thereby increasing the understanding and retention levels of everyone in the course.

WORKSHEET

GIVING PRESENTATIONS AND LEADING DISCUSSIONS

Answer the following questions.

1. What do I know about my audience?

   _____

   _____

   _____

   _____

   _____

2. What is the core organization of my presentation?

   _____

   _____

   _____

   _____

   _____

3. What nonverbal behaviors do I want to increase? What do I want to avoid?

   _____

   _____

   _____

   _____

   _____

4. What technology will I use?

   _____

   _____

   _____

   _____

   _____

WORKSHEET continued
---

5. How will I make transitions?

_____

_____

_____

_____

_____

6. How will I introduce a discussion?

_____

_____

_____

_____

_____

7. What facilitation methods do I want to pursue?

_____

_____

_____

_____

_____

8. What special techniques can I use to stimulate discussion?

_____

_____

_____

_____

_____

◆   ◆   ◆

"One of Mel's favorite conclusions was to group participants in a circle and give one person a large ball of yarn. Before passing the yarn to someone across the circle each participant would relate an "ah-ha" moment, an application step, or key learning point. After everyone had contributed a learning point from the workshop, the crisscrossed yarn became a visible symbol of how connected the group had become. Active learning at its best!"

Jean Barbazette
The Training Clinic

Chapter Fourteen

Facilitating Structured Activities and Promoting Team Learning

*T*his chapter has two goals. One is to offer advice on facilitating structured activities used throughout an active training program. These activities typically utilize small-group formats *for short periods of time.* The other is to offer advice on promoting team learning. This endeavor involves placing participants in small groups or teams *for an extended period of time.*

STRUCTURED ACTIVITIES

In Chapters 5 and 6, we examined alternatives to formal presentations as well as several experiential learning approaches. Because these kinds of structured activities play a central role in active training programs, you will need to develop an array of facilitation skills to make them effective learning experiences. Listening to a presentation, watching a demonstration, or even participating in a discussion demands less effort and risk than does taking part in a role play, an exercise, or a project. Consequently, one of your basic responsibilities as a facilitator of experiential learning is that of *motivating participation.* Since it is difficult to get participants to do exactly what you want them to do, especially if any of your activities are complicated, you also need to become an expert at *directing participants' activities.* As an activity unfolds, the dynamics of the training group can impede success, so you will need to be comfortable with *managing the group process.* In the middle of any activity, energy may begin to flag and your task becomes one of *keeping participants involved.* Finally, at the activity's end, its meaning may be unclear. You now need to involve the participants in *processing the activity.*

Without the necessary skills in each of these areas, these mistakes commonly occur:

1. **Motivation:** Participants aren't invited to buy into the activity or sold on the benefits of joining in. Participants don't know what to expect during the exercise.

2. **Direction:** Instructions are lengthy and unclear. Participants cannot visualize what the trainer expects from them.

3. **Group process:** Subgroups are not composed effectively. Group formats are not changed to fit the requirements of each activity. Subgroups are left idle.

4. **Energy:** Activities move too slowly. Participants are sedentary. Activities are long or demanding when they need to be short or relaxed. Participants do not find the activity challenging.

5. **Processing:** Participants are confused and/or overwhelmed by the questions put to them. The trainer's questions don't promote the goals of the activity. The trainer shares her or his opinions before hearing the participants' views.

How can you avoid these mistakes? Many of the skills you need can be explained best in the context of a case situation. Imagine the following.

EXAMPLE: You have been asked to create a two-day training program on interpersonal effectiveness. You have pulled together materials from other communication skills classes that you have taught previously and have redesigned some key pieces to fit the group you expect. Today is the first time you have tried out the newly designed program.

So far, the session is going very smoothly: there are no latecomers and the total group comprises eleven participants—a comfortable number. Introductions were straightforward and the participant completed the first activity, a needs assessment survey, individually. You followed up the survey with a brief presentation that tied in the needs assessment to the overall learning goals for the course. It's now 9:45 and time for you to facilitate the first structured activity, a small-group exercise called "Making Connections."

The exercise calls for the group to form trios and discuss questions that relate to interpersonal communication skills. After the first question, two of the three group members will rotate to join new groups and discuss another question. The goals for this activity are for participants to learn more about each other and to practice basic interpersonal skills such as communicating clearly and listening effectively.

Motivating Participation

Your participants need to be interested before they will feel motivated to join in and take the exercise seriously. Getting participants to buy into an activity is essential to the success of your planned exercise, especially if it involves risk or effort. Here are some ways to motivate participation:

1. ***Explain your objectives.*** Participants like to know what is going to happen and why. Don't assume that they know your objectives. Make sure they do.

   "Right now I'm going to ask you to take part in an activity called 'Making Connections.' This activity should help you to get to know other members of our group a bit more than you were able to during our brief introductions. In addition, this activity will allow you to practice clear communication and effective listening."

2. ***Sell the benefits.*** Tell participants what's in it for them. Explain what benefits they will derive back on the job as a result of the activity.

   "We often meet new people and introduce ourselves to each other. Usually, getting acquainted provokes some anxiety. This exercise should help you to feel comfortable enough to really get to know someone."

3. ***Convey enthusiasm.*** If you sound motivated about seeing them engaged in an activity, participants will internalize some of your enthusiasm.

   "This activity is a good one; I think you are really going to enjoy some of the questions that I have planned for you to ask each other."

4. ***Connect the activity to previous activities.*** Explaining the relationship between activities helps participants to see the common thread in your program.

   "On the survey you just completed, many of you identified overcoming shyness as one of your goals. During our first exercise, you will get some immediate practice in conversation skills."

5. ***Share personal feelings with participants.*** Explain why you have found the activity (or one like it) valuable to you.

"I know that I can be reserved at times. It's nice to have a structured exercise designed to reduce the anxiety involved in meeting people."

6. ***Express confidence in participants.*** Tell participants that you think they'll do a good job with the activity or that they are now ready to tackle a new challenge.

"Now that you've already met each other at least once, you should have no problem asking each other questions that are a bit more detailed. Let's go ahead and get started."

Directing Participants' Activities

Incomplete or unclear instructions can spell disaster for a structured activity. If you do not take the time to explain exactly how the exercise should be completed, participants may spend more time asking questions about what they were supposed to be doing than actually taking part in the activity. Although you need to be careful not to sound like a grade school teacher, don't be afraid of oversimplifying; there is always someone who needs clarification and repetition. Here are four tips for making sure that the group understands your directions.

1. ***Speak slowly.*** Processing instructions to a complex activity is harder than listening to a presentation. Slow down so that participants can follow you.

"Before we begin the exercise, I'd like to take a few minutes to explain exactly how this activity will take place. Please let me know if I am speaking too quickly."

2. ***Use visual backup.*** If appropriate, write directions on a slide or flip chart and allow participants to refer to this visual information as you explain it.

"As you can see from this slide, I will be asking you to discuss four separate questions with other members of the group."

3. ***Define important terms.*** Don't take for granted that every participant will understand the key words in your instructions the same way you do. Explain important directions in more than one way.

"As you see, the first question is 'What are your strong points in communication?' In thinking about how you'll respond to this question, remember that communication has two parts, the speaking end and the listening end. So include your strong points in both of these areas.

"We will be forming new trios whenever there is a new question to be discussed. When I ask you to rotate out of your trios, I am, in effect, asking your group of three people to split up and join other members of the group to form a new trio."

4. **Demonstrate the activity.** Sometimes it is important for participants to have a mental picture of what they are to do. Provide a brief sample of what the activity will look like. Use yourself and/or a few participants to illustrate the instructions.

"Now that the first trio has been completed, we're ready to rotate. Each of you has been assigned a number—0, 1, or 2. The 0s will stay where they are but the 1s will advance one trio (clockwise) and the 2s will advance two trios (clockwise). Let's have a sample group try this out so that you understand what I mean. John, Kathleen, and Mary were together in a trio. Because he is a 0, John will stay where he is, while Kathleen will move one group over there [point] and Mary will move two groups over there [point]. Have I been clear? [Avoid saying, "Do you understand?"]

When a trainer's directions are ineffective, a few basic flaws are generally responsible, singly or in combination. Here are several tips for giving effective directions:

1. Explain the big picture first, then describe each of the parts that form the whole activity.

2. Try out your instructions in advance on a colleague or friend. Ask the listener if anything seems unclear.

3. Redesign your slides so that instructions are at the top of the screen and are printed in bold type.

4. Take notes when facilitating an activity for the first time. Watch for any problems that come up and either alter the design or make the next group of participants aware of any pitfalls to be avoided or preparations to be made.

5. Give the group detailed directions for one part at a time.

Clear, easily followed directions prepare your participants for the transition from trainer-led training to the independent learning that takes place in structured activities. Many trainers overlook the importance of verifying understanding before an activity begins, only to find that the participants are confused, frustrated, or misguided. A design that you have worked hard to perfect in advance is worth a few extra moments spent on clear directions up front.

Managing the Group Process

Most structured activities involve subgrouping. Small groups give participants an opportunity to discuss ideas and ask questions in greater detail than is possible in a large-group format. Group movement also accommodates the diverse personal learning styles of your participants, many of whom may feel more comfortable speaking in a small group than they do when all of the participants are together.

Managing this process of forming and monitoring subgroups is difficult because you cannot completely control how participants will behave in smaller units. Also, some participants may not be as comfortable, at least initially, in subgroups as they are when the full group is together. Here are some suggestions to maximize peer interaction and productive work.

1. ***Form groups in a variety of ways.*** In order to separate acquaintances or randomize group composition, assign numbers to participants after they have seated themselves and then form groups corresponding to those numbers. Or allow participants to choose their own partners when you want to encourage friends to work together. When you want to achieve a certain composition, form groups according to specific criteria (for example, by gender or department).

   Count the number of participants as soon as you believe that you have full attendance. Then determine how large your subgroups will be by finding a number that easily divides into your total number of participants. Twelve is the easiest number of participants to work with; a group of this size can be divided into subgroups of two, three, or four members without your having to join the last group to make it even.

2. ***Mix teams and seat partners.*** Mixing up groupings offers the participants the chance to get a broad range of opinions and adds interesting variety to their discussions. Keep teams and seat partners together for long periods only when you need continuity.

   Set place cards in new locations in the training room to change seating patterns and create new seat partners.

3. *Vary the number of people in any activity based upon that exercise's specific requirements.* The smaller the group, the more opportunities there are for each participant to contribute. Work with the number of participants in your course to create groups whose sizes fit your design's requirements. If possible, try to keep work groups to six people or fewer to maximize individual participation. Include yourself if subgroup adjustments have to be made.

The "Making Connections" activity calls for trios, yet there are only eleven participants in the course. In this instance, the trainer can join with the participants as a contributor to form four groupings of three people each.

4. *Divide participants into teams before giving further directions.* Ask participants to move to their new locations first, and then describe the particulars of how to conduct the exercise. Many trainers have to repeat directions for an activity because the participants forget them by the time subgroups are formed.

Say, "Before I go over the directions for this exercise, I'd like you first to get settled in your project teams. So please go to your tables now."

5. *Ask groups of five or more to elect a facilitator or timekeeper.* Larger groups can be difficult to keep on track and on time. A facilitator for each group relieves you of that burden.

Say, "I'm going to ask one person in each group to volunteer as a timekeeper. We need to keep each round of discussions to just five minutes in order to stay on schedule today."

6. *Give groups instructions separately in a multipart activity.* Subgroups may finish their assignments at different times. Instead of waiting for all groups to finish one section of a multipart activity, quietly give the next set of directions to each subgroup when it is ready to move on.

Say, "I see that you have completed the first round of questions. For your next assignment, please complete this conversation skills rating that we will be discussing as a whole group when everyone else is finished."

7. *Keep people busy.* If one subgroup finishes all its work well in advance of the other groups, be ready with a "let's take this one step further" question. You are letting the members of the faster group know that they are going to be able to report their findings on the second question to other groups.

Say, "Here is a follow-up question on delegating authority. Since you've finished the exercise, why don't you take a few minutes now to discuss your response. Perhaps you can tell the other groups about it."

8. *Inform the subgroups how much time they have.* State the time allotted for the entire activity and then periodically announce how much time remains. Visit subgroups to see how much they have accomplished. When you are about to stop a group activity, give the participants a warning.

Say, "You'll have ten minutes to do this activity. Make sure each person gets a two-minute turn.... You should be about halfway around the group by now.... There are two minutes left.... Please wrap up your discussions now so that we can get back together as a full group."

A trainer who quietly and smoothly manages group process is rarely noticed; the chaotic atmosphere of the training course will give away one who does so clumsily. For example, an activity that calls for the participants to work together in pairs is awkward if the instructions are only, "Pair up with the person seated next to you" (on the left or the right?). You can facilitate these pairings far more efficiently by pointing out two participants at a time and saying, "You two are a pair, and you two, and you two...." It is simple moves like these that give the participants a clear indication of what to do.

Keeping Participants Involved

Your job is not over once the participants have been organized into groups and begin working on a structured activity. You may find yourself redesigning an activity on the spot if it seems to be too long, short, simple, or complex for a particular situation. Altering a training design to fit the time of day and the mood of your participants helps to keep the energy level of your training group up and active. Redesigning also adds interest and fun. Go with what is happening in the classroom if it meets your training goals. If an activity or exercise yields an unexpected surprise or draws an unusual response from your participants, make a training moment happen by weaving that surprise response into what you are trying to achieve educationally. The ability to be flexible within the design of a planned activity adds energy to the exercise for both you and your participants. Here are some other guidelines for sustaining group energy.

1. ***Keep the activity moving.*** Don't slow things down by speaking slowly, endlessly recording participants' contributions on flip charts, or letting a discussion drag on too long.

   Usually, more energy is generated when participants have to complete an activity within a specific time. Keep time frames short and move things along at a brisk pace.

2. ***Challenge the participants.*** There is more energy when activities create a moderate level of tension. If tasks are too easy, participants will get lethargic. Emphasize the importance of a challenging activity and encourage participants to really think about their answers or try out new behaviors.

   Say, "Now, I've got a tough role-playing situation for you. After trying it out here within your training group, you'll be prepared for anything that might happen back at home."

3. ***Give positive reinforcement to participants for their involvement in the activity.*** Show interest in the participants as they engage in the activity. Don't stand off or busy yourself with other things. Give the impression that you are really interested in how they are doing and praise success.

   Say, "I'm really impressed at the way you're going about this task. You're off to a great start!"

4. ***Build physical movement into the activity.*** Have participants move their chairs, stand up, or use their entire bodies during the activity as a way to wake them up.

   Say, "Since you've been sitting for a long time, how about doing the next segment standing up? I'd like each trio to get up and find a spot in the room to discuss the next question."

5. ***Let your enthusiasm show.*** Genuine feelings of excitement and enjoyment about an activity will inspire like emotions in the participants. Your high energy level can lift up the energy level of the entire group.

   Say, "I can't wait to see how you'll do on the next part of this activity. I think you're going to like it."

Behaviors that energize participants can be easily woven into your facilitation style. Once your active training designs are joined with these behaviors, you'll become both effective and believable as you reinforce participant involvement. Using these behaviors in the session will help you to accomplish your educational objectives while maintaining high levels of energy and interest in your planned activities.

Processing the Activity

When you have concluded an activity, it's quite important for participants to process it by discussing any feelings that the activity elicited and sharing their final reflections and insights. Processing questions help to complete the learning cycle by collating information gathered by the participants during the activity and applying that information within the context of the subject of the training program. Here are some tips to help you facilitate the processing portion of an activity.

1. ***Ask relevant questions.*** Often, trainers think they are processing activities merely by asking participants questions such as "Did you learn from the activity?" or "Was it worthwhile?" Be careful, however, not to ask too many processing questions at once. Usually one to three questions are all a group can handle at a time. Here are some examples of processing questions that encourage participants to go beyond simple answers and invite responses related to training goals:

   • How did you go about doing this activity?

   • What were your concerns?

   • On a scale from one to ten, how well did you think you did on this activity? What went well and what needs improvement?

   • What helpful and not so helpful behaviors occurred in your group while you were doing this activity?

   • Who else had the same experience? A different experience?

   • What conclusions can you draw from this activity?

   • How did this experience apply to your work situation?

   • What struck you while doing this activity?

   • What do you understand better about yourself or your group as a result of this exercise?

   • What skills can you transfer from this activity to your own work or home environment?

   • What behaviors would you like to change as a result of this activity?

2. ***Carefully structure the first processing experiences.*** A high percentage of activities invite processing in an active training

program. Knowing this, it makes sense to familiarize your participants with processing activities in the early phases of the program. The first time you process an activity with a group, ask only one or two simple questions and keep the discussion time brief. It is probably a good idea to direct the processing as well. For example, you might present a question and then go around the group, obtaining a short response from everyone. Later on, less direction will be necessary.

One way to structure the processing of an activity is to use incomplete sentence stems. Say, "One thing I thought was worthwhile about this activity was…"

3. *Observe how participants react during the processing.* The most valuable and productive processing occurs when all participants feel comfortable expressing themselves. If participants begin to give responses that are personally critical of other members of the group, step in by modeling behaviorally specific information and deal with any personal confrontation in a positive manner. Through your own behavior, you can help the group to establish an open forum that promotes the expression of personal views without personal criticisms.

Say, "I didn't perceive Mark as being as hostile in this role play as some of you are suggesting. What I heard was a loud voice and some pointed feedback to the employee. I imagine that you were very annoyed with his procrastination. Is that true, Mark?"

4. *Assist a subgroup that is having trouble processing an activity.* If you have asked subgroups to process an activity and one group finishes well before the time you have allotted expires, it's likely that they have experienced difficulty processing and have wrapped up their reactions too quickly, without probing below the surface. You can help them take a more in-depth look at the implications of an activity by asking them to share with you what they have discussed and then extending the discussion by probing further.

Say, "I see that your group has finished. Would you mind if I join in for a while? Tell me what some of your thoughts were."

5. *Keep your own reactions to yourself until after you've heard from the participants.* Let the participants know that you respect them for their opinions. The processing time is primarily their opportunity to discover what can be learned from the activity. Your insights may be welcomed, but save them for the end.

Say, "I noticed a number of interesting behaviors watching this project team at work. But before I mention them, let me hear your reactions."

TEAM LEARNING

It is one thing to place participants in groups for short, structured activities. It is another thing to place them in teams for longer periods of time. For example, you might decide to form permanent teams that last throughout the life of a training program. Or you might use teams extensively but change their membership a few times during the session. You might even form teams that have assignments beyond the boundaries of the training room.

Team learning has many benefits. Participants develop a bond with their learning teammates that may motivate the team to sustain collaborative learning activity through complex, challenging assignments. Further, participants in learning teams are willing to accept greater responsibility for their own development precisely because they have a sense of ownership and social support, which is often lacking in short-term groups. However, team learning also has its drawbacks. Chief among them is the fact that the trainer has less instructional control than when using short-term groups.

Have any of these things ever happened to you when you have been in learning teams and/or used them in your training?

- *Confusion:* Team members don't know what to do because they didn't understand or follow the directions.
- *Tangents:* Team members don't stick to the topic and get off task.
- *Unequal participation:* Some team members dominate; some remain quiet.
- *One-way communication:* Team members don't listen or respond to each other.
- *No division of labor:* Some team members don't pull their own weight, let the team down, and are not dependable.
- *Superficiality:* The team is done before you know it, breezing through the assignment in the fastest way possible and staying on the surface rather than digging below it.

Chances are you have experienced nearly all of these problems. When they happen, participants and trainers alike get turned off to team learning. What can you do differently?

Composing Learning Teams

The first consideration in promoting team learning is the size and composition of the teams. The most productive work teams range in size from two to six members. Small teams work faster and can manage and coordinate their work with greater ease. Teams that are larger than six members have the advantage of greater knowledge, skill, and perspectives, but often get bogged down in group process issues that prevent them from moving forward. They are difficult to organize and it can be especially difficult to pull the work of a large team together. If you decide to use large teams, realize that they need more structure, more formal meetings, and clearer roles for each member than small teams.

There are few hard-and-fast rules about composing learning teams. Any of the following can be considered:

- *Random assignment:* Form teams arbitrarily (for example, counting off or grouping by insignificant criteria such as birthday or first initial). This randomness often gives participants the sense that they are expected to work well with everybody in the course.

- *Diversity:* Form teams by deliberately varying the background, job function, gender, age, or style characteristics of its members. Diverse teams take longer to get started but often succeed in the long run because of the richness of their resources.

- *Homogeneity:* Form teams by assigning members with equivalent job experience, knowledge, or skill. Homogeneous teams organize themselves quickly and obtain immediate results.

- *Prior acquaintance:* Form teams by keeping together people who have worked with each other previously. Participants tend to be comfortable with each other and may have team skills that will transfer to the new situation.

- *Self-selection:* Allow participants to form their own teams.

Building Learning Teams

Once you have formed learning teams, it's a good idea to have them experience some initial team-building activities such as "Predictions" (see Figure 3.3), "TV Commercial" (see Figure 3.4), and "YouTube Introductions" (see Figure 3.5). Such activities help teams to get to know each other rapidly and build a degree of team cohesion early.

Since the teams will be working together for some time, the next order of business is to set expectations and ground rules. One way to begin this process is to ask the teams to write a brief vision statement that expresses their hopes for what the team learning experience will be like. You might want to start off by asking individual team members to list potential components of the vision statement using the format shown in Figure 14.1.

FIGURE 14.1 HOW I'D LIKE OUR TEAM TO BE

What do you hope your learning team experience will be like? Jot a few wishes down in the spaces below:

How I'd like our team to be . . .

_____

_____

_____

_____

_____

_____

Next, ask team members to share their lists, combine ideas, and formulate a brief vision statement that will focus the learning team's efforts.

Besides asking teams to set their own expectations, you might want to set some trainer expectations as well. One of the best ways to do this is to demonstrate how an effective learning team functions. If you can, make a brief video that shows an effective learning team in action. Or invite a small group of participants to role-play an effective team. During their role-playing demonstration, either join the group and model successful facilitation behaviors or coach the group as they struggle to perform a team learning task.

Setting specific ground rules helps teams to decide how they must function in order to reach their goals. You can ask teams to brainstorm potential ground rules or provide them with a checklist such as the one found in Figure 14.2.

FIGURE 14.2 OUR GROUND RULES

Below are ground rules that are helpful to learning teams. Check the four most important to you.

_____ Start on time with everyone present.

_____ Get to know members who are "different" from you.

_____ Let others finish without interrupting them.

_____ Be brief and to the point.

_____ Be sensitive to gender, race, and ethnicity.

_____ Be prepared.

_____ Give everyone a chance to speak.

_____ Be fully present.

_____ Rotate facilitating and other responsibilities.

_____ Reach decisions by consensus.

_____ Make sure that team meetings are "processed" from time to time.

If teams are going to be effective, some crucial jobs have to be done. If no one does them, the teams will drift aimlessly without achieving much. To make this point, you might want to share a well-circulated story:

> A team had four members called **Everybody, Somebody, Anybody,** and **Nobody.** There was an important job to be done. **Everybody** was sure that **Somebody** would do it. **Anybody** could have done it, but **Nobody** did it. **Somebody** got angry about that because it was **Everybody's** job. **Everybody** thought **Anybody** could do it but **Nobody** realized that **Everybody** wouldn't do it. It ended up that **Everybody** blamed **Somebody** when **Nobody** did what **Anybody** could have done.

Then ask teams to consider assigning themselves (preferably on a rotating basis) some of these important jobs:

- *Facilitator:* facilitates learning team sessions
- *Timekeeper:* allocates and monitors time needed and spent
- *Note taker:* keeps a record of ideas, conclusions, and achievements

- *Checker:* sees if all members are doing what they are supposed to
- *Investigator:* finds things out and brings information back to the team

Team building is not complete without promoting an awareness of group process from the beginning. Teams that go about their business without ever reflecting on how well they are doing eventually flounder. Ask learning teams to discuss their progress from the outset to build the kind of awareness that keeps the team from going off the deep end. Point out that all teams have problems and that if they are not brought to the surface, they won't go away.

Use any of the following processes:

- *Helpful versus unhelpful:* What behaviors have we used thus far that are helpful? What behaviors are unhelpful?
- *In hindsight:* If we had a chance to do that over again, what should we do?
- *What's going right or wrong?* What's going right in the team? What's going wrong?
- *Stop, start, continue:* What should we stop doing? Start doing? Continue doing?

Involving Participants in Team Learning

Whether your learning teams are small or large, it is crucial to structure team learning when it is first introduced into a training program. Use short, collaborative activities such as those suggested in Chapter 5:

- *Study group:* Give teams some learning material and ask them to explain it to one another.
- *Information search:* Give teams some questions and provide learning material that contains the answers. Have them find the answers.
- *Group inquiry:* Give teams learning material to study. Ask them to put a question mark next to or highlight anything they don't understand.

- *Jigsaw learning:* Give different learning material to different members. Ask them to study the material and teach it to one another.

- *Learning tournament:* Give teams material to master in preparation for team competition.

As learning teams become oriented to team learning and show signs of taking responsibility for their own learning, you can begin to give them tasks that are less structured. For example, you might provide a list of questions that teams investigate through reading, interviewing, and observing between training sessions. Here are some questions given to learning teams in a training program on team development:

1. *Types of teams*: What types of teams exist in the workplace? How are they structured?

2. *Goal setting*: How should teams set and clarify goals?

3. *Tools*: What group process tools exist for generating ideas, diagnosing problems, strategizing, planning projects, and making decisions?

4. *Conflict management*: What strategies exist for managing conflict in teams?

5. *Role division*: What roles are needed in teams? What leadership and facilitation skills are critical? How do teams share responsibility and promote individual accountability?

6. *Team development*: What stages do teams go through and what helps them move from stage to stage?

Or you might ask learning teams to do some collaborative problem solving, as in the following example.

EXAMPLE: In a course on process mapping, teams were given the following assignment:

As a group, figure out how to do a process map of the current ordering process in your organization. Then develop a new process and map it.

Consider giving learning teams the responsibility of preparing and teaching a training module.

EXAMPLE:　In a course on creative thinking, individual teams were given the following training assignments:

1. Teach others four different kinds of brainstorming techniques.
2. Teach others about "reframing" and "perspective shifting."
3. Teach others how to use "mind mapping" to create novel solutions.

Finally, you might want to devise team self-study materials and form self-directed learning teams as mentioned in "The Delivery of Active Training" in Part One of this book. This represents a convenient, cost-efficient, and effective way to deliver training. The theory is that if organizations allow work teams to manage their own work, why not challenge trainers to have teams manage their own learning? If you take up this challenge, keep the following in mind:

- It requires skill and commitment to learn in this mode. Train participants how to function in a self-directed learning team before putting them on their own.
- Do a trial run, directing the team at first and then relinquishing control.
- Have the team either elect a facilitator or decide to take turns.
- Serve as a "help desk" throughout the learning team's activities.
- Monitor and check what's happening so that you can provide any necessary support.

WORKSHEET

FACILITATING STRUCTURED ACTIVITIES

Evaluate your effectiveness at facilitating a structured activity by responding to these questions the next time you are training. If you believe that the activity fell short of your expectations in any of the categories listed, work to improve those areas the next time you present the same exercise to another training group.

1. Motivation
   a. Did you give the participants an overview of the activity before starting?
   b. Did you explain why you were doing the activity?
   c. Did you show how the activity connects with the other activities that preceded it?

2. Directions
   a. Did you speak slowly and/or provide visual backup?
   b. Were the instructions understandable?
   c. If appropriate, was the activity demonstrated?

3. Group Process
   a. Did you divide participants into subgroups before giving further directions?
   b. Were changes in groupings managed smoothly?
   c. Did you keep idle groups busy?

4. Energy
   a. Did the design move at a good pace?
   b. Was there something challenging about the activity?
   c. Were participants reinforced for their involvement?

5. Processing
   a. Were the processing questions related to your training goals?
   b. Were participants' reactions discussed before your own?
   c. Was the activity tied into the overall learning goals for the course?

PROMOTING TEAM LEARNING

Evaluate your effectiveness at promoting team learning by responding to the following questions the next time you use this training approach.

WORSHEET continued
---

1. Composing Teams
   a. Did you keep the teams as small as possible?
   b. How did you compose the teams?
      - Random assignment
      - Diversity
      - Homogeneity
      - Prior acquaintance

2. Building Teams
   a. Did you use initial team-building exercises to break the ice?
   b. Did you invite teams to build a vision statement?
   c. Did you clarify your own expectations, preferably by demonstration and coaching?
   d. Did you invite teams to create ground rules and job responsibilities?
   e. Did you promote awareness of group process issues early on?

3. Involving Participants in Team Learning
   a. Did you use short, collaborative activities to introduce team learning?
   b. Did you lessen structure as teams became more mature and give them greater control over their own learning?

◆　◆　◆

"For years, I have used the Mel Silberman *Active Training* book for a class in training and development at Maryville University. It is a very practical, user friendly guide to designing active learning experiences."

Barb Crockett, MS, PHR

Chapter Fifteen

Concluding an Active Training Program

Some trainers teach until the last moments of a program and then conclude by passing out an evaluation sheet. An active training program should not end in such an impersonal and noneducational manner. Don't settle for an ordinary conclusion; you can take many positive actions to bring your program to a meaningful close.

One of the many possible options for concluding an active training program is to leave plenty of time at the end of your program for *reviewing program content*. Another alternative is to invite participants to express any lingering *questions and concerns* about the course content. A third possibility is to engage them in some form of *self-assessment* of what they now know, what they now can do, and what attitudes they now hold. A fourth course of action is to focus the group on *back-on-the-job application*. A fifth approach is to provide an opportunity for participants to *express their sentiments* toward each other. We will consider each of these steps in this chapter.

REVIEWING PROGRAM CONTENT

Reviewing the program with participants can take many forms. On the simplest level, you can ask them to *recall* the information and ideas that have been covered. If the program contained several experiential activities, you could encourage the participants to *reminisce* about what they've been through together. You might also request that they *rehearse* one more time the skills they've learned. Finally, you could call upon them to *reconsider* their opinions about the training topic. Here are some tips on reviewing program content from these different angles.

307

1. ***Recall***: Use games, exercises, quizzes, or tests that challenge participants to recall facts, concepts, and procedures they have learned. If you wish, use the format of a TV game show such as "Jeopardy," "Who Wants to Be a Millionaire?," or "Wheel of Fortune." You might allow a study period in which participants prepare for recall exercises individually or in groups. Utilize team competition to energize the review process.

   EXAMPLE: In advance of her final session, a trainer prepared a set of questions and their corresponding answers, putting each on a separate index card. The questions referred to previously covered material. After shuffling all the cards together, the trainer dealt one card to each person, then told the participants to walk around and match questions with answers. When the participant completed the process, they read each question aloud one at a time for the group to answer. After each group response, the holder of the answer card would corroborate the answer or disagree with it.

2. ***Reminisce***: Gather the group together to review memorable experiences that occurred in the training program. Ask them to share how these experiences affected them personally and professionally. Use an approach such as a fishbowl discussion or mental imagery exercise to add extra energy to the reminiscing.

   EXAMPLE: At the end of a two-day team-building program, a trainer gave participants a blank sheet of paper and told them that it was time for their "final exam." The challenge was to write down, in order, the many activities they had experienced during the session. After each participant had finished, answers were compared until the correct list was jointly achieved. With the list in hand, participants were asked to reminisce about these experiences, recalling moments of fun, cooperation, and insight. The discussion was an intimate exchange that brought a wonderful, emotional closure to a special program.

3. ***Rehearse***: Arrange an opportunity for participants to demonstrate all the skills they have learned in one final performance. Use methods such as role playing, simulations, written tasks, or projects as vehicles for rehearsing these skills.

   EXAMPLE: For a training program in family therapy techniques, four groups were each assigned a family type based on the model of family functioning taught by the trainer. Each group was given the task of role-playing a family of the type assigned to it coming to its first therapy session. The role play was to include a demonstration of techniques for beginning therapy with such a family. This assignment had the virtue of integrating all the cognitive and behavioral learning featured in the training program. The four therapy sessions created a powerful ending to the program.

4. *Reconsider*: At a program's conclusion, participants may have altered their views about many of the topics examined during the program. It can be useful, therefore, to allow time to discuss these shifts in perception. Use methods such as panel or case study discussions to allow participants to reconsider their opinions and attitudes.

   EXAMPLE: At the beginning of a workshop on delegation skills, managers were asked to write down on index cards one of their fears about delegating responsibilities to their employees. The cards were then passed around the group. When participants read an item that was true for them, they were asked to make a checkmark in the upper right-hand corner of the card. After circulating, each card was returned to its originator. At the end of the workshop, the cards checked most frequently were read aloud. The participants were then asked to reconsider their fears in light of the workshop. A discussion was held using a "call-on-the-next-speaker" format to allow the group to exchange opinions without prompting by the trainer. It was an enlightening way for participants to conclude the workshop.

OBTAINING FINAL QUESTIONS AND CONCERNS

When a program is about to conclude, participants are often reluctant to raise final questions or concerns because they don't want to appear to be delaying the program's end. This is unfortunate, since identifying these questions and concerns is a valuable closing exercise *even if there is little time left*. Leaving with some unanswered questions and concerns invites further reflection by participants after the program is over. Here are some techniques for your consideration.

1. Prepare a list of questions you would like the participants to take away with them. Clarify each question and then, if there is time, ask participants to select a few they want discussed before the program ends.

EXAMPLE: At the end of a seminar on the Myers-Briggs Type Indicator, the trainer distributed a final handout asking participants in what ways each of the people in the following pairs might differ when interacting with the other:

Trainer	Learner
Salesperson	Buyer
Therapist	Client
Manager	Employee
Paid administrator	Board president

2. Hold a final question-and-answer period. Hand out blank index cards and request that each participant write down a question. Then answer as many of these questions as time permits.

EXAMPLE: Using this approach, a trainer received the following questions at the end of a train-the-trainer program:

- How much should I charge for one day of training?

- How can I handle questions about how qualified I am to conduct the training?

- How do I get participants to be comfortable with active learning processes when they are only familiar with a passive approach?

- How can you give directions without sounding like a teacher or boss?

- What do I do when no one wants to volunteer for a role-playing activity?

- Is there any way to perk up a group that is extremely tired?

3. Write the following on a flip chart: "One thing that still concerns me about [fill in the training topic] is…" Using a go-around format, ask each participant to complete the sentence. (Encourage participants to pass if they do not have something to share at that moment). Listen to the concerns without response.

EXAMPLE: At the end of a program on conflict management, participants supplied the following endings to the sentence stem "One thing that still concerns me is…"

- How to handle a really aggressive person

- Whether I can listen effectively in the heat of a conflict

- What to do if there is a complete stalemate
- How to communicate that my intentions are cooperative
- Using role reversal techniques; they seem silly
- How to pick the right time to confront someone

4. Break participants into small groups and ask each group to record their final questions and concerns on flip chart pages. Display the items and request a volunteer to edit them into a final list. Send the list to participants after the program is over.

    EXAMPLE: Administrative assistants attending a half-day purchasing program split into groups of four and came up with several remaining questions. They then edited their subgroup contributions into this final list of questions:

    - Can I still order supplies if the system is down?
    - Where can I find a list of the item numbers for both stock and nonstock supplies?
    - Who else besides my manager can approve entries for my department's cost code?
    - What if the warehouse sends me the wrong supplies? How do I make sure that my department isn't charged for orders that are filled incorrectly?
    - What if I have problems when I try using the system for the first time? Is there someone I can call for help?

5. Hand out two index cards. Ask each participant to complete the following sentences:

    Card 1: I still have a question about _____.

    Card 2: I can answer a question about _____.

    Create subgroups and have each subgroup select the most pertinent question and the most interesting answer from the cards of its group members. Then ask each subgroup to report the question it has selected. Determine if anyone in the full group can answer the question. If not, as the trainer, you should respond. Also, ask each subgroup to report the answer it has selected. Have the subgroup share it with the rest of the group.

    EXAMPLE: Subgroups in a session on coping with change selected the following questions and answers.

Questions

I still have a question about…

- How to cope with my fears about all the new technology involved with my job
- What I can do to reduce the stress of adjusting to a new manager
- How to determine what I can control or influence and what I can't

Answers

I can answer a question about…

- The difference between limiting beliefs and empowering beliefs
- Why people resist change
- How to use change to your advantage

PROMOTING SELF-ASSESSMENT

If your program has been meaningful to participants, they have undergone some degree of affective behavioral and cognitive change. A fitting way to end a program is to engage participants in activities that allow them to evaluate their progress. The following suggestions may assist you in this process.

1. Ask participants to complete a questionnaire or test that provides feedback about their current functioning in areas related to the training.

   EXAMPLE: At both the beginning and the end of a bank training program, participants were given a self-scoring test on consumer lending products, business accounts, individual retirement accounts, and brokerage. Each participant was then asked to evaluate his or her results and assess areas of strength and weakness.

2. Design a way for fellow participants to give each other feedback and then ask them each to develop a personal profile based on the feedback they receive.

   EXAMPLE: Participants in a team-building program filled out an index card for each member of their work team describing their reactions toward this individual. Each participant was then given all the feedback cards commenting on her or his performance and asked to summarize the data and present the summary back to the team for clarification.

3. Create one or more statements that assess participant change. Examples might include the following:

- I have changed my views about _____ as a result of this training session.
- I have improved my skills in _____.
- I have learned new information and concepts.

Ask the participants to stand in the back of the training room, clearing away the chairs or desks by moving them to one side. Create a rating scale from 1 through 5 in the front of the room by using the blackboard or posting numbers on the wall. Explain that a statement will be read to the group and that after hearing each one, participants should stand in front of the rating number that best matches their self-assessment. Use the following scale:

1 = strongly disagree

2 = disagree

3 = not sure

4 = agree

5 = strongly agree

As each statement is read, participants should move to the place in the room that best matches their self-assessment. Encourage participants to assess themselves realistically. Point out that several factors might create little or no change, such as previous knowledge or skill level and the need for more practice or time. After lines form in front of the various positions, invite some participants to share why they have chosen that rating. Underscore their honesty.

EXAMPLE: At the end of a session on customer service skills, the trainer prepared the following statements and showed them one at a time to the group:

- I have learned new information about how to deal with irate customers.
- I have changed my views about the importance of how I speak to others.

- I have improved my listening skills.

- I have learned better ways of phrasing negative statements.

- I understand that asking questions is not an interruption but an important part of my job.

- I know the appropriate procedure for transferring a call to my manager.

Participants were asked to assess themselves according to the instructions given previously.

4. Ask participants to write a short essay in response to the question, "How do you see yourself now as a result of this program?" Invite volunteers to read their essays or have participants exchange essays in small groups.

EXAMPLE: At the end of a workshop on parenting adolescents, one parent shared the following:

> "I am learning not to take my son's behavior so personally and not to blame myself for the unsettled nature of our relationship. He's going through a lot and so am I and that's to be expected. I think I'm now able to do a better job at sticking to the issue when we have conflicts and not getting sidetracked. I need to develop fewer but well-chosen rules with clear, enforceable consequences. Perhaps I need to give up control over little things and accept behaviors that don't make a big difference at this stage such as what he eats for breakfast. I think I can make sure that my firmness doesn't cause him to 'lose face.' Finally, I now can share my feelings and opinions with him without lecturing or sermonizing. Once I started doing that, it was easier for us to talk. I think I've come a long way."

5. At the beginning of a training session, ask participants to write down how they hope to be able to use the training on the job. Here are some ways to structure this exercise:

- Ask participants to list their own learning goals for the session.

- Ask participants to list recent successes and failures.

- Ask participants to list ongoing problems, assignments, or issues in their work.

Set aside some time periodically to allow participants to read their initial statement and consider what value the training has had for them thus far. At the end of the session, ask participants to assess whether their investment of time and effort in the training has been worthwhile in light of their initial comments. If you wish, also ask participants to assign a percentage that describes their return on investment (ROI) in the training. For example, a participant might indicate that he received a 75 percent ROI.

EXAMPLE: In a training program on presentation skills, participants were asked to list the things they would like to improve in their presentations. A combined list was displayed. Participants wanted to

- Be less nervous in the beginning
- Use presentation media more effectively
- Maintain better eye contact with the audience
- Rely less on notes
- Improve their pacing
- Begin with a "hook"
- Speak with less of a monotone
- Stimulate discussion and questions
- End with a strong conclusion

At the end of the program, participants were asked to assess the improvements they had made to determine the value of the session.

FOCUSING ON BACK-ON-THE-JOB APPLICATION In Part Four of this book, you will be introduced to several activities—such as discussion of application obstacles, contracting, self-monitoring plans, and action planning—designed to support the transfer of training skills to real-life situations. These are excellent conclusions to a program because participants leave with an eye to the future. Unfortunately, participants are often weary near the end of a training program and are reluctant to participate in such activities. Anticipating this, a trainer can take some steps to get past the obstacle of fatigue:

1. If possible, ask participants to prepare application ideas in advance. This way, you can use the last moments of the program to share plans rather than to create them.

2. Keep these activities brief and move at a quick pace. Don't dwell on your advice to participants. Make your final remarks memorable but to the point.

3. Lend some drama, inspiration, or excitement to the activities by the way you conduct them: Bring participants together into a tight group huddle, invite participants to stand up and announce their plans, encourage applause when appropriate, have participants address envelopes to themselves so that contracts can be sent to them later as reminders, or create a buddy system for later support and follow-up.

EXPRESSING FINAL SENTIMENTS

In many training programs, participants develop feelings of closeness for other group members. This is especially true if the participants have met for a long period of time and have taken part in extensive group work. They need to say goodbye to each other and express their appreciation for the support and encouragement they have received during the training program. There are many ways to help facilitate these final sentiments.

1. Assemble participants for a *group photograph*. As you are about to take their picture, express your own final sentiments. Then invite one participant at a time to take a final picture of the group. As this is happening, applaud the participant for his or her contributions. Text each participant the group photo.

2. Develop an *artistic product* that affirms the value of the group and each individual member. Make a group collage, design a group shield, or create a Facebook page with pictures of the group members.

3. Create a *closing circle* and invite participants to express their final sentiments and share what they learned in the program, the experiences they appreciated, and their future intentions. Encourage participants to comment as the spirit moves them.

4. Symbolically draw the training program to a close by forming a *web of connections*. Use a skein of yarn to literally and symbolically connect participants. Begin by asking everyone to stand and form a circle. Start the process by stating briefly what you have experienced as a result of facilitating the training program. Holding onto the end of the yarn, toss the skein to a participant on the other side of the circle. Ask that person to state briefly what she

or he has experienced as a result of participating in the training program. When that participant is finished, the skein is tossed to someone else. Have each participant take a turn at receiving the skein, sharing reflections, and tossing the yarn on, continuing to hold onto his or her piece. The resulting visual is a web of yarn connecting every member of the group.

5. End with *celebration*. Let participants celebrate their accomplishments with food and awards.

WORKSHEET

CONCLUDING AN ACTIVE TRAINING PROGRAM

Jot down ideas for concluding your training program under the categories below.

Reviewing program content:

_____

_____

_____

_____

Obtaining final questions:

_____

_____

_____

Promoting self-assessment:

_____

_____

_____

_____

Focusing on back-on-the-job application:

_____

_____

_____

Expressing final sentiments:

_____

_____

_____

_____

◆   ◆   ◆

Part Four

Extending the Value of an Active Training Program

No formal training program, by itself, can lead to long-lasting learning and change. It takes more than the completion of a training program, even one that contains all the features described in this book, for participants to truly acquire knowledge and skill or to change from previous patterns of behavior. Really effective training may provide a solid *start* in a process of learning and change, but it doesn't represent its *end*. What follows after the training program is over is critical to the success of that program.

Here are just a few of all too common events that occur that can undermine an active training program:

- The skills learned in the training program are not applied and practiced back on the job.

- The values taught in the training program are not reinforced by the organization in which participants work.

- Ongoing mentoring, coaching, modeling, or even just support and encouragement from managers and co-workers are lacking.

In Part IV of *Active Training*, we will examine how serious training requires steps that extend its value beyond the actual program. As we will see, some of these steps need to begin before the training actually starts and during the training program itself. The remaining steps need to occur both at the end of the training program and

319

for several weeks and months thereafter. If a training program is to achieve real results, everyone involved—participants, their managers, and trainers—has to continue working long after the formal sessions are over. What happens before, during, and after the training ensures the transfer of learning from the classroom to the job.

This process also makes measuring results possible. If there is no follow-up to training, there is no opportunity to gather the data that assesses whether the training had any outcomes beyond satisfying its participants. With follow-up, however, one can find out whether the training program is being applied successfully. This is important because training programs can no longer be approached as "events" that, by themselves, engage and inform, but ultimately lose their impact days after they are over. Training today is held accountable for doing more than exposing people to new ideas or repeating old, but valuable ones that have gone astray. There is an expectation that what was learned has been retained, applied on the job, and hopefully made a difference in what the greater organization is trying to achieve.

While good follow-up to training not only helps evaluation efforts, a commitment to evaluate training results helps training follow-up. That's because the act of measuring training results encourages the use of what has been learned in the training. Therefore, when everyone knows that the training program is being held accountable for results, people put more effort into making the follow-up to training a success. As Jack Welch, former CEO of General Electric, said, "You get what you measure."

The first of the two chapters that constitute Part Four examines how an active training program goes beyond an *event* that ends in the classroom and becomes part of a *process* of learning and change. The second chapter looks at options and tools for assessing the impact of the training.

Chapter Sixteen

Providing for Back-on-the-Job Application

Many training efforts never get off the ground because they are not integrated into the workplace. What truly separates effective from ineffective training is the explicit attention given to back-on-the-job application. Without it, the benefits of even the best learning events are not realized.

The application phase is often the most neglected part of a training design. It can be difficult in both design and implementation, but it is critical. Happily, there are many ways to design your program so that the training sticks and back-on-the-job application occurs. These suggestions will cover three time periods: *before the training event begins, while it is in progress,* and *after it concludes.*

PRIOR TO THE TRAINING PROGRAM

Training produces value when it is applied to the organization's work. A critical part of your job is to ensure that participants transfer what they have learned from classroom to job. Start by pre-training participants' supervisors. When they receive such training, supervisors are able to serve not merely as managers but also as mentors, coaches, role models, and encouragers. When training sessions are followed up with on-the-job support, up to a 300 percent return is realized on every dollar invested. Conversely, little retention of skills occurs after training if management fails to reinforce it.

Of course, this step may initially be expensive, time-consuming, and hard to come by. This is an instance where virtual training programs can be extremely beneficial. If you cannot pre-train supervisors, you will frequently have the chance to brief them about the training their employees are receiving. In such briefings, it is important for you to discuss the following:

- The objectives of the training program
- The course outline
- The kinds of training activities utilized in the program
- Course materials
- Suggestions for facilitating further practice and application of skills

This approach works well if you have built your training program with organizational objectives in mind. That way, management will trust that learners will find a connection between their new skills and the organization's goals and priorities.

Another way to make supervisors your allies is to enlist their cooperation with regard to any pre-course preparation you may ask of their employees. Giving the participants time off from their regular responsibilities to read advance materials or complete pre-course assignments is a real contribution. It is even better when supervisors sit down with their employees and help them define a personal case problem or two to bring to the training program. This problem then becomes the basis for real-life problem solving in your instruction. Here is such a case.

EXAMPLE: For a course on managing difficult employee behavior, the trainer requested participants write brief descriptions of two incidents in which subordinates acted irresponsibly. These incidents were to be discussed in small groups during the program and were also to serve as a basis for role-playing exercises. The trainer asked participants to select incidents in consultation with their own supervisors. After the training program, they would be able to share with their bosses what they had learned.

Prior to the training program, it is also possible to ask participants and their supervisors to select a project to undertake as a result of what the participants learn. If you do this for a virtual training session, be sure to be very clear in your written directions and offer assistance and clarification by phone or email. When participants come to the training program with a project in mind that has already been discussed with upper management, back-on-the-job application is built into the program design.

Of course, the best way to obtain management support is to invite supervisors to conduct training programs for their own team. Once a rarity, this possibility is becoming more frequent. Participants report that manager-led training is successful as long as managers are well prepared to conduct training on their own (Betof 2005). In many instances this may be your role—to help managers prepare.

DURING THE TRAINING PROGRAM

As you teach new skills, you can do certain things to promote retention and on-the-job application. A first tip is to *allow enough practice time for skill mastery.* Some trainers have a tendency to move quickly from skill to skill without enough rehearsal. For example, they may give participants the opportunity to role-play conducting a hiring interview and provide (or have peers provide) feedback on their performance but neglect to provide a chance for participants to redo the role play based on the feedback received. Some degree of overlearning is required in order for participants to feel confident about exercising a new skill. Skill mastery is like the process of breaking in new shoes. At first, it feels unnatural but, with enough wear, the shoes begin to feel comfortable. Confidence grows even more when participants master exercises of increasing levels of difficulty. Eventually, they feel that they truly own the skill. Here is a case in point.

EXAMPLE: In a training program on conflict mediation, participants practice mediation skills in a variety of situations. Experience has shown that when role-playing practice is limited to certain types of clients, learners often have difficulty applying the skills in real life, where clients vary considerably. Because of this, a conflict mediation trainer designed a series of role plays that included a broad range of clients. Participants underwent two days of video-recorded practice before seeing real clients under supervision. Frequently, role plays were redone after video feedback. Participants were pleased by the ample opportunity to practice and felt confident that they were ready for the real thing.

Participants are more apt to use skills back on the job if they have been able to practice them realistically. The more similar the training situation is to the back-on-the-job situation, the more likely it is to last. Even re-creating the physical environment of the job can be helpful. For example, call center training is greatly enhanced if recording of actual customer calls are used and the training takes place in an actual call center.

As participants learn new skills, they should be encouraged to express their attitudes about the skills being taught and their feelings about their performance. Paradoxically, participants are less likely to resist changes if they have the chance to express their reservations and trepidations about them. Some trainers hard-sell the value of the skills, ideas, and procedures they are advocating. It is far better to encourage participants to draw their own conclusions. Ultimately, they are the ones who will decide whether to use what you have taught them. Here is a case example in which this process was encouraged.

EXAMPLE: Using a fishbowl design, a trainer invited participants to examine their feelings about the company's performance appraisal system. One-third of the group was asked to participate in the first fishbowl discussion. The trainer suggested that they begin by describing their positive and negative reactions to the system. After ten minutes, a second third was brought into the fishbowl to react to the discussion of the first group. Then the final third replaced their predecessors and wrapped up the discussion. By providing ample time to air viewpoints, the trainer gave a clear message about his respect for the participants' views.

A final tip can be implemented if you are able to arrange for time back on the job in between training sessions. *Give assignments to be completed in the participants' own work settings.* When you resume the training, you can ask participants to share how well the real-life practice went and to pose any questions they may still have about the skills they have been learning.

EXAMPLE: In a course on overcoming shyness, the virtual trainer requested that participants complete between-sessions questions. The questions required the participants to identify one situation that occurred between sessions in which they attempted to be less shy than usual. Also required was information about who else was present, what the participants said and/or did, what (if anything) they wished they had done instead, how they felt during the situation, and how they felt after the situation.

AT THE END OF THE TRAINING PROGRAM

Before ending the training program and after it concludes, you can employ several strategies to encourage application back on the job.

Self-Assessment

Ask participants to evaluate what they have learned about themselves, including their knowledge, behavior, and attitudes. Taking stock of oneself is a great motivator of change. A wide variety of techniques can help participants with their self-assessment. Make use of questionnaires, post-tests, and final role-playing performances. Activities such as the following ones can be appropriate.

EXAMPLE: At the end of a one-week management development program, participants evaluated the extent to which they saw themselves along three style spectrums: (1) *directive* versus *delegating*, (2) *well planned* versus *spontaneous*, and (3) *challenging* versus *nonthreatening*. For each spectrum, they were asked to stand up and place themselves in a line according to how they viewed themselves. For example, if they saw themselves as more directive than other participants, they went to the head of the line. By contrast, if they saw themselves as more delegating than others, they went to the rear of the line. Participants who did not identify clearly with either choice were to place themselves somewhere in the middle. Each physical continuum was discussed, with participants disclosing their reasons for placing themselves where they did and commenting on the self-placement by their peers. Finally, they were asked if they wanted to change their "place in line" and to indicate what they would need to do back on the job to achieve this.

EXAMPLE: At the beginning of a virtual customer service training program, the trainer assigned participants to form small groups in a breakout room and asked each group to develop a list of guidelines for new customer service representatives. The trainer compiled the list and emailed it to each participant between sessions. The participants' initial list included the following:

- Get people in and out quickly.
- Don't eat in front of customers or chew gum.
- Don't talk on your cell phone.
- Smile.
- Refer an irate customer to the manager.
- Adhere to company policy.

At the end of the training session, the trainer displayed the initial list and asked the participants to produce a new, improved list. Again, in the same small breakout groups, they produced this list:

- Tell people what you can do, not what you can't.
- Whenever possible, give people choices.
- Put yourself in the customer's shoes.
- Go the extra mile.
- Use the customer's name.
- Try to solve the problem yourself.
- Acknowledge the customer immediately.

Job Aids

Job aids include checklists, worksheets, and a variety of other forms that may be in electronic or paper format. These aids provide a structure that helps participants remember and apply what they learned in the course. Job aids are most effective when they are explained and tried out first in the course itself.

EXAMPLE: Participants in a management training program were given the checklist in Figure 16.1 to use in preparing their upcoming interviews with problem employees. This could also be emailed to participants after the session or posted to a group site.

FIGURE 16.1 CORRECTIVE INTERVIEWS CHECKLIST

1. Begin on a positive note.
2. State your purpose.
3. Identify the changes desired.
4. Obtain and listen to the employee's point of view.
5. Get agreement.
6. Involve the employee in generating solutions.
7. Have the employee summarize corrective actions.
8. Express support and encouragement.

EXAMPLE: Participants in a course on project management were urged to remember Murphy's Law when they were back on the job: "If something can go wrong, it will." For this reason, participants were given the Project-Protection Chart (see Figure 16.2) to use as a job aid in predicting and responding to what might go wrong. It asks the project planner to do the following:

1. Identify what is likely to go wrong with elements of the project.

2. Identify how and when the project planner will be informed that something is wrong.

3. Identify what, when, and how something will be done if something goes wrong.

FIGURE 16.2 THE PROJECT-PROTECTION CHART

Project: _____

Project Element	What Is Likely To Go Wrong?	How and When Will I Know?	What Will I Do About It?	When Will I Do It?	How Will I Do It?
Quality					
Cost					
Timeliness					
Other					

Reentry Advice

Any training program might end with a closing session on reentry advice. Such a session should present some realistic first steps for applying the training on the job. First steps might include setting up a meeting with one's supervisor to discuss the training program and how to use it, consciously identifying tasks that would use skills learned in the program, or networking with others who have taken the course or similar courses to compare experiences and applications.

EXAMPLE: As a program on improving technical training skills was ending, the training consultant advised the employees of a large retail organization to begin observing each other's work. She urged the group to adopt this practice as the best way to build support and continued reinforcement of what they had learned in the training program.

EXAMPLE: Participants in a virtual training program on business writing skills were urged to request writing assignments from their supervisors that would enable the participants to practice the skills learned in the training program.

OBSTACLE ASSESSMENT

Future planning must include a realistic assessment of the obstacles to applying training. Just as any dieter will have a hard time resisting a midnight snack, so a participant subjected to the pressures of his or her job may slip back into old ways of doing things. The most common obstacle is a lack of support from peers, supervisors, or others on the job. Another common obstacle is the lack of time to apply new skills consciously, assess how they've been used, and get feedback from others. In addition to offering reentry advice, a training program should build in time for participants to discuss some of the obstacles they expect to meet and ways to overcome them.

EXAMPLE: A stress management trainer was so concerned about the obstacles to carrying out the techniques he had taught participants that he decided on an unusual strategy. Instead of giving his usual pep talk at the end of his course, he asked participants to predict the circumstances of their first moment of faltering. Using a mental imagery approach, he encouraged participants to visualize the scene in great detail. He then asked them to develop positive images of coping with the situation that they would be able to keep in their mind's eye when the predicted negative scenario began to unfold in the actual work setting.

EXAMPLE: At the end of a team-building course, teams were asked to identify "threats" to their future effectiveness. Using a SWOT (strengths, weaknesses, opportunities, and threats) analysis, teams were challenged to convert these threats into "opportunities" for future development.

PEER CON-SULTATION

One of the best designs I know to bring together the learning from a training program and to encourage back-on-the-job application involves peer consultation. Participants are arranged in small groups for the purpose of discussing a specific back-home issue for each member. After each issue is clarified, the client (the participant with the issue) receives advice from the consultants (the other group members). This process gives participants the opportunity to summarize and apply the knowledge and skills they have gained and to try out their new expertise.

EXAMPLE: At the end of a workshop on managing cultural diversity, participants were formed into quartets. Each participant took turns being a client with a specific problem (based on her or his own work situation) concerning racism or sexism. The job of the other group members was to recall and select concepts and action ideas examined earlier in the workshop that might apply to the problem posed by the client. By taking part in this process of peer consultation, participants were able to prove their expertise to one another and to pull together the contents of the workshop.

EXAMPLE: At the end of a workshop on managing change, peer consultation was used in the following way. Each participant was asked to develop a plan to effectively handle a change in his or her work unit. Then participants were paired with someone from a different work unit who served as a "peer consultant." After the workshop was over, partners consulted with each other on the progress of their respective change management plans.

Peer Teaching

An excellent way to master new ideas and skills is to try to teach them to someone else. Teaching others is also bound to increase one's own commitment to actually using what is being taught. Consequently, there is considerable benefit in encouraging participants to present to others what you have taught them. This can be done within the program by assigning participants to different projects and having them present their findings to others in the training group. Participants may also be able to present the material to peers back on the job who have not yet received the training.

EXAMPLE: Half the members of a sales staff were given training in how to build rapport with different types of clients. Each participant was then paired up with a salesperson who had not received the training. Pairs were expected to meet with each other three times to share the ideas and skills gained from the training. The trained salespeople did such a good job that it was unnecessary to conduct a program for the other half of the staff.

EXAMPLE: A similar approach was used in an ERP class. Participants were invited to teach the techniques they learned in the class to colleagues who had not yet taken the class.

SELF-MONITORING

A well-known technique in behavior modification is to ask clients to monitor their own behaviors. For example, in a weight loss program, clients might be asked to note everything they eat on the assumption that increased awareness will bring about greater self-control. Likewise, you could suggest to participants that they closely monitor their own behavior back on the job as a way to make training benefits last. Keeping a personal journal or blog is one way to perform self-monitoring. The use of ready-made checklists is another approach. Whatever tools are chosen, they ideally should be tried out before the training program ends so that participants can gain comfort with the procedure and understanding of it.

EXAMPLE: At the end of a 60-minute virtual business-writing module, the trainer asked participants to design their own checklist for monitoring their future business emails. A checklist was provided to participants as a working model. The trainer assigned members to breakout rooms, each of which developed a series of checklist questions covering such areas as organization ("Have I used subheadings?"), conciseness ("Do I make my point in the fewest words possible?"), sentence and paragraph length ("Do I use too many choppy sentences?" or "Are my paragraphs short?"), redundancy

("Do I repeat ideas instead of elaborating on them?"), phrasing ("Have I used antiquated phrases like 'pursuant to your request'?"), passive language ("How tentative is my language?"), tone ("Is my style conversational or stuffy?"), spelling ("Is the email free of spelling errors?"), and grammar ("Do my subjects and predicates agree?"). Each group uploaded its checklist to the group's shared site. The assignment before the next module was to create a personal checklist that included the most important questions.

EXAMPLE: In a session on time management, the facilitator asked the participants to brainstorm reminders to help them manage their time more effectively back on the job. Using the sentence stem "Remember to…" the participants came up with the following reminders:

Remember to…

- Make a "to-do" list every day
- Make an appointment with myself
- Track actions and ideas on my smartphone
- Set priorities based on importance, not urgency
- Download articles and documents to my tablet to take with me when I travel
- Skim books and articles quickly, looking for ideas
- Answer most voicemails and emails right on the item itself
- Delegate everything I possibly can to others
- Consult my list of lifetime goals once a month and review them if necessary
- Save trivial matters for a three-hour session once a month

Participants were then asked to select the three reminders that they felt had the most relevance to them and to place them on a card to be posted in their work space.

Contracting

A popular method for promoting the application of training is a simple written expression of the intent to change one's behavior in some respect or to undertake a particular action appropriate to the goals of the training program. The contract can be made with oneself or with others (a co-participant, the trainer, one's boss, or a colleague). The format of the contract can be formal ("The undersigned hereby commits himself to...") or informal (a letter to oneself). Often, trainers will offer to collect the contracts and send them back, by regular or email, to participants for review in one month. Pairing participants who commit themselves to exchanging contracts and supporting each other is an excellent way to conduct this process. Following up with e-mail, a phone call, or a get-together helps to cement the contract.

EXAMPLE: The peer contract shown in Figure 16.3 was used in a career exploration seminar.

FIGURE 16.3 PEER CONTRACT

As a result of our training on career exploration, I want to incorporate the following ideas:

1.

2.

3.

4.

Signed _____

I will follow-up with the above person in one month.

Signed _____

Date _____

EXAMPLE: At the end of a facilitation skills workshop, the trainer asked participants to write a letter to themselves indicating what they had learned about facilitating team meetings and how they were going to apply it. Here is one participant's letter:

> "I hereby resolve to be less directive in conducting team meetings. I will ask open-ended questions and allow team members to give complete answers without interrupting them. If no one answers

immediately, I will be patient and not jump in to fill the void created by silence. I will avoid giving my direct opinion immediately. When asked a direct question, I will direct it back to the team members to answer before I respond. I will make a real effort to facilitate group interaction instead of controlling the meeting."

Action Plans

A more detailed tool for future application is the action plan. In this approach, participants define appropriate outcomes and the steps to achieving them as a result of the training program. Obstacles are anticipated as well. In a work setting, an action plan is often utilized as a mechanism by which participants and their supervisors agree on a project that has benefits for the organization. An action plan can also be viewed as a self-motivational tool for employees without specific monitoring by supervisors. Figure 16.4 shows a typical action plan used in many training programs.

FIGURE 16.4 DEVELOPING AN ACTION PLAN

---

1. List three actions you would like to undertake as a result of this program.

   a.

   b.

   c.

2. Choose the action that you would plan to do first and enter it below.

3. List the potential roadblocks to implementing this action:

4. Discuss with your partner how you might overcome these roadblocks.

5. Describe in detail the action you will undertake and the steps you will take to ensure that it will happen.

Action plans push writers to be clear about what they are going to do. In the form in Figure 16.5, learners are asked to specify the actions they want to take in the next month to develop people skills.

FIGURE 16.5 A CHECKLIST OF ACTIONS

Look over the following list and select one action from each category that is the most important for you to take in the next month.

TO UNDERSTAND PEOPLE BETTER:

- Ask more questions
- Avoid labeling
- Look beyond surface behavior
- Evaluate how I compare to another person (style, gender, age, culture)

TO EXPRESS MYSELF MORE CLEARLY:

- Think before I talk
- Provide more/less detail
- "Give up the microphone"
- Be straightforward and direct

TO ASSERT MY NEEDS BETTER:

- Get clearer about what I want
- Say no when I must
- Speak up and ask for what I need
- Remain calm and confident under fire

TO EXCHANGE FEEDBACK BETTER:

- Invite others to give me feedback
- Listen to the feedback others give me
- Don't withhold feedback I can give
- Offer suggestions instead of criticism

TO BECOME MORE INFLUENTIAL:

- Temporarily drop my agenda and connect
- Find out more about the opinions of others
- Explain the benefits others may obtain
- Give people time to mull over my advice

FIGURE 16.5 continued

TO RESOLVE CONFLICTS MORE EFFECTIVELY:

- Bring concerns out into the open sooner
- Find out what the other party needs
- Seek solutions, not victory
- Persevere despite initial negative reactions

TO BECOME A BETTER COLLABORATOR:

- Find out what teammates need
- Express appreciation
- Use the talents of others
- Keep others informed about my activity

Figure 16.6 reproduces an elaborate example of action planning used in a management development program. It involves a serious commitment on the part of the participant and others in the organization to apply what has been learned in the training program and simultaneously to benefit the organization.

**FIGURE 16.6 ACTION PLAN DESIGN
AND DEVELOPMENT GUIDELINES**

DIRECTIONS FOR USE

Sometimes a shortcoming of management development programs is the absence of a tool to measure effectiveness. The only true measure of impact is the degree to which the participants return and use the skills learned in the program. In order for this to happen, two conditions must be met:

1. The participant must work on a plan of action that spells out the specific steps for implementing change.
2. This plan is shared with the mentor and manager and supported by them.

This ACTION PLAN is designed to assist participants in meeting these two conditions, thereby enabling both them and XYZ Company to realize a return on the investment made through participation in the program.

FIGURE 16.6 continued

SUBJECT

Many topics are covered in this module. Select a project (one of those covered or one of your own) on which you will focus. As you complete your ACTION PLAN, try to be as specific as possible in stating your subject. For example, if you were writing an ACTION PLAN for communication, "Written Communication" would be too broad. A more specific subject would be "Developing a Highlight Report Format for the Department."

Within the subject you have selected, state your purpose or reason for selecting it. This will be a brief description of your intent or goal. Using the example of "Developing a Highlight Report Format," the goal might look like this: "Highlight reports contain numerous details. They need to be organized so that the details appear in a logical sequence. After obtaining permission from my manager, I plan to format one of my manager's highlight reports using an eye-opener, transition one, supporting details, transition two, and action conclusion."

Goals are stated in broad terms; objectives are quite specific and should include measures by which your progress toward them can be determined. Objectives are the things you must achieve (deadlines, performance indexes, and so on) in order to meet your goal. Building on the same example, the objective might look like this: "To spend one day formatting a highlight report that can be used as a model for subsequent highlight reports."

To achieve your goal, you must schedule activities to move toward it. This section is your blueprint and timetable for reaching the goal. Following our previous example, the activities list might look like this:

Activities	Time
1. Meet with mentor to explain my ACTION PLAN	1. One morning next week, two hours
2. Meet with my manager to explain my ACTION PLAN and obtain three latest highlight reports written by manager	2. One morning next week, two hours (after meeting with mentor)
3. Read over my manager's highlight reports	3. Two hours following week
4. Develop a format for organizing a highlight report	4. Two hours same week as item 3
5. After obtaining necessary highlight facts, data, and so on, write an actual highlight report for my manager	5. Four hours before report is due

---

FIGURE 16.6 continued

As you carry out your schedule of activities, problems or barriers inevitably occur. Sometimes these can be anticipated in advance. Other times they may not. This section of the plan asks you to list and number all problems, present and potential, that you foresee as barriers to completing your activities.

Next, state how you plan to deal with each problem, numbering each solution to agree with the problem it addresses. Following the example, this section might look like this:

Problems	*Solutions*
1. Manager may not be able to get me all the facts and data needed to complete the actual highlight report	1. Work directly with manager in writing highlight report

---

Resources

Some ACTION PLANS are easy to carry out, requiring no resources other than your own time. Others may need help to be implemented (from your manager, other professionals, other managers, and so on). This section asks you to detail other sources you are depending on.

Costs and Benefits

Some activities you plan may involve a cost to the organization. If you don't know actual costs, estimate them. For example, the cost of completing our sample ACTION PLAN includes "Word Processing Services from Support Staff." Then list the payoffs you expect to realize from carrying out the ACTION PLAN. Some may be intangible (improved morale, a systematic approach, an increase in performance, better customer service, and so on). If possible, estimate the dollar value of your benefits, both tangible and intangible. For example, one benefit of the plan is "developing a format usable in writing highlight reports."

Commitment

Finally, the last section asks you, your mentor, and your manager to make a commitment to carry out the plan. As described in the directions, you will review the plan with your mentor and agree upon any changes. Then you will want to review the plan with your manager.

FIGURE 16.6 continued

Next you, your mentor, and your manager should sign the plan confirming your intent to carry out the plan. You should set one or more dates for reviewing progress.

Source: Training Management Corporation, 600 Alexander Road, Building 2, Princeton, NJ 08540. Reprinted with permission.

Follow-Up Questionnaire

A clever strategy for raising participants' consciousness about the training program long after it is over is to use a follow-up questionnaire. It also serves as a way to stay in touch with participants.

Here are the steps for this approach:

1. Explain to participants that you would like to send them a follow-up questionnaire one month from now. The questionnaire is intended (a) to help them assess what they have learned and how well they are doing in applying the training and (b) to give you feedback.

2. Urge them to fill out the questionnaire for their own benefit. Ask them to email their replies to you. You may also consider using SurveyMonkey or Zoomerang or another questionnaire service provider.

3. When you develop the questionnaire, consider the following suggestions:

    • Keep the tone informal and friendly.

    • Mix the questions so that those that are easiest to fill out come first. Use formats such as checklists, rating scales, incomplete sentences, and short essays.

    • Ask about what they remember the most, what skills they are currently using, and what success they have had.

    • Offer participants the opportunity to call you with questions and application problems.

Figure 16.7 contains an example of a follow-up questionnaire sent to participants after a virtual training program on stress management.

FIGURE 16.7 FOLLOW-UP QUESTIONNAIRE

Hello! How are things going? I hope you have had the opportunity to work on your management of stress. As I promised, I'm sending you this questionnaire to help you review and assess your ability to obtain the goals you are seeking. By sending this questionnaire back to me, you will also help me to evaluate the impact of the training program. Thanks!

1. Please rank the situations below in order of difficulty to you. Use the following scale: (1) least difficult to (5) most difficult.

   _____ Managing time effectively

   _____ Keeping physically fit

   _____ Maintaining healthy nutritional habits

   _____ Staying relaxed

   _____ Being able to say "no"

2. Briefly describe a recent stressful situation in which you managed things effectively: _____

   _____

   _____

   _____

3. Describe a recent situation in which you did not manage stress effectively and regretted it: _____

   _____

   _____

   _____

   _____

4. Please circle the strategies below that you have found useful:

   a. Identifying negative self-thoughts and distortions

   b. Scheduling in fun, relaxation, and recreation

   c. Delegating responsibility to others

   d. Striving for realism, not perfectionism

5. Check one of these statements:

   _____ Please call me. I'm having difficulty with _____.

   _____ Everything's going well. There's no need to contact me.

FOLLOW-UP COACHING AND SUPPORT

Organizations recognize that follow-up coaching helps to extend the value of training. This has been especially true in leadership training programs where the development of key leaders is critical to the organization's future success. These individuals receive private coaching by so-called "executive" coaches who consult intensively with their clients, often focusing on those barriers that prevent them from achieving their maximum potential. Although expensive, this service can provide a strong return on investment. Other levels of the organization can benefit from coaching as well. Although not as common, group coaching is another option for personnel who are not traditionally seen as coaching clients. In small groups, participants have the opportunity for continuing practice of vital skills and for discussion of common obstacles for success. For example, after a four day program on project management tools, participants were offered an additional four to six weeks of weekly group coaching sessions. Those who chose to attend were 95 percent more likely to use the project management tools taught in the training than those who did not attend.

Peer support groups, sometimes called peer coaching have also proven to provide useful training follow-up. Most meet on a regular basis, perhaps monthly over lunch, to continue to work on course skills or issues they've encountered at work. When successful, peers support each other, from providing small suggestions on how to handle difficult situations to undertaking joint initiatives that improve the quality of their work context. For example, a support group was formed after attending a training program on meeting management. They not only shared common problems, such as how to equalize participation at meetings, but also organized a process whereby peers observed each other's meetings and provided feedback and recommendations for best practices.

WORKSHEET

PROVIDING FOR BACK-ON-THE-JOB APPLICATION

Now is your chance to think about strategies for back-on-the-job application of your training program. Use the worksheet to guide your planning.

Strategies Prior to the Program:

_____

_____

_____

_____

Strategies During the Program:

_____

_____

_____

_____

Strategies at the End of the Program:

_____

_____

_____

_____

_____

◆   ◆   ◆

"Over the years, when developing training worldwide, individuals would tell me that people learned differently in their country. Yet I always helped them see that people, everywhere, learn by DOING! Active learning methods help people practice DOING in a safe environment."

Lisa Owens
Training Design Strategies, LLC

Chapter Seventeen

Evaluating an Active Training Program

*E*valuating a training program is often seen as a final step, but, in actuality, it starts the process of design and delivery. That's because it provides the data that allows for the continuous improvement of the training program. When you learn how participants have been impacted by the training, you have the opportunity to assess how well the existing program works and what modifications may be necessary to make it more effective. In reality, evaluation begins at the design phase. The objectives identified should lead to the results desired and that is what is evaluated.

Evaluation is important. It takes time, but it is essential. Professional trainers build in time to measure results to ensure everyone knows what in the training program should be changed, what kinds of assistance participants may need after they return to their jobs, and what obstacles still exist that prevent transfer of training.

Most trainers subscribe to the model advanced by Dr. Donald Kirkpatrick (2005) that there are four levels of evaluation of a training program:

Level 1, Reaction: Learner attitudes toward the training opportunity, such as a satisfaction with involvement or what was learned

Level 2, Learning: Knowledge and skills learned, such as being able to state the best practices or for having new skills for tasks on the job

Level 3, Behavior: Changes in execution and implementation of skills learned and practiced on the job

Level 4, Results: Quantifiable results that demonstrate an impact that training has on the organization

EXPANDING THE FOUR EVALUATION LEVELS

Over time, Dr. Kirkpatrick's original work has evolved. Jim Kirkpatrick, Don's son expanded the original work by creating the New World Four Levels (see Figure 17.1). This model emphasizes identifying results (Level 4) up front and underscores the need to focus on collective efforts of the training department, supervisors, and senior leaders to accomplish return on stakeholder expectations. This return on expectations (ROE) should not be confused with the common use of ROE meaning "return on equity," which is determined by comparing net income to shareholders' equity. According to the Kirkpatrick model, ROE offers indicators of value through a holistic measurement of both qualitative and quantitative measures from a program or initiative with formal training typically being the cornerstone.

FIGURE 17.1 THE NEW WORLD KIRKPATRICK MODEL

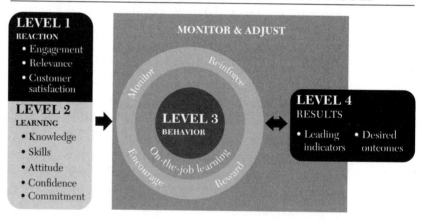

To achieve return on expectations, learning professionals must ask questions to clarify and refine the expectations of key business stakeholders as they attempt to satisfy the stakeholders and convert their expectations into observable, measurable business or mission outcomes. ROE is like turning the Kirkpatrick four levels upside down, because you need to ask questions in Level 4 first. These questions might include:

What will success look like to you?

What will participants do with what they learn?

How will this training effort affect our customers?

What impact will participant development have on our bottom line?

How will you know we are achieving the goal?

What is your goal?

In addition, the New World Kirkpatrick model emphasizes the need to partner with supervisors and managers to encourage them to prepare participants for training and to play a key role after training by reinforcing the learned knowledge and skills. All of these steps are completed during your design.

EXAMPLE: A pharmaceutical company was evaluating the training it was giving to sales representatives. During the design phase the trainers asked leaders in the organization:

- What skills do you want employees to perform?
- What desired outcomes should the company see due to these new skills?
- What indications will you have that the new skills will produce the results you desire?
- What will your customers experience based on these new skills?
- What data will you use for these measures?

Here are some indicators the company used to evaluate each of the four levels.

Level 1, Reactions to the training program:

- Participants were satisfied with the relevancy of the training.
- Participants thought that the training program covered the promised objectives.
- Participants said that the trainer encouraged participation and questions.

- Participants wanted more opportunity to role-play during the training program.

Level 2, Learning:

- Participants could state the features and benefits of the company's top-selling drugs.
- Participants were able to use clinical studies to reinforce benefits.
- Participants demonstrated how to quickly bridge from their opener to the main topics of the sales call.
- Participants knew the difference between fact questions and priority questions.

Level 3, Behavior or on-the-job application:

- Participants described to physicians how the product met a specific, stated physician need.
- Participants established rapport with physicians in their sales calls.
- Participants planned their use of visuals in advance of their appointments.
- Participants used more open questions than closed questions in their sales calls.

Level 4, Business results:

- Participants increased sales each week over a four-week period.
- Physicians reported increased satisfaction with the service received from representatives.
- Participants made more sales calls than in previous weeks.
- Participants' retention increased over the prior year.

A thorough evaluation of your training program might involve all four levels: *reaction, learning, behavior,* and *results*. Each level of evaluation has value in its own right, but it is the combination of evidence that truly assesses how effective the training has been.

Level 1: Reaction

The most common kind of training evaluation is that of Level 1. It is easy, fast, and inexpensive when compared to evaluation efforts at other levels. When your program has ended, you will naturally want to find out if the training met the participants' expectations. Try to obtain a picture of participants' reactions to the training program as a whole as well as a sense of their response to the various parts.

　　　　Figure 17.2 presents the kind of form typically used to obtain these data quickly.

FIGURE 17.2 TRAINING EVALUATION QUESTIONNAIRE

Course Title: _____ Date: _____

1. Circle the number that best represents your reaction to the program.

   a. I feel prepared to use what I learned.

   (never)　　　1　　　2　　　3　　　4　　　5　　　(often)

   b. The program was relevant to what I need on the job.

   (never)　　　1　　　2　　　3　　　4　　　5　　　(often)

   c. The training program has motivated me to implement what I learned.

   (never)　　　1　　　2　　　3　　　4　　　5　　　(often)

   d. The program achieved the stated objectives.

   (never)　　　1　　　2　　　3　　　4　　　5　　　(often)

   e. The trainer encouraged participation and questions.

   (never)　　　1　　　2　　　3　　　4　　　5　　　(often)

2. What did you find most useful in the program?
3. What do you still need to be successful on the job?
4. What suggestions do you have to improve this program?

　　　　You could consider asking participants to download the survey while in the session and email it to you or to email it to you after the session. There are two drawbacks with these ideas. Emailing response decreases the anonymity. And waiting until after the session will dramatically decrease the number of responses you receive—often by more than half. If you prepare it ahead of time, you could email everyone in the session a link to a provider such as SurveyMonkey, which eliminates the issue of anonymity.

A less standard way to obtain participants' reactions is to use a semi-projective technique. Provide a blank piece of paper with the following instructions on the top:

> Imagine that a coworker (or friend) of yours was thinking about attending this program. He or she asked you, "What has this program been like for you?" How would you respond? Please take the next ten minutes to write your response below.

The beauty of this technique is that you will usually obtain a deeper and more personal response than a questionnaire could elicit. The drawback, of course, is that it is much more difficult to quantify or summarize the results. The following is an example of one person's response to a program on counseling techniques:

EXAMPLE: "This program provided me with a different look at what I had been doing. At first, I was bewildered. I was so much into crisis counseling— trying to solve the problem by applying Band-Aids without too much thought as to how I could help make a difference down the road. I will be different in the future. Now, I have some powerful techniques that, with practice, will remove the rush, the uncertainty, and, yes, the sometimes wishy-washy techniques I have occasionally used. This program helped to refresh a weary soldier!"

Level 2: Learning

Besides finding out how participants viewed the training program, you need to know what attitudes, knowledge, and skills they acquired. The most common way to measure learning is the use of tests. It's not easy to construct a test that is both *reliable* and *valid*. A reliable test is one that gets similar results time after time. A valid test measures what it purports to measure and not something else. So, take time to get feedback about your test items as well as pilot them before using them with your actual participants. With the objectives of active training programs in mind, *be sure to go beyond testing factual recall.* See if participants can state the information in their own words, give examples of it, and apply it in a variety of situations. Without this information, it is impossible to determine whether or not the training achieved real learning as opposed to memorization.

To further substantiate that test results prove that learning occurred, it is desirable (although not always practical) to test participants' knowledge, attitude, and skill before the training begins as well as after. With such a baseline, it is easier to state the changes that occurred as a result of the training program.

Besides testing, you can obtain some evidence that learning has taken place by any of the following:

- Performance on job-relevant tasks at the end of the training program, usually involving in-basket exercises, games, case studies, or role-plays.
- Interviewing participants to see how they would respond to job-related problems.
- Project assignments that require participants to integrate what they learned.

Don't overlook the value of asking participants directly about what they learned and how it will be applied. Self-report does not constitute proof but it provides some indication that learning occurred. The simplest approach is to use a questionnaire or interview and ask participants questions such as these:

- What tools, skills, or ideas do you now have that you did not have at the beginning of this program?
- What have you learned that you can put to immediate use?
- What have you already practiced outside of the session?
- What intentions or plans do you have as a result of the program?
- What do you want to learn next?

Level 3: Behavior

The easiest way to assess if your training had led to on-the-job application is to survey or interview participants once they return to their jobs. Questions to consider are:

- How have you used the things you learned in the training program?
- How has the training program helped you perform better at work?
- What specific steps can you take to continue or improve the use of the skills and knowledge you learned from the training program?

Although self-reports of participants may have value, there is every reason to confirm participants are actually doing on the job what the training objectives were seeking. Post-training performance may be evaluated by observing their actual job performance or obtaining feedback from supervisors or other key informants. A procedure that combines participant self-report and supervisory feedback can be utilized. You might do this by asking participants to complete a follow-up form at the end of a program that contains statements about how they plan to implement the training (see Figure 17.3). In three to four weeks, send follow-up instructions (see Figure 17.4). Then, at each participant's option, the work statement and a supervisor's follow-up form (see Figure 17.5) can be sent to the participant's supervisor for evaluation.

FIGURE 17.3 WORK STATEMENT FOLLOW-UP FORM

Describe situations in which you plan to apply this material and tell when and how you plan to apply it. Be specific.

Course	Course Implementation Goals	*(Do not write in this column)*
I. _____ _____ _____	Situation: _____ My plan to apply: _____ _____	A _____ B _____ C _____
II. _____ _____ _____	Situation: _____ My plan to apply: _____ _____	A _____ B _____ C _____
III. _____ _____ _____	Situation: _____ My plan to apply: _____ _____	A _____ B _____ C _____
IV. _____ _____ _____	Situation: _____ My plan to apply: _____ _____	A _____ B _____ C _____

Please address the attached envelope to yourself; it will be returned to you in three to four weeks.

FIGURE 17.4 FOLLOW-UP INSTRUCTIONS

Please review the course content. Then review what you had planned to apply.

You may now place checkmarks in the third column of the work statement. If you were able to apply your plan successfully, check the "A" space. If you were partially able to apply your plan and are still working on the implementation, check "B." If you were not able to apply your plan successfully, check "C" and explain what obstacles stopped your application.

Obstacles that prevented successful application:

Please feel free to make any additional comments about the workshop or yourself in the space provided below:

FIGURE 17.5 SUPERVISOR'S FOLLOW-UP FORM

[Name] was a participant in a workshop dealing with [subject]. During the last three to four weeks, s/he has attempted to implement the ideas or skills listed on the enclosed sheet labeled Work Statement. Please review what s/he has written.

Did you observe any change? You should place checkmarks in the third column of the Work Statement. If you were able to note a change, any change, please check "A." If you were able to note some effort to change, check "B." If you were not able to note a change or an effort to change, check "C."

Were you able to offer your support to this person as s/he attempted to implement actions?

Please feel free to add any additional comments:

Level 3 data can also be obtained by any of the following:

- Performance appraisals of participants
- On-site observation of sample participants on the job
- Checklists of key behaviors that are completed by unbiased informants
- Interviewing supervisors

Examples of Level 3 measures, listed by Barksdale and Lund (2004), include:

- Process measures (for example, participants follow a new business process back on the job)
- Productivity measures (for example, participants' errors are reduced)
- Cost measures (for example, participants identify methods to reduce costs)
- Revenue measures (for example, participants increase their referrals to other products)
- Safety measures (for example, participants follow safety procedures)

One of the challenges of Level 3 evaluation is to provide evidence that the behavioral changes of participants were a result of the training program and not the results of other factors. This is difficult to "prove." If this is a requirement for you, Bobrow (2005) recommends the following questions to ask of any Level 3 study:

- How many people were in the study? (The more people involved in the study, the more confidence in the results.)
- Was there a control group? (If people not involved in the training program changed as well, the training program may have not been necessary.)
- How large was the performance improvement? (Small changes in behavior may not warrant the time and expense of the training program.)
- Was the improvement sustained? (Behavior occurring immediately after the training may not continue several months later.)

Level 4: Results

Assessing the business results of training may be the most difficult to do. Typically, Level 4 evaluation requires time-consuming activities such as focus groups, strategic interviews, and observation. However, if you use the ROE model suggested earlier, your stakeholder will have told you what "results" they expect. It could include things such as a reduction in turnover in a specific department, increase in sales, or decrease in absenteeism. In addition to asking for stakeholder expectations, data may already exist in your organization. Here are some examples:

- Employee satisfaction surveys
- Organizational and team morale scores
- Number of customer complaints
- Employee retention; lost time
- Sales revenue
- Cost per sale
- Safety ratings
- Customer service ratings
- Work flow and efficiency data
- Awards from outside sources
- Operating costs
- Compliance versus violations
- Accuracy studies
- Consistency
- Product defects

Note in the previous lists items that not only impact on the organization's "bottom line" by increasing sales, profits, revenues, market share, and so forth but also impact on "organizational effectiveness" indicators such as employee morale. As Spitzer (2004) points out, "One of the greatest dangers of the 'bottom-line' definition of impact has been the tendency to reduce everything to financial terms. This is a dangerous practice because it tends to trivialize many nonfinancial measures."

Of course, evidence from these kinds of Level 4 data doesn't constitute proof that the training was responsible for organizational results. Besides the use of control groups, evaluation guru Jack Phillips (1996) recommends other alternatives such as trend-line analysis. As he explains, "In this approach, a line is drawn from current performance to future performance, assuming that the current trend will continue even without the training. After employees receive training, the post-training performance is compared to their performance predicted on the trend line. It's reasonable to attribute any improvement over the trend-line prediction to training." Phillips also suggests other approaches such as participant, supervisor, and expert estimation, as well as input from customers and subordinates. The more evidence you provide, the more your Level 4 claims will have clout.

ROE emphasizes that formal training events by themselves do not deliver significant bottom-line outcomes. It does not emphasize using estimates, assumptions, and empirical financial formulas to try to isolate the effects of training. However, it does acknowledge that the results always come from a variety of factors, and if you do not measure and know which factors aided in the transfer of learning to behavior and subsequent results, you will not be able to take any credit for the success. So, although ROE does not attempt to isolate outcomes related to training, it does place emphasis on validating that the transfer of learning to on-the-job behavior is related to training.

DESIGNING EVALUATIONS

As you can see, training evaluation requires the same careful design as the training program it assesses. Attention must be paid to three central decisions:

1. **Focus**: What elements are being evaluated? Data can be gathered concerning any of the following:
   - Participants' reactions
   - Participants' knowledge, skills, and attitudes
   - On-the-job application
   - Organizational results

2. **Tools**: What means are used to collect evaluative data? Any of the following can be utilized:
   - Questionnaires
   - Observation
   - Tests

- Reports
- Interviews

3. *Timing*: When are data collected? Any of these times are possible:

- Pre-training
- During training
- End of training
- Follow-up period

Finally, remember that evaluation of an active training program is not only about outcome but also about process. Evaluation efforts should address what is happening in a training program as much as whether it is making any difference. Why is process evaluation so important? Quite simply, *without good records of what happened during a training program, it is not always clear what needs changing if the outcome evaluation is disappointing.* Try to keep a log of the events during the learning program, how participants responded, and what your own reactions were as well. Or invite others to watch the proceedings and make observations about the program as it is being experienced. By doing so, you will be an active participant in your program.

OBTAIN FEEDBACK ALONG THE WAY

Actually, you won't want to wait until the end of your session to learn about your participants' needs and satisfaction. You can design your active training program to obtain feedback and data on an ongoing basis so that you can make adjustments before it is too late. Even observing participants' behavior gives you clues about their satisfaction. Do they smile? Do they seem alert? Involved? Do they ask questions?

Behavioral cues are often good barometers; however, they give you incomplete feedback. You could fill in the gaps by guessing how the participants think and feel, but although these guesses might be accurate, it is more likely that they will be influenced by your fears (if you are anxious) or your ego (if you are too assured). Verifying your impressions is the only way to obtain accurate and detailed feedback.

There are two major ways other than observation to obtain ongoing group feedback: orally and in written reports. Obtaining oral feedback is a challenge. It can be time-consuming. Obtaining written feedback is usually quicker and less threatening. However, you will not be able to immediately clarify the information you receive if you want to probe further. Both oral and written feedback activities must be well designed. You may also want to use a survey provider such as Zoomerang or SurveyMonkey to gather data quickly. Another option is to use instant survey tools such as polling available through platforms like Adobe Conference. Here are some of the best techniques.

1. ***Reaction surveys***. Create brief questionnaires and give them to participants at an appropriate moment. Items can be presented in different formats:

Short Essay

Please respond in writing to the question "What would you suggest to improve this portion of the session?"

Checklist

Check the words that describe your reactions to today's session:

____ Slow-moving

____ Illuminating

____ Overwhelming

____ Practical

____ Well organized

____ Engaging

Sentence Completion

Complete the sentence beginning "Something I am still confused about is…"

Ratings

Use the following scale to rate how valuable you found today's session.

(high) 5 4 3 2 1 (low)

Rankings

Rank each module by placing the letter A beside the one that was the most relevant to you, B beside the next most relevant, and C beside the least relevant.

___ module 1

___ module 2

___ module 3

2. **Anonymous remarks**. Write a question on a blank flip-chart sheet or a whiteboard, and ask participants to respond to it—on the flip chart, on the board, or on blank index cards—during breaks. Here are some possible questions:

> What one word best describes your reaction to today's session?
> What will you remember from today?
> What was the most important thing you learned today?

3. **Oral survey**. Survey reactions by asking participants to share their feedback on the program out loud. Ask for volunteers to contribute or go around the group if you want to hear from everyone. Here is a good set of questions to pose:

> What would you like more at our next session?
> What would you like less of?
> What would you like to continue?

4. **Informal interview**. Casually solicit participant feedback at breaks and at lunch or schedule an evening rap session to discuss participants' feelings about the program in a relaxed manner. Ask questions such as these:

> How does this material resonate with what you need?
> How well does this material relate to your situation?
> What needs to be clarified?
> Are we ready to move on to the next section?

If you are conducting a virtual learning session, you can use all of these to gather evaluation data as well.

WORKSHEET

EVALUATING AN ACTIVE TRAINING PROGRAM

Jot down ideas for evaluating a current training program. Use the worksheet below to guide your planning.

QUESTIONS TO ASK YOUR SPONSOR ABOUT RESULTS:
Final Evaluation:

___Reactions (Level 1)

___Learning (Level 2)

___Behavior (Level 3)

___Results (Level 4)

INTERIM FEEDBACK:

◆   ◆   ◆

Part Five

The Evolving Role of Trainers

*N*ew roles. New realities.

Rapid technological change; new, tougher competition; a demographically changing workforce; increased globalization; higher customer expectations; employee expectations; a constantly increasing rate of change: An incredible number of pressures are placed on organizations today. Every one of these pressures faced by our organizations requires the attention of training and development professionals. Where there are new challenges, there is a need for new knowledge and skills. And that's our role.

The role of trainers has been changing and will continue to change. Our profession has struggled with what to call ourselves and how to define our role. Even our professional association has changed its name from the American Society for Training and Development (ASTD) to The Association of Talent Development (ATD).

Our role has changed. It did not wait for us to either name or define it. Effective training may provide a solid foundation for helping our organizations overcome the challenges and pressures they face, but there is so much more. We are called to take on more responsibilities and to find ways to relieve the pressure our organizations face. We are a part of the fabric that makes up our organization. We touch every part of the organization, so it is no wonder our roles and responsibilities have expanded.

Part V is all new content for the *Active Learning* book. The two chapters in this section address two topics: new roles and new business realities for the training profession.

In Chapter 18 we examine some of the new roles we have inherited most recently. We will: examine onboarding and leading change, viewing lots of ideas and see why both of these are a perfect fit for those of us who develop talent in others. Coaching managers to be developmental managers is an interesting task because you will be modeling exactly what you want them to learn to do. Mentoring programs are critical for leadership success. If your organization does not have a mentoring effort, expect to be asked to start one. Internal consulting takes your role as a trainer one step deeper into helping your organization be successful. Finally, understanding the difference between team skills training and conducting a team building intervention is addressed; both are important for different needs. Trainers need to be able to do both.

In Chapter 19 we explore the business realities we face as we do our jobs. Many of these challenges have been around for some time. They aren't going away, so we'd better get good at them. Doing more with less, globalization, and multiple generations in the workforce each has a role in defining how we do our work, as well as how we help the workforce do its work as well. From a business perspective we'd better hone our skills for working with those in the C-suite, our vendors, and subject matter experts who hold the key to gaining content for so many of our training events.

Entire books have been written about each of the dozen topics within these two chapters. This means that we are barely scratching the surface of the topics as well as how and why they are important to you. You will find experts mentioned throughout the chapters whose books should satiate your desire for more information.

"The brilliance in Mel's work lies in its simplicity...simply focus on the learners. Being invited to help update Mel Silberman is pretty heady stuff!!"

Kathy Shurte
Florida Department of Transportation, District Four

Chapter Eighteen

Expanded Roles for Trainers

Yes, change is the only constant in today's world. A successful training professional embraces change and welcomes the new roles that come with it. How do you stay on top of this? Beverly Kaye, author of *Love It Don't Leave It: 26 Ways to Get What You Want at Work*, says that you need to be alert to everything that's happening in the world of work. Identify the trends and challenges in the workplace. Talk to people. Identify opportunities to enrich your skills. Stay on top of what's happening in your industry. Predict what will happen.

Even without knowing what will happen in the future you can continue to work on your own development. Share your needs and hopes for continued development. Broaden your skills and knowledge. Learn to be flexible and to watch for opportunities to learn new skills. Learn everything you can about your industry. Set goals and build development plans for your future.

So what about the roles that are upon us now? Although there are many, we have selected six to explore more deeply in this chapter. Onboarding is close to the typical "learning event" with the caveat that it is always with your newest employees—the ones you will want to ensure have a good first impression. The other five roles are not usually thought of as typical training or learning department roles. If you begin thinking of your role as a "talent developer," however, you will see how each of these fits into your new job description. Let's examine each of these new roles.

ONBOARDING How your organization welcomes new employees creates the important "first impression." This is the time to ensure that your company puts its best foot forward. Long-term employee engagement is based on the right fit and that starts with your onboarding process.

Does your organization email a packet of intimidating forms to complete? Maybe herd everyone into a room to complete the forms? Send them around the building to get signatures from department heads? Is that really the way you want to welcome the people that you hope will buy into your culture, become committed, engaged long-term employees? Probably not.

Well, it is no wonder that this role, being responsible for your organization's onboarding process, now falls to you. You understand what it takes to draw people in, to create involvement, to engage participants, and to provide an active learning experience.

Start with that premise—an active learning experience. Add to it all the other ingredients that make the workplace a pleasant place to be:

- Ensure that employees receive the information they need to help them integrate into the workforce. Try to focus on what they "need" to know, not everything that would be "nice" to know.

  EXAMPLE: Many organizations create neat little packets and beautiful binders full of everything-you-want-to-know-about-our-company. That does not lend itself to "active learning." A Midwestern promotional products company holds a new employee orientation every month. They put the new employees into teams of three or four and set them off on a scavenger hunt, looking for things such as the EEO office, the best-selling sandwich in the cafeteria, and the name of the copyright attorney. Along the way they meet people, find their way around the building, and learn much about the organization. Of course there are prizes involved, and the best part is that they become a part of two teams—the small team of new employees and the corporate team.

- Ensure that employees understand how their role fits in the organization.

  Build new employees' self-esteem by recognizing the value they bring to the organization and the importance of the role they have in the organization.

EXAMPLE: One multinational organization established stations that represented each of the key departments. The stations were set up in its large conference room and staffed by individuals from the department. Participants went from station to station in pairs and talked to people of each department. They learned three key things: the key issue or project the department was currently addressing; where each department fit in the organizational chart; and how their job at the company fit into the other department and the role they played in the current project.

- Introduce new employees to other employees, including management and their department coworkers. If the company president or the department director is out for the day, use technology.

EXAMPLE: In one organization the president Skyped into the general information sharing meeting and then followed this up with a text message welcoming the new employees.

- Ensure that new employees feel welcome, that they feel like they are a part of the team, and that they leave knowing they made the right decision.

EXAMPLE: A federal government agency that operated on an abundance of acronyms conducted an acronym BINGO event during the onboarding. It accomplished several things. New employees worked in teams to find clues throughout the agency building that led them to the acronym meaning. They learned more about the organization's mission, its organizational structure, the location of many of the departments, and the names of other employees. Through meeting others in the organization they started to feel a part of the action. In the end, by making fun of itself and all its acronyms, the agency established a basis for its culture which was that they work hard but have fun.

Onboarding is not an event; it is an entire process. It isn't over once the original event has ended. Many organizations ensure that new employees are assigned a "buddy" or "coach" who will help them find answers and feel welcome.

This is an important new role and you can see how an active training background helps to plan and design an effective orientation. A positive orientation leads to a higher level of employee engagement right from the start.

LEADING CHANGE

You may have designed a change management effort for your organization. If you have, you know how important active, involved participation is to the success of the project. This is why your role is critical to helping lead change in your organization.

Almost everything you do in your daily work supports change in one way or another. You are probably responsible for designing change management training to help others understand change. All change processes use a four to seven step change model to ensure that everything is addressed in order.

As an example of what a change model includes, let's look at one that has six steps. Each of the six steps requires completing distinct and specific tasks and we can determine a trainer's role in each step. Change is rarely a nice, neat, linear process as presented in any model. Change is led by people; it is conducted by people; and it is the people who must ultimately change in order for an organization to change. It is this aspect of "people" that makes change not only exciting, but also unpredictable. And of course your understanding of people demonstrates why it is a critical new role for you.

The change model provides a process that can be used to facilitate an organization through a change effort. Change comes in many formats: developmental change, transformational change, or opportunistic change. Change may be large or small. The change model is generic and may be used with any type of change intervention including structural, process, cultural, M&A (mergers and acquisition), growth, downsizing, cost cutting, and others. Your organization has probably experienced at least one of these. Each step presents tools and techniques that will help you hone your skills as a change agent or a change leader.

Step 1, Challenge the Current State. The first step addresses the recognition that something can be different, a preferred future that dares the status quo to innovate. This step is usually initiated by someone at or near the top of the organization who identifies a need for change. It may be externally generated, such as an impending industry regulation or a customer demand. Or it may be internally generated, such as a high percent of retirement-eligible personnel on the horizon, technology upgrades, or a merger. This step addresses the question of "why?" As a trainer your role is to help leaders clarify what the change is and the best way to approach it. You will also be there to remind them to communicate or to help gather data.

Step 2, Harmonize and Align Leadership. The first two steps of the change model address Kurt Lewin's "unfreezing" concept, ensuring that the organization begins the process of unlearning its current habits. Included in the unlearning process in Step 2 is aligning the organization's leadership to understand the organizational need and to identify a way to focus on the challenge from a systems perspective. It is also leadership's responsibility to begin to model and communicate a consistent message to the rest of the organization about what will happen and what is the reason it is happening. This step addresses the question of "what?" As a trainer your role may be to analyze your organization's readiness for change or to facilitate discussions among leaders. You may be tapped for your ability to provide a process to select team members. One organization used the Decision Matrix for Selecting Team Members in Figure 18.1.

Step 3, Activate Commitment. As the planning phase moves into the design phase, teams are formed to begin the design, considering what to maintain, what to change, how to get employee buy-in and involvement, and a host of other events to ensure that everything has been considered before implementation begins. Leadership continues to build a strong united front ensuring commitment to the initiative. The facilitators of change may be required to learn or invent new tools and techniques to develop the implementation plan that will help everyone understand how the change will occur. This step answers the question of "how?" As a trainer you may begin to train the change management team or train others in their roles. You may be asked to facilitate the creation of the change management team's charter, or you may be asked to address resistance to change.

Step 4, Nurture and Formalize a Design. Many organizations skip the first three steps and begin their change effort at this point. They decide a change must take place and then begin to create the change. They find, however, that stumbling blocks begin to spring up in their paths to prevent the desired change. This step encourages change agents to use tools to formalize the design: conduct a risk assessment, select appropriate metrics, and utilize a number of implementation tools. As a trainer you work with many tools that can help the change process: risk assessment tools, force field analysis, and others. You may also be needed to explore aspects of the organizational system.

Step 5, Guide Implementation. The fifth step is the action step. The organization is busy keeping the implementation moving forward. The organization will begin to see some short-term gains, an important result because it provides proof that what was intended with the effort is beginning to bear fruit. Using the short-term gains as a springboard, the organization will want to identify ways to increase motivation to accelerate the implementation. You may be called upon to provide conversation starters throughout the organization.

FIGURE 18.1 DECISION MATRIX FOR SELECTING TEAM MEMBERS

Assign a letter from A to F, to each person you are considering for the team. Use the following rating scale:

    1 = Never
    2 = Rarely
    3 = Sometimes
    4 = Usually
    5 = Always

Criterion	A	B	C	D	E	F
Select the right people:						
• Offers executive-level support						
• Is an informal leader						
• Possesses required expertise and knowledge						
• Is credible throughout the organization						
• Capable leader and manager						
• Respected and trusted by other executives						
From the right areas:						
• Fulfills cross-section representation						
• Respected by all stakeholders						
• Represents the most critical area						
• Ability to allocate resources						
With the right attitude:						
• Positive						
• Trusting						
• Problem solver						
• Enthusiastic						
• Persistent						
• Team player						

Source: ebb associates, (2007).

Step 6, Evaluate and Institutionalize the Change. Once the implementation has been completed, many organizations are off to find other dragons to slay. It is essential to encourage people and the organization to accept the desired change and to permanently institutionalize the variations in processes, different products or services, new philosophy, or whatever was intended to be changed. This step embeds the change into the organizational culture and transforms it to become the new reality—the way it is. This step also encourages the organization to prepare for continuous change. As a trainer, your expertise in evaluation tools will be tapped in this step.

EXAMPLE: A global scientific research organization had experienced a director for almost eight years who had not kept abreast of the changes in the world. Once it was discovered by the home office on the other side of the Atlantic, much damage had been done. The director was very personable and the staff was unaware of how far behind the field office had become. The home office sent its best trainer to support the change efforts of the newly appointed director. The trainer designed data gathering tools, established and trained a change management team, facilitated exploratory groups, provided templates for the redesign, encouraged employees to get involved in focus groups, and created monitoring tools to ensure that the change would be institutionalized.

The key to successfully managing change is strong, effective communications. As your organization moves through a change management effort, you will find many of your skills are critical to its success.

COACHING MANAGERS

Have you ever had managers tell you it was your job to develop their people? They are only half right. Developing people, closing the skill gaps in the workforce, and increasing knowledge must be a partnership between you and managers.

Given that managers may not have thought about it this way in the past, you will most likely need to get them started and coach them along the way. You will need to clarify their role as a developmental manager and show them how to embed development into the work the employees are doing.

Managers will tell you they are too busy—they can barely get their real work done, so how can they be expected to "do your job too?" Wendy Axelrod, author of *Make Talent Your Business: How Exceptional Managers Develop People While Getting Results*, assures all trainers that it is possible to "graciously guide" them with some of these ideas.

- Help managers learn how to think about developing their employees as they plan work assignments. This is a matter of a mindset shift. It requires managers to think about the long term. What could be completed over the next half year if employees were given a chance to be developed?

- Show managers how to think differently. If managers can begin to think about what needs to be accomplished and connect it to what needs to be learned they will turn the work into the development tool. Managers need to hold employees accountable for both the performance results and their development.

    EXAMPLE: One finance manager tells his staff members that every project has one finish line but two ribbons: one ribbon for results, and one for development.

- Work with managers to analyze which employee skill improvements would best fulfill the ability to accomplish more. Help managers select developmental assignments that align with anticipated results, not simply stretch assignments that are easy because they are available and visible.

- Help managers rethink how they delegate work. Benefits occur when managers learn to reshape an everyday work assignment to include a developmental component. Show them how to break deliverables into new smaller stretch tasks that will expand employees' expertise.

All this requires honing skills for managers. It requires that you put a coaching plan in place to bring the managers up to speed. In fact, you are modeling exactly what you are requiring of managers.

MENTORING PROGRAMS

The word "mentor" originated in Greek mythology. In Homer's *Odyssey*, King Odysseus arranges for his trusted friend and advisor to act as guardian for and to nurture and protect his son, Telemachus, while Odysseus is away to fight the Trojan War. The guardian's name is Mentor. Mentor guides and advises Telemachus on his journey to find out what happened to his father.

Today, we understand the word mentor to mean "a trusted counselor or guide" (Merriam-Webster 2011). There are at least two people in a mentoring relationship, and both can gain valuable new knowledge, insight, and skills as a result of participating in this endeavor.

According to Halelly Azulay, 71 percent of Fortune 500 companies have mentoring programs. A Sun Microsystems study of more than 1,000 employees over five years found that mentors were promoted six times more often than those not in the program; protégés were promoted five times more often than those not in the program; and retention rates were much higher for protégés (72 percent) and mentors (69 percent) than for employees who did not participate in the mentoring program (49 percent) (Insala 2011).

Mentoring is not limited to those whose employers offer a formal program. In our highly connected world of social networking, new mentoring relationships are emerging as a result of savvy employees (and their employers) making connections and joining groups that give them access to potential mentoring matches. Eager learners and seasoned veterans who are willing to be mentors can easily connect and begin a consensual, mutually beneficial mentoring relationship. Anyone can start a mentoring relationship.

As a training and development professional, developing employees through mentoring is another role you may be expected to complete. In this role you may:

- Create a matching process to locate and match mentor/protégé partnerships
- Design readiness surveys for mentors and protégés
- Design and conduct a mentoring training program
- Determine how to create mentoring opportunities for employees around the globe
- Identify ways to use social media tools to facilitate mentoring matches
- Create an evaluation plan to measure the success of the mentoring program
- Determine a balanced diversity approach for the program

EXAMPLE: A consulting firm that provided services to retail stores was experiencing a loss of good people. During their exit interviews a "lack of development" and "unclear about how to get promoted" was often cited. The organization's Talent Development department customized a mentoring program including training, marketing, and a mentor/protégé matching process. They engaged experts to discuss topics such as Risk Communications, Preparing for Senior Level Position, Emotional Intelligence, the Generation Gap, and Negotiation Skills. These sessions were only open to mentors and protégés. They wrote a 45-page Mentor Guide and provided training for new partnerships. They currently maintain a roster of senior leaders as potential mentors and list dozens of individuals who are willing to mentor other employees. They track partnership objectives and email discussion starters to mentors and protégés to stimulate discussion. Evaluations and discussions show a high satisfaction level with the program as well as an increased retention rate of 64 percent over the six year effort. The company believes the key to success is in creating the best match which begins with their Mentor Partnership Agreement displayed in Figure 18.2.

FIGURE 18.2 MENTORING PARTNERSHIP AGREEMENT

Mentor Partnership Agreement

Mentor Name	Department Level	Telephone

Protégé Name	Department Level	Telephone

What we believe the company expects of us . . .

Logistics: How often shall we meet?   Who will initiate contact?
Where shall we meet?   How else can we connect?
How much time shall we make available?   Our first meeting will be:

What the Protégé expects from this partnership:

What the Mentor expects from this partnership:

FIGURE 18.2 continued

Guidelines that will help us work well together:

Objectives:

How we will address issues that may arise, e.g., conflicts between us;
one of us is not getting what we think we should; one of us thinks we
are mismatched; gender, racial or cultural issues:

We agree that our discussions are confidential:

Protégé Signature   Date

Mentor Signature   Date

© 2007 ebb associates inc, used with permission.

INTERNAL CONSULTING

Internal consulting is a unique training and development role. An internal consultant's in-depth knowledge of the organization may create times when it is difficult to be neutral. In addition, internal consultants may be pressured to take on unreasonable projects, make inappropriate changes, or reveal confidential information.

Despite these dilemmas, internal consultants have an exciting job. They are called upon to facilitate high-level meetings, to mastermind change efforts, to take a systems approach for future projects, and many other exciting high-level projects.

Bev Scott and Kim Barnes see new internal consulting roles emerging including:

Performance Consultant: An expectation for increased performance contributed to the growth of this role. It is a combination of the whole system focus of the organization and the understanding and techniques of skills training. A performance consultant partners with clients to identify and address performance needs.

Trusted Advisor: Leaders face rapid change, environmental complexity, competitive global markets, and rapidly changing technology. In the midst of this turmoil, they must focus on maintaining cultural alignment and meeting the expectations of customers and employees. Internal consultants may serve as a sounding board to leaders. The trusted advisor is a confidant and provides authentic communication and reaction.

Change Leader: As organizations continue to cope with a changing business environment, facilitators are required to guide the implementation and support of change or innovation initiatives. (See Leading Change in this chapter.) Internal consultants may be asked to guide the process and be the driving force of a change initiative.

What does it take to be a successful internal consultant? First and foremost it requires that you gain the trust and credibility of everyone in the organization: leaders and employees. You must be a generalist, competent in a broad range of applications, but you must also be seen as an expert in several areas to ensure credibility. The checklist in Figure 18.3 is based on work by Scott and Barnes. It will help you think about your strengths for this role.

FIGURE 18.3 INTERNAL CONSULTING COMPETENCIES

Place a checkmark in front of each of the competencies you possess as an internal consultant.

___ Collaborates with Others

___ Establishes Credibility

___Takes Initiative

___ Maintains Detachment

___ Markets the Value of a Specialty Expertise

___ Demonstrates Organizational Savvy

___ Is Resourceful

___ Understands the Organization

Adapted from Scott and Barnes, 2011.

BUILDING TEAMS

Human beings make up organizations, create the culture, and determine the total effectiveness of their organizations. This effectiveness is dependent upon how well these human beings work together as a group. Indeed, human beings do almost everything in groups. We grow up in families, learn in classes, play on teams, socialize in clubs, travel in car pools, and work in departments. Working as a team is how we get things done.

We all recognize the interdependence of people and the need for cooperation to accomplish group goals. These groups are most effective when they communicate well and function as a team. Unfortunately employees may cognitively "know" the importance of teamwork, but may not practice what they know. We may appreciate good communication, but may not realize how our personal communication may inhibit understanding by our co-workers. Past history and expectations of a group may also prevent it from functioning as an effective team.

Teamwork is on the lips of every organization that is future-oriented. Organizations are doing more with slimmer budgets. They must find ways to release the untapped talent of their employees. Teamwork has been one of the most basic and successful approaches. And all of this is dependent upon good communication.

Team Skills

But what are the characteristics of a successful team? The characteristic of high performing teams encompasses a list of many characteristics. Foundational team characteristics include things such as setting clear goals, clearly defined roles, open and clear communication, and effective decision-making. Other critical skills are knowing how to balance participation, valuing diversity, managing conflict, and creating a positive atmosphere. Teams are effective when the team members are cooperative and when participative leadership exists.

EXAMPLE: To encourage discussion around the characteristics of a team, a trainer asked a newly forming team to respond to these questions with a true or false. The questions are designed to create discussion and the correct answer to each of them is, "It depends."

1. A team needs a strong leader, even if the leader intimidates some team members.

2. The team should meet only if all members are able to attend.

3. There are often times when individual team members must do what they think is right, even if it conflicts with a team decision.

4. Consensus decisions generally take too much time and result in a watered-down decision.

5. It is healthy for several team members to talk at the same time; it shows team energy and enthusiasm.

6. Teams should take time up front to establish clear roles for each member.

7. It is difficult for a team to succeed when it does not have clear goals.

8. Teams are more successful when they are able to avoid conflict.

9. A team should set aside meeting time to explore member feelings and relationships.

10. The team should not actively try to get quiet members to participate; they will participate when they have something to contribute.

11. In truly effective teams, members have a personal liking for each other.

12. Once a team gets an established way of working, it is unproductive to spend time changing it.

© 2009 ebb associates inc, used with permission.

Team Building

Teams rarely start off great; they learn to be great. And that is what "team building" can do. You can easily "teach ten team skills," but often a team doesn't request this training until it is nearly dysfunctional. At that point your role changes from facilitating team skills training to facilitating team building interventions. You may need to work with teams that are less productive and efficient than they should be (sometimes dysfunctional!) in order to create a functioning team.

A team building intervention begins in much the same way active training starts. You will gather information. A good way to start is to use a questionnaire similar to the one in Figure 18.4.

FIGURE 18.4 YOUR DEPARTMENT TEAM BUILDING QUESTIONNAIRE

Please take 15 minutes to respond to the following questions. You may return your responses by email (ebbxxx@ebbinc.com) or fax (757/400-1313) by 1600, Friday 31 October.

1. What's it like to work in your department, e.g., fun, frustrating, challenging, other?

2. How do you describe communication in your department?

3. How could communication be improved in your department?

4. What do you believe the top three priorities should be for your department?

5. What is the best part of working in your department that you would like to retain?

6. If you could make one or more improvements in your department, what would they be?

7. How difficult or easy has it been to adjust to consistent staff attrition?

8. Rate your team on the following on a 1 to 7 scale with 1 being low and 7 high. Add a comment to explain your rating if you wish.

___ Teamwork

___ Morale

___ Communication

___ Level of trust among colleagues

___ Level of trust between employees and management

___ Conflict management

___ Feedback to each other

___ Service to your customers

___ Vision direction for the future

___ Improving processes ●

___ Clear goals

___ Defined Roles

9. The organization is like a _____, because . . .

Other comments:

_____

© 2013 ebb associates inc, used with permission.

The data you gather from the questionnaire, interviews, or other methods is fed back anonymously to the team to use during intervention activities. You will also open a team building intervention in much the same way you open an active training event. Identify an activity that ensures that everyone speaks at least once. The Team Warm-Ups in Figure 18.5 give you a few ideas.

FIGURE 18.5 TEAM WARM-UPS

I am most like a _____ on a team.
For fun, I like to . . .
If I could be any animal, I would be _____ because . . .
My dream vacation is . . .
The last book I read was . . .
On Saturdays, I usually . . .
The turning point in my life was . . .
I feel best when people . . .
Five things I want to do in the next five years include . . .
One thing I recently learned on the job is . . .
The slogan on my favorite T-shirt says . . .
Something you may not know about me is . . .
I once won a . . .
To me, teamwork means . . .

© 2007 ebb associates inc, used with permission.

Each of these roles expands your responsibility, your opportunities, and your development. Embrace the changes that each bring to you.

WORKSHEET

NEW ROLES ACTION PLAN

Consider the six roles presented in this chapter. What do you know, what do you need to learn, how will you learn it, and who can help you learn about your new role? Complete the table with this information.

New Role	What I Need to Learn	How I Will Learn	Who Can Help Me
Onboarding			
Leading Change			
Coaching Managers			
Mentoring			
Internal Consulting			
Building Teams			

◆ ◆ ◆

Mel Silberman changed my life—professionally. In fact, I remember vividly the specific incident that triggered the change.

Very early in my doctoral program at Temple University, I enrolled in Mel's instructional design course. One of the course requirements was to design, develop, and present a mini training session to our fellow classmates as well as others outside the program. By the time I participated in what was known as the "PEP Potpourri," I had been a successful training and development practitioner for nine years (first as a corporate training director and then as an external consultant). For my session I chose a topic that I had been delivering for several years to my clients: "Interpersonal Communication." I thought to myself, "This is going to be a piece of cake." In the ninety-minute session, I included every interactive method I could think of: assessment, case study, role play, group discussion. The day arrived, I facilitated my session without a problem, and I was confident all participants were involved. As Mel called me into the hallway to give me feedback, I remember smiling and thinking, "He's going to tell me I was a 'star.'" The smile quickly disappeared. Mel began by saying, "It was a great performance, Karen, but it was about you, not about them." I honestly have no idea what he said after that, but it was not at all what I expected.

I cried all the way home and vowed I was going to drop out of the program. After the tears stopped flowing, I spent some time reflecting on what Mel said. Then after I "got over myself" and my ego, I realized he was right. I thought about the message he said repeatedly: "It's not what you give them; it's what they take away that counts." When I made that shift in my head, it made a major difference in the way I delivered training and the way my audiences responded. I, like hundreds of others, became a Mel disciple.

Mel gave me a wonderful opportunity by asking me to co-author the first edition of *101 Ways to Make Training Active*. In fact, it opened doors for many other book authorship opportunities. I have spent the past twenty-two years of my career promoting active training techniques through my teaching, writing, and speaking, and I will continue to do so.

Mel was much more than my teacher, advisor, and co-author; he was my mentor, colleague, and friend. He truly made a difference in my life.

Karen Lawson
Lawson Consulting Group, Inc.

Chapter Nineteen

New Business Realities for Trainers

*T*he world changes and with it comes new challenges. Many of the challenges our organizations face are the same ones we face as trainers.

Your organizations will look to you and your colleagues to help resolve the latest challenge of the day. Our profession must have answers to address these needs. What is your department's latest encounter? Doing more with less? Yes, that's one your organization is addressing. Globalization? Working with many generations in the workplace? Yes and yes. You will need to learn to work with the C-suite to better understand these issues from their perspective, so this chapter provides you with some ideas.

If this sounds as if your job is becoming more business oriented, you are right. Facing business realities is what this chapter is all about.

Examples in this chapter are in the form of tools, checklists, and ideas for how you can be more successful addressing the realities of the day. Even though these realities are business oriented, each also has a training element that requires your active learning tools and techniques.

This chapter addresses:

- Doing more with less
- Globalization
- Working with multigenerational workforces
- Working with the C-suite
- Vendor management
- Working with subject matter experts

379

DOING MORE WITH LESS

The cry to "do more with less" is nothing new. As trainers we are tuned into the challenges our organizations face. We understand this business reality, whether it is "new" or a repeated reality of years past. This battle cry is heard in every organization. We need to accept it as a permanent business reality.

Finding ways to continue to provide services to your organizations' growing list of requirements may seem daunting at times. What can you do?

Begin by ensuring excellent communication with your organization's leadership. What are their priorities? What are the top priorities in the strategic plan? Where will you obtain the best return on investment? This discussion and the resulting information are critical for you to learn what roles will make the greatest difference, what tasks are priorities, and how can you make technology work for you?

Embrace New Roles

In the previous chapter we introduced new roles. When done well every one of those roles is a good investment because they ultimately save the company time and money. It is your job to ensure that "active learning" continues to be the focus.

- Onboarding ensures that employees get off to a good start with the information and tools to make them productive right from the beginning.

- Leading change allows you to share tools and methodologies that can help move the change along faster, with fewer delays, and better results.

- Coaching managers to develop their employees multiplies your efforts with each manager helping to develop other employees.

- Mentoring programs can retain good employees, keep them engaged, and encourage them to invite other good employees to work for your employer.

- Internal consulting can prevent single leaders and departments from indecision or worse—making poorly thought out decisions that impede progress.

- Building teams means that you can help align everyone to work in exactly the same direction.

You see that these new roles can have a great impact and a multiplier effect on your organization. Can you do all of them? Well maybe not, but with your senior leaders' input, select the one that broaches the greatest issue facing your organization.

Prioritize Training and Development Tasks

You may need to focus on doing fewer things. Trainers may not be able to say, "How do I get these 10 programs delivered?" Instead, your question becomes, "Which of these 10 programs will get delivered?" and "What can we stop doing?" Some training efforts that were deemed essential last year may not be viewed the same this year. You may need to focus on doing fewer things well—doing the *right* things with less.

Communication is the best way to begin to prioritize. Address these issues with your senior leadership. The data you have been collecting over the years will help to support results, establish priorities, and determine budgets.

As trainers we discuss the difference between "must know" and "nice to know." This is one of those times when it is critical to cut out the "nice to knows" in your programs. Making these decisions must align to corporate strategy.

Use Technology Wisely

Chapter 10 presented an overview of e-learning tools available to you. If travel budgets are reduced or time away from your organization isn't as liberal as it once was, think about all the tools you have at your disposal that weren't available just a few short years ago. Think of this as a positive challenge. Identify all the ways to train and develop the people in your organization.

This is a great time to review the training program that is offered most often to determine how you might be able to use blended learning to its best advantage. This will require some redesign but it is also a great developmental opportunity for someone in your department—maybe you. How can you use Skype or Google Hangout to reach employees in other cities or countries? Would one of your classes lend itself to a Virtual World scenario? Can you send small nuggets of information, just in time to employees via their mobile devices? Will several short virtual classroom modules provide the same learning as a physical session? Could you invite your CEO or a panel of senior leaders to conduct a panel discussion in lieu of a particular topic? Can presentations be recorded for future use? Can you create peer coaching groups or virtual buddies to continue the learning? How can you establish a networking group after a shortened class to continue learning? What job aids can you deliver using social media tools? Can you create an online book club?

The ideas are endless. Your resources are not. Tap into technology.

EXAMPLE: A research and development firm recently had its travel budget cut. The scientists and engineers were devastated. They counted on attending conferences, symposiums, seminars, and other scientific gatherings around the world to stay in touch with the newest science and innovations in their fields. They called upon their training department who worked directly with conference and seminar organizers to produce a solution that combined video conferencing, Skype, social media tools, virtual meetings, and other options. In at least one instance it turned out to be a better solution because all the parties were together for one conversation that was more productive than tracking individuals down individually. Did the PhDs embrace the solution instead of conferences? Not entirely. As soon as budgets returned to normal travel also returned to its previous levels. On the other hand almost everyone agreed that learning about other communications options has increased their productivity between conferences.

You can address doing more with less: embrace change, prioritize programs, and use technology wisely. Every organization is facing the same challenges. Plan to overcome this business reality successfully in your organization.

GLOBAL-IZATION

Globalization offers companies exciting growth opportunities; it also introduces a complex array of challenges. The challenges, mostly focused on a lack of the right infrastructure, affect all parts of the organization. Managing global organizations isn't a new challenge, but the accelerating shift of economic activity from Europe and North America to Africa, Asia, and Latin America creates new challenges. Global organizations struggle to adapt to the tension in managing strategy, people, costs, and risk on a global scale. In the end many organizations are willing to work through these struggles because there are clear strategic benefits: the ability to access new customer markets, new suppliers, and new partners.

So how does this create a requirement for trainers? Your work in globalization experiences the same challenge and excitement that your organization faces. The broad supply of skills, knowledge, and experience available within the global workforce represent an invaluable asset to your company. On the other hand, utilizing these assets effectively is difficult. For example, if your company is like most it has a vast amount of corporate knowledge gained in various ways. Unfortunately, few companies are good at transferring lessons learned from one emerging market to another. Trainers have the tools to gather, compile, and redistribute lessons learned.

Cultural differences make it difficult to tap into the talents around the world. Managing workforces that are separated by thousands of miles, international time zones, and diverse cultures can be a challenge. Your organization must be able to create an infrastructure that maintains the diversity of international teams while also empowering local employees. From a positive perspective, technology has made possible new forms of international coordination within global companies and potential new ways for them to flourish in these markets. Trainers who have experience or expertise in organizational development can be supportive in this arena.

EXAMPLE: A multinational organization used a consultant to create a list of corporate objectives that were presented in white papers, in virtual classroom settings, as job aids, and built into the mentoring program. These objectives were identified and the materials drafted by a team whose members were from three different continents. The objectives included things such as building a common language, building cultural awareness diversity, clarifying the corporate behaviors and competencies required for global success, defining objectively-measured work standards, and establishing consistent roles across locations. The team met twice each week using the company's video teleconferencing service.

Increased competition for local talent may result in skills shortages in key functions. This creates increased demand for effective planning processes allied to dynamic resource management capabilities. While the tools exist to support these activities, the trick is to review intelligence from a consolidated global perspective. From a positive perspective, technology has made possible new forms of international coordination within global companies and potential new ways for them to flourish in these markets.

Many companies find deploying and developing talent in emerging markets to be a major challenge. Few organizations have figured out how to tailor recruiting, retention, training, and development processes for different locations. This is another area where trainers can assist their organizations.

The literature suggests that few global organizations have developed the talent required for their emerging markets at the same rate as their expected growth. Again, another role for trainers and this one is a perfect fit. Many of the technology ideas discussed throughout this book and especially in Chapter 10 highlight ways to deliver learning solutions around the globe—sometimes at the same time.

WORKING WITH MULTI-GENERA-TIONAL WORK-FORCES

Four generations in the workforce. We all experience it. We all work within this mix. What do you need to know about the mix that ensures the best results? Four primary generations: Traditionalists, Baby Boomers, Generation X, and Millennials.

As a trainer you have two issues to address. The first is to ensure the entire workforce appreciates the diversity each group brings. The second is to ensure that the Millennials are developed and ready to take on leadership responsibilities at a much earlier age than typical in the past.

Generational Challenges

You have a great opportunity to bring the generations together through your training programs. Focus on the similarities rather than the differences among generations. The group that garners the greatest attention seems to be the Millennials, those employees born between 1981 and 2000.

Complaints from Millennials about the rest of the workforce include that they are not open to new ideas, work in siloes, aren't accessible, are slow to adapt new technology, insist on rigid schedules, and use political games for gain.

Complaints about the Millennials from the rest of the workforce include that they don't follow rules such as dress codes, are not diplomatic, complain too much, do not show respect, expect promotions and incentives without earning them, and do not turn their phones off during discussions.

Certainly there is some truth on both sides. Helping everyone to appreciate the diversity that the other generations bring is a first step. Help everyone identify the similarities, for example, everyone wants to do work that makes a difference, desires consistent feedback, and wants to know what is expected of them.

The situation is not as bad as some would make it seem. But you can address these challenges by thinking through the differences as you design and deliver training. Think about the individuals you train who fall into each of the four generational categories. How do they demonstrate the attitudes, behaviors, and expectations of their generations? What experiences have they had that led them to where they are? What challenges do they create as you design or deliver training? What can you do to address these challenges to become a more effective trainer?

Prepare Millennials for Leadership Roles

Generation X, the generation sandwiched in between the Boomers and the Millennials, is half as large as the Boomer generation. This means that as the Baby Boomers retire, less than half of the positions will have experienced workers to fill behind. This means nearly 80 million Millennials will have early promotion opportunities and will require an accelerated rate of training and development services.

Although we don't have enough space here to share all that this means in this chapter, we do have a few tips for designing and delivering training to Millennials.

- Clarify expectations. Millennials want to know what is expected of them, how they will be evaluated, and how the knowledge and skills they are acquiring relates to their performance evaluations on the job.
- Take advantage of their tech savvy. Millennials' electronic capabilities are amazing. They have never known an educational environment that was not subject to constant and consistently changing technology. They view learning and technology as going hand-in-hand. In your classroom use Twitter® to share the results of a small-group discussion. Online, provide links to additional resources that learners can access while taking training if they want to learn more. Implement gamification where possible. Design content so learners can access it on their laptop, iPad, or other device.
- Coach along the way. Millennials appreciate opportunities for coaching, require feedback, and appreciate advice. Using mentors or senior associates during or to follow up after training is a practical approach.
- Look for networking options. Capitalize on the Millennial's affinity for networking. They are comfortable with teams and group

activities, but your Millennial employees also like to network around the world electronically. Use social media to continue to enhance their skills fast.

EXAMPLE: A Midwestern supplier of agricultural feed and seed found it was having a hard time holding onto its college graduate employees. It seemed that they would spend a year to eighteen months learning the organizational systems and then leave. During exit interviews, some said they did not have enough learning opportunities. The company established a Millennial Learning Team made up of senior leaders and Millennial employees. Trainers facilitated discussions to identify innovation options for the company. Implementation and funding of these ideas was given to teams of Millennials as opportunities for active learning and development. One of the results was a virtual corporate university that highlighted the use of gamification, videos, and social tools for continued learning. Employees uploaded content and the company created videos the related directly to corporate needs. Participants won certificates, awards, and corporate accolades for all aspects of their efforts.

The loss of Millennials is not a unique phenomenon. Millennials post their resume electronically on web job boards viewed by millions of employers. They can be loyal employees, but they keep their options open.

Circumstances are different in the world and what has been successful in the past may not be successful today. About half of the Millennials are currently in the workforce. This means you have some time to gear up but not much. Your organization expects a plan for how you will address this exciting business reality.

WORKING WITH THE C-SUITE

So you've designed award-winning training programs. You've delivered economical and effective onboarding processes. You successfully meet every challenge that internal consulting presents. You may have built, coached, and mentored strong internal teams from the ground up so that these groups work like a well-oiled machine. You may have led managers to relish developing their employees so that they see it as their role. You've led change, overcome generational differences, and implemented mentoring programs that get results.

However, if you cannot articulate your achievements, how you've impacted profitability, and your vision for the future, you will not succeed.

What does it take to communicate with the C-suite? What is their focus? Take it from Dianna Booher (2012), the first thing you need to do is to understand how members of the C-suite think.

Executives want to know the most important element of your message first. Dianna says, "Make your bottom line your opening line." If you are a trainer and you need to be prepared to state your viewpoint, offer your recommendation, or deliver the headline (good or bad) first. Executives are an impatient lot. They want to know the message up front and are happy to fill in the details later.

Plan your message in advance. Make it concise and to the point. Too many people take too long to get to the point, and when they do they fill in with too much information. Sift through all the content to find the nuggets that will resonate with your C-Suite audience. Identify what is critical to them.

Make your message strategic. Strategic ideas get approved and funded. Support the strategy with just enough detail to demonstrate that your plan is sound.

Ask provocative questions. Your message should not just "tell" but should also invite thinking from your audience. Booher states that stimulating questions generate more support. What questions can you ask to pique interest from your audience?

Take a stand. Know exactly where you stand, what your recommendations are, and how you will make that known.

Create a memorable story. Be sure that your facts tell a story—a memorable one. Use an analogy, a prop, or quote. Tap into your active learning experience to identify the successful methods you use to convince your learners. The more memorable your story the more likely you will receive funding for your project.

EXAMPLE: A trainer needed to make the point of how money was being wasted by not requiring team building in areas where teams were dysfunctional. She asked the executive team to identify dysfunctional behaviors they'd observed and wrote them on a white board. Next she turned to the CEO and asked if he had a $20 bill. He reached in his pocket and gave it to her. She waved the $20 bill in the air and asked the team if each of the items written on the white board was costing the company $20. They all chuckled and agreed that each was in excess of $20. Her next move made her point. She reviewed each of the points listed by saying, "So late reports are costing us at least $20." "And missed deadlines for customers are costing us at least $20." She went through each item and as she said each one she ripped the

$20 bill in half, then in half again, and again until she was through the entire list when she threw the mangled bill in the air and sat down. Needless to say, she received her funding.

The next time you are invited to the C-suite to present your plans for the following year or to justify why a blended learning approach would be better, use the C-Suite Communication Checklist in Figure 19.1 to remind yourself of the strategies that will make you more successful.

FIGURE 19.1 C-SUITE COMMUNICATION CHECKLIST

C-SUITE COMMUNICATION CHECKLIST

Before your next C-suite encounter, test your message against this checklist.

☐ I will open with the big-picture message statement, my bottom line.

☐ I have selected only critical information nuggets to present a concise message.

☐ I will deliver a strategic message supported by only details that will sell my idea.

☐ I have defined several provocative questions.

☐ I take a stand on my issue.

☐ I have created a memorable story.

Adapted from Booher, 2014.

VENDOR MANAGE-MENT

Does your training department use vendors? Most do. Know why you are hiring a vendor because if hired for the right reason, it can be a very wise decision. How can vendors be a good investment?

- Vendors have the experience, expertise, and time that employees may not. Organizations have difficulty hiring enough good people to keep up with normal, ongoing tasks. Organizations turn to vendors to fill the knowledge and time gap for special projects that arise. Vendors bring experience and expertise from past projects and other organizations.

- Vendors provide flexibility. Vendors can be brought in for short-term projects. Unlike hired staff who require ongoing paychecks, benefits, and severance packages, vendors serve their purpose, and are gone.

- Vendors offer a fresh, objective point of view. With hundreds of other projects under their belt—and valuable experience in dealing with an array of situations and personalities—vendors are able to provide unbiased, fresh ideas.

- Vendors are more efficient. Vendors are more efficient for three reasons: 1) they bring experience with similar problems with them; 2) they have the luxury to focus solely on the assigned project or problem; 3) they do not need to deal with the organization's internal politics or attend meetings.

- Vendors may be proof of honest endeavor. When other parties are involved, a consultant may serve as a sign that an organization is trying to correct an existing problem.

Once you settle on the purpose and the need, finding a vendor that fits your organization's culture is an important task. Find someone that comes with good references, who understands your problem, and whom you believe you will be able to work with and build trust with.

Vendor management has been left up to department heads in the past, but the responsibility for hiring, monitoring, and sometimes firing vendors has been pushed down the organizational ladder to the trainer level.

Are you ready for this responsibility? Here are a few tips to make the relationship work.

- **Keep the lines of communication open.** Be completely open and candid with the vendor. A vendor can only be as good as the information she has. Explain the business goals so the vendor understands how the work ties to what's important for the organization. Request progress reports and be available for meetings.

- **Be a model client.** Demonstrate goodwill by giving referrals, offering more work, and limiting demands. Be sure the vendor is paid on time.

- **Build a partnership for the long term.** Demonstrate trust. Thank them and provide recognition. Go to lunch or coffee to learn more about them personally. Learn more about their businesses. Invite key vendors to help you strategize.

- **Demonstrate respect.** Be reasonable. Plan in advance and provide adequate lead time. Respect their time and resources.

You can see that each of these tips tap into your "active learning" skills as well. To be successful a vendor relationship must be an "active" business reality. If not it will fail.

WORKING WITH SUBJECT MATTER EXPERTS

Subject matter experts (SMEs as they are commonly called), have become a critical business reality for trainers. We require their thoughtful and wise advice to ensure that the training we design and deliver is accurate, current, and focused.

SMEs may assist with several tasks, but the one that comes to mind initially is the expert who is a technical expert. The individual is focused on the content and is not overly involved or interested in the other aspects of the training design. A technical SME is brought into the process to provide content knowledge and to ensure that the content details are current and accurate. This SME will help you identify what must be included and what is not necessary.

If asked, this SME can also provide input about whether the content is more appropriate for an asynchronous learning event, an instructor-led physical classroom, or a virtual classroom. If you ask questions correctly and give a few examples this SME might be able to provide insight about how social media could be used as follow up or when a performance support app could be developed.

When selecting a SME, you will of course be looking for experience. Consider a couple of things with experience:

- The SME's experience must be relevant to the content you are designing.

- The SME's experience must be deep; ensure that the SME can drill down into the content to communicate details that may only arise on occasion.

- The SME's experience should be timely; to be truly helpful to you, the SME should be intimately involved with your topics now, today.

- The SME's experience should be local—that is in the same location, same country, same factory, or whatever is the standard for the content.

You've found the perfect SME. She has all the experience you need. How do you ensure that the relationship is productive and positive? Start by providing a clear definition of roles and responsibilities. Who will do what? How? When is it due? If you can plan this together, all the better. It helps toward building a positive working relationship. Pay close attention to the SME's needs. The more you can work around your SME's schedule the better.

Communicate frequently with your SME. Keep the person informed between various groups and follow up regularly between times. Integrate the SME on your design team. Everyone wants to be a part of the team—and not just some add on. Allowing everyone on the team to act as partners improves communication and builds a shared feeling of commitment, accountability, and appreciation.

Speaking of appreciation, remember to say thank you—often! Few people get too much appreciation at work. Send a card when your SME goes out of the way to reach a deadline or comes up with a brilliant idea for your training. Email the SME's supervisor, too. You can share positive comments about the SME and thank the supervisor for allowing the SME to work on your project.

Finally celebrate. Celebrate at the end of the project. If the project occurs over a long period of time, celebrate project milestones.

The bottom line is that you want to find the best SME available to you. Once you find your SME, do everything you can to build and maintain a positive and productive working relationship.

There are many reasons why your organization might be tapping into SMEs more: limited budget for external experts, greater technology requirements, or increasing immediate requirements that don't allow enough time for the training department to get up to speed. Whatever the reason, you are likely to work more frequently with SMEs in the future.

WE'VE REACHED THE END— OR IS IT THE BEGINNING?

We have concluded this book with two chapters about how your role is changing. But in reality, it isn't changing at all—it is simply expanding.

A trainer's role always has been, always will be to develop people using the principles of active learning. Our job is to foster an enthusiasm for learning—lifelong learners we call it in the profession. Our job is to give employees the tools to improve themselves personally and professionally. Remember training is not about us as trainers; training is all about the people, your participants, your learners. Our role is expanding in magical ways to be even more helpful to others.

It's the end of the book, but hopefully will be the beginning of a successful active training experience for you.

WORKSHEET

Each of these business realities affect your ability to provide the best talent development opportunities that meet employees' needs and your organization's requirements. Take time to consider each of these and what you need to do to continue to deliver active training.

DOING MORE WITH LESS

- Defined for my situation:
- Additional information I'll need:
- My next step:

GLOBALIZATION

- Defined for my situation:
- Additional information I'll need:
- My next step:

WORKING WITH MULTIGENERATIONAL WORKFORCES

- Defined for my situation:
- Additional information I'll need:
- My next step:

WORKING WITH THE C-SUITE

- Defined for my situation:
- Additional information I'll need:
- My next step:

VENDOR MANAGEMENT

- Defined for my situation:
- Additional information I'll need:
- My next step:

WORKSHEET continued

WORKING WITH SUBJECT MATTER EXPERTS

- Defined for my situation:
- Additional information I'll need:
- My next step:

◆   ◆   ◆

References

Axelrod, W. and J. Coyle. *Make Talent Your Business: How Exceptional Managers Develop People While Getting Results*. San Francisco: Berrett-Koehler, 2011.

Azulay, H. "Assessing Readiness for a Mentoring Partnership" in *The Pfeiffer Annual: Training*, ed. E. Biech. San Francisco: John Wiley & Sons, 2013.

Barbazette, J. *How to Write Terrific Training Materials: Methods, Tools, and Techniques*. San Francisco: Pfeiffer, 2013.

Barbazette, J. *Instant Case Studies*. San Francisco: Pfeiffer, 2004.

Barksdale, S., and E. Lund. "How to Differentiate between Evaluation Levels 3 and 4" in *The 2004 Training and Performance Sourcebook*, ed. M. Silberman. Princeton, NJ: Active Training, 2004.

Betof, E. *Leaders as Teachers*. Alexandria, VA: ASTD Press, 2014.

Biech, E. *101 Ways to Make Learning Active Beyond the Classroom*. Hoboken, NJ: John Wiley & Sons, 2015.

Biech, E. *ASTD Handbook: The Definitive Reference for Training and Development*. Alexandria, VA: ASTD Press, 2008.

Biech, E. *The ASTD Handbook for Workplace Learning Professionals*. Alexandria, VA: ASTD Press, 2014.

Biech, E. *Thriving Through Change: A Leader's Practical Guide to Change Mastery*. Alexandria, VA: ASTD Press, 2007.

Biech, E. *Training and Development for Dummies*, Hoboken, NJ: John Wiley & Sons, 2015.

Blanchard, K. *Situational Leadership II*. Escondido, CA: Blanchard Training & Development, 1997.

Bobrow, W. "How to Evaluate Training Programs" in *The 2005 ASTD Training and Performance Sourcebook*, ed. M. Silberman. Alexandria, VA: ASTD, 2005.

Booher, D. *Communicate With Confidence: How to Say It Right the First Time and Every Time*, revised and expanded ed. New York: McGraw-Hill, 2012.

Booher, D. *Creating Personal Presence: Look, Talk, Think, and Act Like a Leader*. San Francisco: Berrett-Koehler, 2012.

Booher, D. "Securing Executive Support: Presenting to the C-Suite" in *ASTD Handbook: The Definitive Reference for Training and Development*, ed. E. Biech. Alexandria, VA: ASTD Press, 2014.

Bozarth, J. *Social Media for Trainers*. San Francisco: John Wiley & Sons, 2010.

Brislin, R. *Intercultural Interactions*. Thousand Oaks, CA: Sage, 1986.

Bruner, J. *Toward a Theory of Instruction*. Cambridge, MA: Harvard University Press, 1966.

Christopher, D. *The Successful Virtual Classroom*. New York: AMACOM, 2015.

Clark, R. *Evidence-Based Training Methods*. Alexandria, VA: ASTD Press, 2014.

Eikenberry, K. "Effective Listening: Better Relationships and Improved Results" in *The Best of Active Training*, ed. M. Silberman. San Francisco: Pfeiffer, 2004.

Gilbert, T. *Human Competence: Engineering Worthy Performance—ISPI Tribute Edition*. Washington, D.C.: International Society for Performance Improvement, 1996.

Hermann, N. *The Hermann Brain Dominance Inventory*. Lake Lure, NC: Hermann International, 1995.

Huggett, C. *The Virtual Training Guidebook: How to Design, Deliver, and Implement Live Online Learning*. Alexandria, VA: ASTD Press, 2013.

Insala "Mentoring Benefits." Retrieved from www.mentoringtalent.com/mentoring-benefits.asp#tabs, 2011.

Jensen, E. *Brain-Based Learning*. Thousand Oaks, CA: Corwin Press, 2008.

Kaye, B. *Love 'em or Lose 'em: Getting Good People to Stay*. San Francisco: Berrett-Koehler, 2012.

Kirkpatrick, D. *Evaluating Training Programs: The Four Levels*, 3rd ed. San Francisco: Berrett-Koehler, 2005.

Kirkpatrick, J. D. and W. K. Kirkpatrick. *Bringing Business Partnership to Life*. Newnan, GA: Kirkpatrick Publishing, 2013.

Knowles, M. E. Holton, and R., Swanson. *The Adult Learner*, 6th ed.. Oxford, UK: Butterworth-Heinemann, 2005.

Levin, H. *Innovations in Learning: New Environments for Education*. Mahway, NJ: Lawrence Erlbaum Associates, 1996.

MacKenzie, R. A. *The Time Trap*. New York: AMACOM, 1972.

Maslow, A. *Toward a Psychology of Being*. New York: Litton Educational Publishing, 1968.

McKeachie, W. and M. Svinicki. *McKeachie's Teaching Tips*. Boston: Houghton Mifflin, 2006.

Mosley, D. C., L. C. Megginson, and P. H. Pietri, Jr., *Supervisory Management*. Cincinnati: South-Western, 1985.

Mundhenk, L. "Developing Career Resilience: New Career-Management Strategies for the Twenty-First Century" in *20 Active Training Programs, Vol. 3*, ed. M. Silberman. San Francisco: Jossey-Bass/Pfeiffer, 1997.

Phillips, J. "Was It the Training?" *Training & Development,* March 1996, 28–32.

Pike, R. *Creative Training Techniques Handbook*, 3rd ed. Amherst, MA.: HRD Press, 2003.

Quinn, C. *Designing mLearning*. San Francisco: Jossey-Bass/Pfeiffer, 2011.

Scott, B. and B. K. Barnes. *Consulting on the Inside: An Internal Consultant's Guide to Living and Working Inside Organizations*, 2nd ed. Alexandria, VA: ASTD Press, 2011.

Silberman, M. "Coaching and Counseling: Two Ways to Guide Employees" in *20 Active Training Programs, Vol. 1*, ed. M. Silberman. San Francisco: Jossey-Bass/Pfeiffer, 1992.

Silberman, M. "Negotiating to Win/Win: Conflict Resolution in Personal and Professional Relationships" in *The Best of Active Training*, ed. M. Silberman. San Francisco: Pfeiffer, 2004.

Silberman, M. and F. Hansburg. *How to Encourage Constructive Feedback from Others: Leader's Guide*. San Francisco: Pfeiffer, 2005.

Simon, S., L. Howe, and H. Kirschenbaum. *Values Clarification*. New York: Warner Books, 1995.

Spitzer, D. "How to Drive and Track Level 4 Training Results" in *The 2004 Training and Performance Sourcebook*, ed. M. Silberman. Princeton, NJ: Active Training, 2004.

Steadham, S. V. "Learning to Select a Needs Assessment Strategy." *Training and Development Journal* 30 (1980): 56–61.

Stieber, W. "Proactive Project Management: How to Be in Charge from Beginning to End" in *The Best of Active Training*, ed. Mel Silberman. San Francisco: Pfeiffer, 2004.

"State of the Industry Report." Association for Talent Development. Alexandria, VA, December 2014.

Stringer, D. "Case Writing 101." *Training & Development* (September 1999): 53–58.

Stolovich, H. and E. Keeps. *Telling Ain't Training*. Alexandria, VA: ASTD Press, 2011.

Thiagarajan, S. *Thiagi's Interactive Lectures*. Alexandria, VA: ASTD Press, 2005.

Trifiletti, D., and R. Alexandri. "Consultative Selling: How to Build Partnerships in Business Relationships" in *The Best of Active Training*, ed. M. Silberman. San Francisco: Pfeiffer, 2004.

Vella, J. *Learning to Listen, Learning to Teach*. San Francisco: Jossey-Bass, 1994.

Whiteling, V. "Stress for Success: Understanding and Managing the Stress in Your Life" in *The Best of Active Training*, ed. M. Silberman. San Francisco: Pfeiffer, 2004.

Wick, C., R. Pollock, A. Jefferson, and R. Flanagan. *The Six Disciplines of Breakthrough Learning*. San Francisco: Pfeiffer, 2010.

Zemke, R., and S. Zemke. "What We Know for Sure About Adult Learning" in *What Smart Trainers Know*, ed. L. Ukens. San Francisco: Pfeiffer, 2001.

About the Authors

Dr. Mel Silberman was Professor Emeritus of Adult and Organizational Development at Temple University for forty-one years, where he was the recipient of the Great Teacher Award in 2000. Mel rose to international prominence for his contributions to the field of training. He received his AB degree in sociology from Brandeis University and his MA and PhD degrees from the University of Chicago in educational psychology.

He was president of Active Training, a provider of a wide range of services that develop instructional skills in any subject matter. He has conducted seminars in active training techniques for hundreds of corporate and governmental organizations throughout the world.

A popular presenter at training conferences, he has appeared before audiences at the American Society for Training and Development, the International Society for Performance Improvement, the North American Simulation and Gaming Association, and *Training* Magazine.

Mel was the author or editor of over thirty books. This book, *Active Training,* has been one of the most widely read texts in the field of training and development. He is also the author of *101 Ways to Make Training Active, The Best of Active Training, The 60 Minute Active Training Series,* and *PeopleSmart.* Mel died in 2010.

Elaine Biech, president of ebb associates inc, a strategic implementation, leadership development, and experiential learning consulting firm, has been in the field over thirty years helping organizations work through large-scale change. She has presented at dozens of national and international conferences and has been featured in publications such as *The Wall Street Journal, Harvard Management Update, Investor's Business Daily,* and *Fortune Magazine*. She is the author and editor of over sixty books, receiving national awards for two of them. Recent publications include: *The ASTD Handbook: The Definitive Reference for Training and Development, Developing Talent for Organizational Results, A Coaches Guide to Exemplary Leaders,* and the *ASTD Leadership Handbook*.

Elaine specializes in helping leaders maximize their effectiveness. Customizing all of her client work, she conducts strategic planning sessions and implements corporate-wide systems such as designing leadership development programs, change management, and mentoring programs. She is particularly adept at turning dysfunctional teams into productive teams.

A long-time volunteer for ASTD (now ATD), she has served on ASTD's National Board of Directors, was the recipient of the 1992 ASTD Torch Award, the 2004 ASTD Volunteer Staff Partnership Award, the 2006 Gordon Bliss Memorial Award, and in 2012, the inaugural CPLP Fellow Program Honoree from the ASTD Certification Institute. Elaine was instrumental in compiling and revising the CPLP study guides and has designed five ASTD Certificate Programs. She was the 1995 Wisconsin Women Entrepreneur's Mentor Award recipient and served on the Instructional Systems Association (ISA) board of directors. Elaine is currently a member of the Center for Creative Leadership's Board of Governors.

Carol Auerbach is an independent training consultant. She has over twenty-five years' experience designing, developing, and delivering corporate training programs for such companies as Mellon Bank, CIGNA Insurance, McCormick & Company, Kellogg's, and IBM. She co-authored the first three editions of *Active Training* with Mel, in addition to co-editing four other training-related books. She is the president and founder of My Future Directions, LLC, a college and career consulting business. Carol has a BA in Economics and English from Duke University and an MA in Educational Psychology from Temple University.

Index